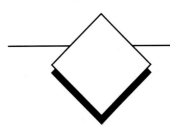

# THE LAST .400 HITTER
## *The Anatomy of a .400 Season*

John B. Holway

Cover design by Tim Kaage.

Library of Congress Catalog Card Number: 91–71684

ISBN 0–697–14129–2

Printed in the United States of America by Wm. C. Brown Publishers, 2460 Kerper Boulevard, Dubuque, IA 52001

10  9  8  7  6  5  4  3  2  1

To Jerry Cooper

# Contents

Introduction September 9, 1941     vi
**Part I:** The Squire of Islamorada     1
**Part II:** The Country of the Past     7
**Part III:** The Kid     13
**Part IV:** The Red Sox 1939–1940     33
**Part V:** The Winter of '41     85
**Part VI:** The Spring of '41     93
**Part VII:** The Summer of '41     165
**Part VIII:** The Autumn of '41     261
**Appendix:** The Math of the .400 Hitter     291
    Williams 1941 Breakdown by Team and City
    Sacrifice Flies and .400
    Against Lefties and Righties     293
    Day Versus Night     294
    At Bats and .400  ·   296
    Walks and .400     298
    Einstein's Theory of Baseball Relativity     302
    Ty Cobb's .420 in 1911     306
    Climbing the Hill     309
    Those Who Came Close     316
    MVP: Does 56 Beat .406?     320
    IVP: Individual Victory Percentage     321
    Teammates Table Setters     321
    GWAB: Games Won At Bat     324
    Offensive Assists     325
    Linear Weights     326
    Ted Williams Batting Record     331
    San Diego Padres 1936–1937     331
    Minneapolis Millers 1938     338
    Boston Red Sox 1939–1941     344

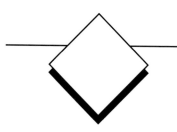

## Introduction
## September 9, 1941

### "The past is another country: they do things differently there."

—the film "The Go-Between"

I'll never forget the sight of Ted Williams in 1941. What 11-year old could?

It was a sunny September Saturday afternoon, September 6, to be exact. My father had taken me to Yankee Stadium, a rare treat after ten long years of Depression. From our box seats in short right field, we watched Williams hitting .411, step up to bat not 40 yards away. He had just turned 23, curly headed, handsome as the movie cowboys he and I both admired, skinny as a fungo bat, and temperamental as a knuckle ball. The blue "9" on his road uniform was toward us. His long skinny legs looked even longer and skinnier because he wore his pants almost to his ankles. He stood glaring at the pitcher over his right shoulder, bat held tight against his left shoulder, working his left elbow nervously up and down as though tightening a wrench. (John Updike said he seemed to be squeezing sawdust out of the handle.) Then Ted brought his hands down and forward with a jerk, almost a samurai sword stroke (Sadaharu Oh would later pattern his swing on *kendo*, or swordsmanship), holding the bat/blade in front of him, pointing it over the left-field roof at a 45 degree angle. Williams held the pose only an instant. Then he brought the weapon quickly back to his shoulder and pumped and glared some more.

When the pitcher finally gave up the ball, Williams gave a quick genuflection, a dimpling of his right knee, and swung. A wickedly skipping grounder headed right at his first base coach, who danced out of the way and let the missile continue straight at us, smacking against the front of our box like a bullet, as we instinctively leaned away.

Checking the newspaper files four decades later, I read that Ted walked his first time up, grounded out, popped up, backed Yankee George Selkirk against the right-field seats for a high fly, and finally singled in a run. As he trotted back to the dugout, his average had dropped to .409. He had three more weeks to go. He couldn't afford too many more 1–for–4 afternoons—even 1–for–3 would be a net loss to his .400 average. Could he keep it up there? Or would he fail, as so many before and since—Rod Carew, George Brett, etc—have done?

Of course Ted didn't fail, though it was a cliff-hanger. He came triumphantly through with one of the finest, most dramatic finishes in batting annals.

Earlier that summer I had seen Joe DiMaggio hit in game #34 of his 56-game streak. Even as we watched, one of the most stunning news events of the 20th Century was taking place, as the German army awaited the signal to invade the Soviet Union.

That was an amazing summer, 1941. The year had begun with the Battle of Britain; it would end with Pearl Harbor. And on the ball field two of the three greatest batting dramas of the last 60 years were played out—Williams' .406 and DiMaggio's streak. (The third of the three of course was Roger Maris' 61 homers in 1961; I also saw three of those 61.)

"Some day," an avid fan once remarked to me, "I'd like to see a .400-hitter in action." My gosh, I thought to myself, four-fifths of all the baseball fans in America today were either not yet born, or were too young to remember Williams' historic achievement. Time has lent a perspective to the event that we didn't have in 1941. In 65 years since 1876 the .400-barrier had been pierced no less than 27 times, or almost once every other year. In 1894 alone it had been done five times; in 1922, three. But in the 50 years since then, no man has been able to do it again. And, unless there is a dramatic change in the game—massive expansion, the aluminum bat, a 70-foot pitching distance, for instance—no one is ever likely to see it again. I wanted to write the anatomy of a .400 hitter so that others less fortunate than I will have the thrill of reliving that now unique event.

# 1

## *The Squire of Islamorada*

More than 40 years after that first, boyhood look at Williams, I drove into the palm-studded driveway of his retreat on the Florida Keys. The home was just off Route 1 behind a chain link fence. The gate was open, and though a small sign said "Private," it did not say "Keep Out," and I took it as a neighborly tip to guests at the hotel next door that this was not the hotel entrance.

Inside the fence Ted's white stucco house snuggled beneath palms. In the wide front yard clumps of beach grass pushed up among the fallen coconuts. A hammock was slung between two trunks. At the rear of the house the Gulf of Mexico lapped at the back door, a boat bobbing gently at a pier. It was a comfortable home, not ostentatious, a place where a man could mix a drink from the sideboard, kick off his shoes, put his feet up on a hassock, and enjoy the fruits of life.

I knocked on the glass patio door, which bore a printed warning: "Absolutely no smoking." No one answered. That night I inquired at a small bamboo bar on the beach, where Japanese lanterns swayed beneath a tropical moon. No, the young bartender said, he hadn't seen Williams yet this autumn, and since Ted usually stopped by for a drink as soon as he arrived, the barkeep surmised that he must still be up north doing his summer fishing.

A week later I returned to Islamorada. Williams' housekeeper, Louise Kaufman, a merry Barbara Bush look-alike from Boston, greeted me hospitably and ushered me into the sitting room. Framed paintings of fish and fishermen hung on the walls. A picture window looked out on mangrove islands in the Gulf. A Japanese translation of Ted's book, *My Turn At Bat*, lay on a coffee table. "Except for the book, you wouldn't know I'm a ball player, would you?" Ted would later point out. "I don't have many mementoes." Those baseball pictures he does have are upstairs in the bedroom. "Maybe because they're kind of sacred to me. This is the first time I've ever said that."

The refrigerator door held a cartoon of a handyman who had put his foot through the seat of a wicker chair. Apparently the game's greatest precision hitter is a klutz around the house. Kaufman humors Ted and deflects his occasional bursts of temperament. "Oh," she smiles at him, "just because you can hit a baseball doesn't mean you know everything."

She listened with interest to my idea for a book on the 1941 season until we were interrupted by the phone. In a few minutes she returned, shaking her head maternally. Ted had called from the airport on his way to Jamaica to say he had forgotten his passport. She smiled and sighed like a mother whose child has forgotten his mittens.

How sorry she was that I hadn't arrived the day before. The World Series was on TV, and since she knew almost nothing about baseball, she had retired early. Poor Ted had been forced to watch the game with no one to talk to. If only I'd been there, she said, how glad he would have been to have some company.

I told Mrs. Kaufman I'd do some scuba diving and return in three days. She promised to prepare Ted and said she'd give him a good report.

When I returned on the appointed morning, Ted's car was gone from the driveway, but a couple of "captains"—fishing boat skippers—were lounging in the yard and began regaling me with lies about how well they knew Ted. In the midst of the tall tales, Williams pulled into the yard in a station wagon and stepped out. The once Splendid Splinter was no longer a splinter; his tennis shorts revealed a paunch in spite of his devotion to exercise. But he was still splendid with the rugged good looks of an Erroll Flynn or a James Garner.

"You the fella that's been doin' all the writin'?" he asked.

He led us into his living room, and while he dabbed at the sweat with the bandana around his neck, the captains continued their act, which now consisted of outdoing each other in insults. Ted tolerated them for a polite interval, as a good host must, then nodded to indicate that it was time to start the interview. The captains took the hint and left.

"Now," Ted said affably, turning to me, "what can I do for *you*?"

For hours over three different visits we talked, as I probed his memory for specific games and pitchers and even pitches. We also ranged over other subjects. Williams dislikes traveling, but to earn some dollars he drags himself off to airports and hotels and baseball card shows. Does he feel bitter about missing out on today's big money?

"Not a bit," he insisted. "You can't look back like that. These modern players are having a tough enough time. They've got everybody and their brother on their ass." And they have to play from the snows of early April to the wintry winds of October. Williams was always a hot-weather hitter and blames the longer schedule in part for the demise of the .400-hitter. "I'm happy doing what I'm doing today. I'm going bonefish fishing tomorrow."

Politically he and I had little common ground. ("I think the Democrats for 50 years have squandered too much," he said. "Reagan's turning it around in the right direction. But I don't think they'll *ever* balance the budget, do you?") Ted may have put George Bush in the White House. In early 1988, when Bush was behind in the polls, Williams stumped New Hampshire, where the Vice-President won his first key victory over Robert Dole and went on to lock up the nomination.

But we quickly forged a bond on the issue of justice for the old Negro leaguers. I had been at a luncheon at Washington's Howard University in 1969, when Williams was given a brotherhood award for his graceful speech urging that the doors of Cooperstown be open to Satchel Paige and Josh Gibson, a wish that came true just one year later. I said he deserved credit for that.

"You're damn right!" he agreed. "You know, they had a movie on Satchel Paige, and they used my quote. And I'm *proud* of that, by God. That was something I did absolutely on my own, 'cause I felt that way for a long time. I used to go to Washington, and they'd tell me where Josh Gibson hit one— goddam, nobody in *our* league hit one any *further* than that!" Josh was playing in Mexico in the summer of '41, and his rival, Satchel Paige, was posting a 7−1 record with the Kansas City Monarchs. They were two of the greatest players in North American baseball history, but at that time I hadn't yet heard of either one of them. There were no blacks on so-called "big league" teams in 1941 of course, and almost none in the stands, and nobody found that strange. Today they are on the field, but the only other blacks in the park are probably either dragging the infield or selling beer. And still no one finds it strange.

Williams and I relived that historic season and entered a time machine back to another era, back to a year poised like a fulcrum between the two biggest adventures of the 20th century, the Great Depression and World War II.

# 2

## *The Country of the Past*

Back in 1941 boys slicked their cowlicks with stickem or spit, played marbles, one o' cat, and roller skate hockey on the street, listened to Jack Armstrong, The Lone Ranger, and Little Orphan Annie on the radio, and watched Hopalong Cassidy and Our Gang at the ten-cent Saturday movie matinee (movies with kissing were greeted with groans).

Nobody wore blue jeans except farmers and workmen, and then we called them overalls. Boys' uniforms were sneakers, argyle socks, and corduroy knickers—except for me. I had to wear short pants, which the other boys considered sissy, because my father, a clothes' horse, thought knickers didn't look good. He and I would fight about the length of my pants as later my son and I would fight about the length of his hair.

We spoke a different language then. Watches had hands, and we said "a quarter to eleven" or "half-past three." Now watches have digits, and we say "10:47" and "3:31," only now my arm is too short to read my watch. Magically transported 50 years forward, we would not have understood today's kids. Jet, Sputnik, VCR—even TV—floppy disk, xerox, fax, cholesterol, AIDS, Ms., NATO, *macho, sayonara*, and DH are concepts incomprehensible to us in 1941. Even old words such as rock, grass, cool, gay, turf, acid, bust, fuzz, hairy, adult, save, wave, turn on, cop out, put down, and "you blew it" have now taken on confusing new meanings. But then we used to say reefers (marijuana), java (coffee), drip (nerd), and tomato (chick). The Los Angeles Dodgers, the Toronto Skydome, and Jackie Robinson would have been as amazing to us half a century ago as an outfielder being paid $26 million for hitting .276—in 1941 Ted was paid $17,500 for hitting .406. Will we count players' salaries in the billions in the year 2041?

Looking back now, the Depression is a one-decade anomaly among nine decades in this century, but then it was the normal way of life for us. We were closer in time then to Wee Willie Keeler's .424 in 1897 than today's fans are to Williams' .406. We were almost as close to the Wright Brothers as we were to Neil Armstrong. World War I was as fresh in memory to people then as Vietnam is to us now. Only we didn't call it World War I—it was simply "the World War." " There was no Veterans' Day, but we did celebrate "Armistice Day" every November 11. My neighbor down the street twitched spastically when he walked or talked, the result of a gassing in France in 1918.

In the Stadium that day almost no one had ever been in an airplane, not even the players. Very few people had ever been to Chicago, let alone California. I considered Pittsburgh the wild west, a land of cowboys and Indians. But you might have found some fans who had fought in the Spanish-American war, the Indian wars, or even the Civil War.

Dwight Eisenhower was an obscure lieutenant colonel in Louisiana then. Jack Kennedy was chasing girls at Harvard. Ten-year old Neil Armstrong, the future moonwalker, was building model airplanes in Ohio. Woody Allen was five years old and pulling girls' pigtails in kindergarten. In Mobile, Alabama Hank Aaron, the future conqueror of Babe Ruth, was four years old, while out in South Dakota, Roger Maris, Ruth's other conqueror, was two days away from his fourth birthday party. Elvis, Ringo, Muhammad Ali, and Nolan Ryan hadn't been born yet.

Nobody in 1941 had ever heard of Iran, Israel, Vietnam, Zaire, or Zimbabwe, none of which had been born either. They were then called Persia, Palestine, French Indo-China, the Belgian Congo, and Rhodesia. When the Japanese bombed Pearl Harbor just three months later, I thought it was in the Philippines, but I wasn't sure where the Philippines were.

I could remember no President other than Roosevelt, and no heavyweight champ but Joe Louis.

The pole vault record had only recently topped 15 feet, and I would be an adult before the four-minute mile was achieved. Yet today most of the 1941 track and field records have long since been demolished—by women. Johnny

"Tarzan" Weissmueller, the world 400 meter record-holder, couldn't even make the Olympic team today—on the women's squad. If his movie mate, Jane, were endangered by ravenous crocodiles, he could splash to her aid in just over five minutes, to find that young Janet Evans had gotten there a minute ahead of him, rescued Jane, and was already swinging away through the jungle, ululating triumphantly.

In 1941 teams played double-headers every Sunday and held ladies' days (free tickets to ladies) every Tuesday. Games started typically at 3 pm. Almost no parks had lights—George Barrow had just vowed that there would never be lights in Yankee Stadium. The average attendance in 1941 was 7,000 per game. Today it's over 28,000, accounting for part of the inflation in salaries. Fans sat in the centerfield bleachers, giving hitters fits trying to see the ball against the white shirts. Players wore heavy flannel uniforms, even in double-headers at 100-degree temperatures. They had numbers but not names on their backs, so you literally "couldn't tell the players without a scorecard," which cost five cents. (Will uniform numbers 50 years from now begin with #30 because all lower numbers have been retired?) In 1941 scoreboards did not give batting averages, nor even hit/error signs and of course didn't shoot fireworks, show instant replays, or blare "Charge!" Instead, boys, such as future commissioner Bowie Kuhn, hung the score each inning by hand. Catchers wore heavy padded chest protectors (has the new steel cup made them obsolete?). There was a little path from home plate to the mound. There were no padded outfield walls or warning tracks. The outfield was littered with the discarded gloves of the team at bat. No one wore batting helmets or batting gloves. There was no protective screen for the batting practice pitcher. Players on deck swung three bats instead of one bat with a weighted "donut." They wore steel spikes on their shoes, not cleats, and chewed tobacco, not gum, spitting constantly. Players played "pepper" before the game, batting the ball to three or four teammates who did tricks with it before throwing it back. Yankee Stadium had a roof, from which gingerbread decorations hung. Cigar smoke filled the stadium, and the smell still triggers memories in me, like Marcel Proust's tea-dipped cookie.

It's still partly true: The only blacks in the park today are probably playing center field, selling beer, or dragging the infield.

Players are faster and bigger today. In 1941 Danny Murtaugh led the National League in stolen bases with 18; today they steal four or five times that many. In 1941, Williams at 6'3" stood head and shoulders above his teammates; if he were in a team photo today, he'd be about average. Then Bob Feller was virtually the only pitcher throwing near 100 miles an hour; now almost half the pitchers do. Hitters then could swing 40-ounce bats or kick their legs up like Mel Ott; they couldn't get away with either against today's flame throwers. Although pitchers get bigger, hitters do not get quicker, and 400-strikeout seasons may be coming before long.

What will the world of our grandchildren be like in the year 2041? Will we be able even to talk to them?

Will players stand seven feet tall or more? Will the world high jump record be over nine feet? The mile record, 3:30? The 100 meters, 8.5 seconds? Will base paths be 95 feet apart? The pitching distance 65'6"? Will teams use three hurlers a game, each going three innings? Will players take "mental steroids" or every team have a "mind coach" trained in psychic science, as they now hire weight coaches?

Will the world see mammoth stadia entirely underground or on the tops of skyscrapers? Will the Tokyo Samurai and the Moscow Bears host a real World Series? Will home run champs be named Jiro Watanabe and Yuri Raskalnikov? Will players' salaries be counted in the billions of dollars? Will a bleacher ticket cost $50? What will a Mickey Mantle rookie card be worth?

Compared to the changes of the last 50 years, nothing is unthinkable.

In 1941 Cooperstown had 17 plaques in it. Today it has more than 200. By 2041 will it have 600? The value of all plaques will be cheapened. One can imagine a father and his young son standing before the bewildering wall. "Dad," the boy asks, "who was Hank Mays?" "You mean Willie Aaron, don't you son?" the father replies gently.

Will a white-maned Jose Canseco, a paunchy Roger Clemens, and a bald Rickey Henderson have become mythic figures at Cooperstown inductions and old-timers games as Williams, and Joe DiMaggio are today?

Ted Williams has succeeded in transcending the years. He still dominates all others on the dais at Cooperstown each summer and is still reverentially deferred to as the greatest authority on hitting in the history of the game. His picture on the cover of *Sports Illustrated* still sells magazines, as it did in 1941 on the cover of *Life*. Williams is the only player in baseball history to dominate two decades, the 1940s and '50s. Only Louis and Muhammad Ali have equalled that feat in *any* major sport. Cobb had been king 1910–19, Ruth 1920–29. No one man has reigned unrivaled over even one decade since then—except Williams, who dominated both the '40's and '50's. With the increase in competition growing inexhorably every year, no one is ever likely to do that again.

Nineteen forty-one was a year of FDR, Hitler, Churchill, Mussolini, and Chiang Kai-shek. Their names leaped off the newspaper pages with an impact that transcended Bush, Gorbachev, or Saddam Hussein. On the playing field it was also a year of mythic gods. DiMaggio and Williams waged a season-long battle for the attention of the fans, for the votes of the writers at MVP time, and eventually for the judgment of the historians.

Those of us who lived through that historic year owe an obligation to tell about it to those, less fortunate, who did not.

## 3

### *The Kid*

*1918–1935*

# San Diego
# Boyhood

◆

Even as a kid in San Diego, Ted Williams said his ambition was to walk down the street and have people turn and say, "There goes the greatest baseball hitter who ever lived."

As a gangly 17-year-old in his first year of professional ball, he was still saying it. His fellow rookie, Bobby Doerr, who would become his best pal on the Red Sox, remembers Ted getting kids to shag balls for him while he took batting practice by the hour, while he grunted and muttered, "I want to be the best hitter who ever lived."

And, says Bob, "I think he was. They threw away the mold when they made him. I didn't see all the great hitters before him, but I don't see how you could get any better."

In later years on the Red Sox, Ted and Bob would pair off on road trips, and when the older guys went out on the town, the two walked miles through the streets together. Williams was what the other players called a loner, but Bobby thinks they didn't understand him.

Ted's father was a weak role model, and his mother, a peppy little Mexican woman, played in the Salvation Army band. His younger brother Danny was constantly in trouble; in later years he was in and out of prison and finally was shot to death, according to one tabloid account. Ted himself does not talk about Dan, except for one laconic reference in his autobiography: "He died tough."

Ted admits he "was not a good student." But I once met his third grade teacher, Ruth Snyder, who recalled her most famous pupil: "He was diligent, and he tried, and he was well-behaved. Ted was always taking care of his little brother out in the school yard." When I repeated this report card to Ted, it pleased him very much.

Williams was born in August 1918 as World War I was ending and spent the first 23 years of his life between the two worst wars in history. For his first 12 years he was a child of the Roaring Twenties. He heard over and over again of the .400 hitters. There were no less than eight of them in the 11-year period, 1920–30, and Rogers Hornsby, Harry Heilmann, and Lefty O'Doul missed by only three points or less of making it 11 out of 11. Like most boys, who pick out their lifelong heroes at puberty, in 1930 the 12-year-old Williams seized on Bill Terry, who hit .401 for the Giants in far-away New York. Perhaps not coincidentally, Terry also had a reputation as a stormy baiter of the press.

Ted spent his teenage years in the dreary Depression. He had been too young—nine—to comprehend the import of Babe Ruth's 60 homers in 1927. But Ruth, Lou Gehrig, and a few other long ball hitters began pushing the .400-hitters out of the game. The big league home run totals climbed from 900 in 1927 to almost 1100, then 1350, and 1565 in 1930. In the first six years of the '30s, Jimmie Foxx, Mel Ott, Hack Wilson, Al Simmons, Chuck Klein, Joe Medwick, Hank Greenberg, Johnny Mize, and a youngster named Joe DiMaggio made home runs the hallmarks of fame.

Ted was a pitcher in high school, over six feet tall but only 150 pounds. Several teams scouted him. The Cardinals were first, but Mrs. Williams said St. Louis was too far away. The Tigers decided he was too skinny. The Yankees offered $400 a month if he could play Class A ball. When the scouts rang his doorbell, Ted remembers hastily covering the sofa seat with a towel, so they wouldn't see the springs sticking out.

But when Hollywood moved its Pacific Coast League franchise to San Diego, Ted's mother decided that was the team for her boy.

*1936*

# Padres Rookie

◆

As a kid of six, my own memories of that year are few. And I recall adults talking about war in Spain and Ethiopia—Franco, Haile Selassie, Mussolini—about the King of England abdicating to marry an American, about Bruno Hauptman going to the electric chair for the kidnapping of the Lindbergh baby, and of President Roosevelt beating Alf Landon.

I also recall that airplanes were mostly the old-fashioned World War I biplanes and still so novel that if we heard one overhead, we all craned our necks to watch it. Sometimes they trailed plumes of smoke spelling out an advertiser's name, and everybody stopped to guess the word before it was finished.

It was not unusual to see men on the corners selling pencils in a tin cup, or turning an organ-grinder while a monkey danced and held out a cup. I remember tramps knocking on the kitchen door for food and then eating an ear of corn under a tree in the front yard. My father, I found out later, went from job to job—last one hired, first one fired. He even sold vacuum cleaners door-to-door, a great blow to his pride. My mother told me she once gave him a scolding for coming home late, only to learn he had walked home to save the nickel in car fare. There must have been many nights when he came home to report that he had lost his job again. Yet we kids never guessed. As Dwight Eisenhower wrote of his own childhood, "We were poor but we didn't know it."

I remember eating a lot of lentils—they were the cheapest thing in the stores. I've never liked them since. Italian kids came around with penknives and dug dandelions out of the lawns to boil. And we all chewed on wild rhubarb like sugar cane.

We ate all the wrong things—when we could afford them: bacon and fried eggs, red meat, salt, plenty of sugar and cream. There were no such things as diet Cokes. Most adults smoked, including ball players who advertised cigarettes, holding Luckies or Camels or Chesterfields. No one jogged, and many adults keeled over from heart attacks. Fifty years from now, what will doctors tell our grandchildren about things we are doing today that have been killing us?

We listened to radio—Kate Smith, "Gangbusters," newsman Gabriel Heatter ("Ah, there's baaad news tonight"), "The Shadow" ("Who knows what evil lurks in the hearts of men?"), and Charlie McCarthy ("I'll clip ya, so help me, I'll mow ya down").

Shirley Temple, almost my age, was big in the movies. I remember Charlie Chaplin's *Modern Times*; unfortunately it was a silent, and I couldn't read fast enough to get to the end of the line before the next scene flashed on; if my mother tried to whisper to me, the other people all went "Shhhoosh!"

Bing Crosby crooned "Pennies From Heaven;" Jeanette MacDonald and Nelson Eddy sang "Indian Love Call," and Gene Autrey, later owner of the California Angels, sang "I'm an Old Cowhand."

Although I don't remember it, baseball inducted its first five Hall of Famers; Joe DiMaggio and Bob Feller made their debuts; Jesse Owens won four gold medals in Hitler's Berlin Olympics, and the German Max Schmeling KO'd Joe Louis in one round.

In 1936 18-year-old Bobby Doerr got his first look at the 17-year-old Williams. Bobby was already in his third year at second base in the league and recalls the day Ted arrived for a tryout, a skinny "148-pound weakling," to paraphrase the famous Charles Atlas body-building ads in the magazines. He was standing around the batting cage hoping for a chance to hit. "Let the kid in," manager Frank Shellenback, the old spitball pitcher, ordered Doerr and the others. "Let the kid in, let him hit a few."

"You don't like to have a young kid come up, take your time in batting practice," says Doerr, who was three months older than "the kid." But when Ted smacked two or three out of the park, the older guys just whistled. "My gosh, who's that kid?" they asked.

"A natural stroke," Bobby recalls admiringly. "A big gangly kid with great ability."

In his first professional at bat, June 27, against a tall Texas right-hander named Cotten Pippen, Ted says, he was so petrified he struck out on three called strikes.

Still Doerr insisted, "This kid will be signed before the week is out." Sure enough, "there's Ted at the depot, pacing back and forth, all excited," waiting to board the train with the rest of the team. He was offered $200 a week and considered himself well paid.

Six days later in Los Angeles Shellenback put Ted in to pinch-hit, and he smacked his first professional hit, a single against Glenn Gabler.

Shellenback left Ted in to pitch. The kid pitched one shutout inning, according to research by Al Kermisch, of the Society for American Baseball Research, then gave up two home run over the short Wrigley Field fence, the second by ex-football player Wes Schulmerich, before Shell came to rescue Ted "to save his life." ("Anyway," Ted told him philosophically, "there's nobody on base.") He replaced Vince DiMaggio, Joe's older brother, in left field for the rest of the game and collected another hit.

In his next 14 at bats, Williams got only one hit. But when Vince was sold to the Boston Bees, a spot opened up in the outfield, and Ted was put in it. He didn't do too well, but then,

San Diego Padres 1937 *San Diego Historical Society-Ticor Collection*

for a 17-year-old, he didn't do too badly, either. He took morning batting practice by the hour and watched the older men closely.

"You ever hear of Moose Clabaugh?" Williams asks. In 1926, according to Bob Hoie of SABR, Clabaugh had hit 62 homers in the East Texas League. In '36 he hit 20 with Portland in the PCL. "A big ol' left-handed hitter," Williams says, "and he'd swing big, and when he hit 'em, they went long, deep to right. He was the type of hitter that I aspired to be." (At the age of 82 Clabaugh went to see Ted in Florida, and "I couldn't have been happier to see him.")

But Williams hit no home runs that rookie year. Lane Field was 350 feet to the right-field foul line and 500 feet to dead center. (Oddly, the backstop was only 12 feet behind the

San Diego's Lane Field *San Diego Historical Society-Ticor Collection*

plate, according to Phil Lowrey, author of the seminal ball-park study, *Green Cathedrals*.) Ted got a lot of doubles and singles there, enough to hit .303 at home.

Unfortunately, however, Shellenback used him mostly on the road, where he batted only .257.

In 42 games that year the kid got a few doubles, some triples, even stole a couple of bases and contributed a few brilliant catches in the outfield. But his batting average, home and away, was only .247 with three games left to play, all in San Francisco. Then Ted got hot and cracked six hits in 14 at bats, to raise his final average to .271, not bad for a teen-ager in Triple-A ball.

Kermisch says Williams finally hit his first home in the playoffs in Oakland, where the fence was a reachable 313 feet. The homer came September 15 against veteran right-hander

Willie Ludolph (21–6 that season), who had blanked the Padres for eight innings before Ted lined a two-run shot so hard that the Oakland right fielder didn't even move. Ted had just turned 18.

---

*1937*

# San Diego Sophomore

---◆---

Amelia Earhart was lost in the Pacific. War erupted in China; I remember a famous *Life* magazine photo of a Chinese baby screaming amid the columns of smoke and debris of war. Newsreels showed the German zeppelin Hindenberg destroyed in a giant fireball near my home in New Jersey.

On the radio Bob Hope first sang "Thanks for the Memory." Eddie Cantor sang "I Want to Spend Each Wednesday With You." Knock-knock jokes were big.

At the movies I remember *Captains Courageous* with Mickey Rooney and Spencer Tracy, Shirley Temple in *Heidi*, as well as *Dead End* and the elephant boy Sabu. The Marx brothers were popular. But the "zany" Ritz brothers were just as funny, I thought, and their movies are never revived today. Ditto big-mouthed Joe E. Brown and his baseball comedy, *Elmer the Great*—his son later became general manager of the Pittsburgh Pirates. One "grown-up" movie, *A Star Is Born*, was over my head, but another, *Lost Horizons*, made a big impression on me when the beautiful young girl turned into an old hag as she crossed the mountains from Shangri-La in a blizzard. Almost half a century later I'd go to Nepal to try to find Shangri-La myself.

Eddie Collins, the Hall of Famer who had played against Ty Cobb and was then general manager of the Red Sox, traveled to San Diego to scout both Bobby Doerr and Ted. Eddie was impressed with Williams' swing and compared him to Shoeless Joe Jackson, who had hit .408 in 1911. Jackson and Williams were in a class by themselves, Collins said later. But of the two, Ted was tops. Collins signed both Williams and Doerr, who had hit .342. Ted always considered Collins "a father to me."

Doerr was promoted to the Red Sox, where he hit .224. Ted stayed in San Diego under Shellenback. As he was through most of his career, Williams was blessed with a patient and understanding manager. Shell had been a star spitballer back in 1920 — the year they outlawed the spitball in the majors. As a result, he never got out of the minors, where he had a fine career, while other, older spitballers, such as Burleigh Grimes and Stanley Coveleskie, were allowed to continue to throw the pitch in the majors and rode it to the Hall of Fame. If the ruling had come one year later, who knows? Shellenback might have been with them. In 1941, as coach with the Red Sox, Frank would continue to pitch patiently to Ted by the hour and probably deserves some of the credit for Williams' .400 season.

Kermisch reports that Ted slugged his first regular-season home run April 11 against Stewart Bolen at Lane Field.

Lefty O'Doul, who had hit .398 with the Phils in 1929, was managing San Francisco, and was quoted in the newspapers as predicting that Williams will be one of the greatest left-handed hitters in the game. "He went out on a limb for me, an unknown kid," Williams said years later. "It made a great impression on me. Lefty gave me many batting tips, but the greatest thing he gave me was confidence." O'Doul's number-one tip was: "Kid, never let anyone change your stance."

Ted adopted his mentor's bat model—medium barrel, small handle, big knob, 33–34 ounces, 35 inches. In an era when Babe Ruth and others were striving to show their *macho* power with 40- and 50-ounce bats, O'Doul and Williams were among the first to realize that bat speed, not weight, was the key to power. Now every slugger uses a lighter bat.

Williams remembers one pitcher telling him, "You know, Ted, you're gonna make over a quarter of a million dollars in this game!"

The irony makes him smile. "Well, you know, a joke of a player's making over 200,000 a year now. See how times just change? God, they tell me inflation's going to be, in another 15 years, exactly double what it is now. Can't hardly believe it. It scares ya."

The kid showed flashes of the temperament that would later make him famous. On July 1 he was abruptly benched for lack of hustle. The next day he atoned with two singles, a double, and a homer.

Ted went on to hit 23 homers— 19 of them at home, and one inside the park. He would hit only three more inside-the-parkers in his life, the last one clinching the pennant for Boston in 1946.

Ted went into a slump in his final series, against the Mission team in San Francisco, but in his final double-header, he slammed four hits, including a home run. It was only the eighth ball in seven years hit over the distant right-field fence there. Unfortunately the Padres lost the game. Meanwhile, San Francisco's little center fielder, Dom DiMaggio knocked six hits in a double-header to knock the Padres out of second place.

But Williams end up with .291 and 98 runs batted in for the season. He continued to hit in the play offs, batting .314, as the Padres swept eight straight games without a loss.

At season's end the Red Sox gave San Diego $25,000 and three players for the kid who was already being hailed as "the second DiMaggio."

---

## 1938
# Minneapolis

$\blacklozenge$

"Nazis," "Austria," "Sudetenland," and "Czechoslovakia" were in the headlines. Newsreels showed British Prime Minister Neville Chamberlain, a thin man with mustache and emblematic umbrella, returning from talks with Hitler and promising "peace in our time."

Joe Louis destroyed Schmeling in one round in their long-awaited rematch.

Older people whistled "Begin the Beguine," but kids preferred the "Beer Barrel Polka" or "A-tisket, A-tasket."

*Snow White*, Mickey Rooney as *Andy Hardy*, and Errol Flynn in *Robin Hood* were the big movie hits I remember. My father whittled down his old wooden golf club shafts so I could have rapiers like Flynn's.

I bought books of cutouts of cowboys for a dime, or my mother drew them for me to cut out, and I entertained myself with them by the hour. I collected Dixie cup lids from ice cream with movie cowboys' pictures on them: Johnny Mack Brown (the Rose Bowl star), Wild Bill Elliott, George O'Brien, and my favorite of all, William Boyd—"Hopalong Cassidy"— with his white hat, white horse, and pearl-handled pistols. (Ted's favorite was Buck Jones.) They all wore tall hats, usually white, with bandanas around their necks, drank sarsa-parilla (a primitive soft drink) in bars, and said, "Shucks, howdy ma'am" to the schoolmarm. My father spent his hard-earned money to buy me holsters and guns.

I was welded to my bike like a cowboy to his horse and still have the scar tissue on my knees and elbows to show for it. Bikes had only one gear, so pumping uphill meant standing on the pedals and weaving, red-faced and puffing, from side to side until we had to get off and walk it up the rest of the way. We put a clip around our pants legs so they wouldn't get caught in the chain; even so, I spent hours of my childhood hopping on one foot and turning the pedal slowly to get my pants free. The trousers perpetually had a greasy, torn-up look around the cuffs.

We also roller-skated on the street. The skates clamped onto our street shoes, and we tightened them with a key from a string around our necks. Or we built scooters of wood, with skates nailed to the bottom, a do-it-yourself skateboard.

Tin soldiers with World War I helmets, leggins, and weapons flooded the toy counters, or you could make your own with a mold, some lead, an electric heating cup, and paint.

There were no supermarkets. We shopped down the street, where the owner, in white apron, with a pencil behind his ear, got you your items off the shelf himself, sometimes with the help of a ladder, then totted up your bill on the back of a brown bag. You got your change in buffalo nickels, liberty dimes, and an occasional Indian head penny. The penny would buy a stamp for a postcard, three of them would buy a first-class stamp or a newspaper.

Gas pumps had glass tops with colored balsa-wood balls that danced around to show that the gas really was flowing. My grandfather had a Model-T Ford that he started by hand with a big crank below the radiator.

By far the most indelible memory of that year was the night before Halloween, when we tuned in late to our favorite radio program, Orson Welles, to hear instead a program of concert music interrupted by news bulletins of strange space ships landing in New Jersey, near where we lived! We kids listened in terror, and I think my parents did too for a while. Now when I play the tape on the car radio to try to fool my kids, they catch on right away—kids are more sophisticated nowadays—but I have never been so scared in my life, except the night a burglar got into our house and was shot dead in the living room by a cop.

Doerr shepherded the 20-year-old Williams to Florida for spring training with the Red Sox. They rode a train across the country with Floyd "Babe" Herman, who had hit .393 in 1930, the year Terry hit .401. Ted and Babe talked hitting the whole trip.

Williams was a cocky stringbean of a kid when he reported to camp. He hailed the veterans as "Sport," and when one player replied with a cold stare, Ted asked, "Who's that?"

"That's Joe Cronin, the manager," he was told. But Ted says all his blustery talk really hid an inferiority complex. He denies a story that, when told, "Wait till you see Jimmie Foxx hit," Ted shot back, "Wait'll Foxx sees *me* hit."

The other players sneered at the fresh busher. The erudite coach, Moe Berg, who spoke seven languages but, they said, couldn't hit in any of them, was riding Ted. "So you're the agitator?" Williams retorted and called Berg "Adge" for short thereafter. The players called Ted "California," a place that all of them apparently considered hilarious. He rewarded them by taking the bait and shouting back insults about their states.

Boston had a solid outfield from the year before—Joe Vosmik (.325 at St. Louis), Ben Chapman (.307), and Doc Cramer (.305). Chapman for one was one of baseball's most abrasive bench jockeys; indeed, he later became famous for giving Jackie Robinson a murderous needling, and slipped a barb into Ted's thin skin whenever he could.

Meanwhile, the Boston front office decided the kid needed more polishing and shipped him to Minneapolis. So Ted— "bitter," "rebellious," and "pugnacious," in the words of writer Bill Cunningham—stood outside the team hotel waiting for the bus to take him to the Minneapolis camp as Vosmik, Cramer, and Chapman walked by. "Heh, California," they jeered, "going somewhere?" Williams' answer has been variously reported, but he apparently said in effect, "I'll be back, and some day I'll make more money than the three of you put together."

Williams may have been disappointed that the Red Sox sent him down to Minneapolis, but it actually may have been lucky for the batting coach at Minneapolis that spring was none other than Rogers Hornsby himself. "Hornsby knew everything about hitting," Ted says. "He never once told me about the mechanics, about the swing, about hands, or the angle of the bat, or anything like that. Nothing." But Rog did give the kid "the single best advice I ever got—'get a good ball to hit.'"

When Williams was criticized in future years for refusing to swing at a ball an inch out of the strike zone, even if his team needed the long ball badly, Hornsby should probably have taken the blame. On the other hand, he may deserve the credit for Ted's .406 year three years after leaving Minneapolis.

Williams' mood soon changed, and he was "tickled to death" to be with the Millers, Dick Hackenberger of the Minneapolis *Star* wrote. He "talked a blue streak" and wanted to know all about duck hunting in Minnesota.

In spite of Hornsby's help, however, Williams got off to a bad start in 1938. He came to bat his first 12 times without a

Nicollet Park Minneapolis *Minnesota*
*Historical Society*

hit (the Millers lost all three games), and when he heard a
train roar past the park, he growled that "that's what I want
to be, an engineer." Three days later, in Louisville's huge Park-
way Field (512 feet to center), Minneapolis baseball historian
Stew Thornley reports, Ted walloped a 425-foot drive to right
for an inside-the-park home run. Then he smashed another
one 500 feet and ran it home as well. "Heh, this league's a
cinch," he beamed.

When he got his first look at Minneapolis' Nicollet Park,
Ted must have leaped with joy to discover one of the shortest
right-field walls in organized baseball, only 278 feet from
home down the line, 328 in the "power" alley. However, the
fence reared 46 feet above the field. Five years earlier Joe
Hauser had smashed 47 balls over it on his way to 69 that
season, Thornley says. The fence helped Williams a little: He

hit 24 homers over it, two of them landing on rooftops a block beyond the park. But he also hit 19 away from home for a total of 43.

The Minneapolis manager, Donie Bush, was a kindly old-timer who had played with Ty Cobb; he was the perfect man to handle Ted, who called him "a lovable little tiger." Williams' new roommate, pitcher Broadway Charley Wagner (the two rookies were both W's alphabetically), says Bush was "a great artist," who let the kid have the reins "and the rope he needed. Didn't put any pressure on him."

After one hitless drought, Williams stomped into the club-house and began tearing it up. Bush gently suggested he go outside and tear a few seats out of the grandstand instead. Ted meekly apologized.

In August, Thornley reports, Williams struck out and tossed the bat as high as the grandstand roof. Then he stalked into the dugout and smashed the water cooler to smithereens with one punch. "It's all in the wrists," he bragged to reporter Halsey Hall. But 16 years later an older Williams realized that the petulant stunt "almost ended my career. Luckily no ligaments or arteries were cut, but he would carry the scars for the rest of his life.

Williams "had his little moods," Wagner smiles, but he got out of them rapidly. Actually, Ted listened to his managers "pretty well," both in Minneapolis and later Boston. "He didn't argue with them, let the manager have his say. He never had a 'splash-in' with a manager. Ted got along with everybody."

Williams likes to tell the story of hitting a double. Bush, in the coaching box, kept chattering to him to be careful, not to take too big a lead. "Don't worry, Skip," Ted called back. "I got here by myself, and I can get home by myself."

"I never had any trouble with Ted," Donie said later. "He was just a kid." And anyway, "you want a lot of fight in your ballplayer."

Williams also liked Bush but admits now that "I didn't listen to him enough."

Ted's exuberance overflowed on the field. He would gallop after fly balls, slapping his rump and crying, "Hiyo, Silver!"

But when Bush looked out to left field and saw Williams with his fists on top of each other, taking practice swings instead of watching the batter, he rolled his eyes upward and "gave up," he said. However, he hastily agreed with Eddie Collins that there was only one man in history with a swing like that—Shoeless Joe Jackson.

"It was a picture swing," says Wagner, later the top scout for the Red Sox. "You don't have to be prejudiced about it: He stopped everyone in the ball park, just with his swing. When he went to bat in batting practice, the whole park got silent as a church. Beautiful swing. A classic swing. Nobody's had it since." And Ted had "so much bump in his bat." He could really crack it. He just enjoyed hitting. Hitting was just a priority in his mind all the time." Ted used to keep Wagner awake nights swinging a bat in front of the mirror.

(Bobby Feller, two months younger than Ted but already in his third year in the majors, also drove his roommate, Roy Hughes of Cleveland, crazy practicing late into the night. Wearing an old-fashioned pullover nightshirt, Bobby threw pitch after pitch into the pillow—plop, plop, plop. "I couldn't hardly go to sleep," Roy laughs.)

Ted was also a physical fitness nut. He was sensitive about his skinny arms and legs, which may be why he wore his baseball pants down almost to his ankles. He was especially envious after seeing Foxx' biceps bulging beneath his short sleeves and hearing the rifle-like "Kee-rack!" of Jimmie's hits. "Mine didn't sound nearly as loud," Ted said wistfully. So he began to build himself up. He took to squeezing a rubber ball wherever he drove or walked. He did push-ups. Then he did finger-tip push-ups. Then finger-tip push-ups

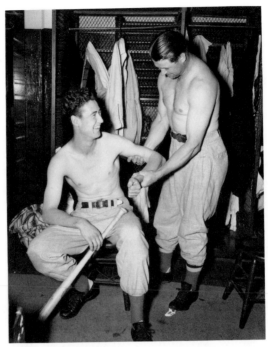

With Jimmie Foxx *UPI/Bettmann*

with his feet on a chair. (Try it.) By the time he got back to the Red Sox he could stand in the middle of the dressing room and challenge anyone to do push-ups with him, including Foxx.

"Ted built up his forearms to tremendous strength, from the tip of his middle finger to his elbow," says shortstop/broadcaster Buddy Blattner, who played against Williams in '38 and received many a lift after the game in Ted's big red Buick.

Reports of Williams' phenomenal eyesight were exaggerated, Ted said. In fact, his brother had hit him in one eye with a walnut, and he never did have full vision. But his hand-eye coordination was super-human. Blattner was a world-class table tennis player and proud of his own coordination. He and Williams joined the Marine Air Corps in 1942. "They'd put you in a chair," Blattner says. Have to keep your hands on your knees. All around were lights. As they put the lights on, you'd have to take your hand from your knee and touch that light cylinder, go faster and faster. Hell, Ted came in and established records that nobody will ever break."

And he liked to talk baseball, adds Blattner, who later teamed with another loquacious partner, Dizzy Dean, on the NBC Game of the Week telecasts in the 1950s. Ted talked velocity, angles—"almost a trigonometry lesson."

Williams liked to talk to everyone at bat, Blattner says. He listened to everybody in the opposing dugout, answered them, laughed, and suddenly realized there were now two strikes against him. "Then he'd dig in."

Ted's liners left the bat with vicious top-spin; apparently he was turning his wrists, hitting over the top of the ball. "If he hits a line-drive over your head," the veterans told Blattner, "pull in your butt, because he hits those sinkers."

Ted led the league in most everything in Minneapolis. In addition to homers, he was tops in batting, .366, and RBI, 142.

The Red Sox figured he was ready to play in the major leagues.

## The Red Sox
## 1939–1940

*1939*

◆

Russia invaded Finland, and the adults gathered worriedly around the radio for President Roosevelt's fireside chats. With his patrician diction, he, along with Churchill, was surely the greatest communicator of this century. Not even John Kennedy or Ronald Reagan could galvanize us with their voices as those two did.

Kate Smith was already making "God Bless America" our second national anthem. In Sunday school we increasingly sang "Onward, Christian Soldiers" and "Stand Up, Stand Up for Jesus." The last two have since been purged from the hymnal as too militaristic, though if we ever get into a World War III, I imagine they'll make a comeback.

I was publishing a neighborhood newspaper reproduced on a gelatin pad and carrying civic news supplied by my mother. We distributed it free and advertised the local movies, and my pay was free passes from the theater managers.

My father taught Sunday school, and his classes were always well attended because he discussed the lesson for 15 minutes then let us talk about anything we wanted to for the last 15 minutes; that usually meant movies or baseball.

The big movies were *Gone With the Wind* (we gasped when Clark Gable said "damn") and *Ninotchka* with Greta Garbo. But my favorites were *Gunga Din* with Cary Grant and Gary Cooper, *Destry Rides Again* with James Stewart, *Jesse James* with Tyrone Power and Henry Fonda, and, best of all, the World War I flying adventure, *Dawn Patrol*, with Errol

Flynn and David Niven; we liked it best because there weren't any girls in it. Kissing scenes were always greeted with groans on Saturday afternoon.

I was also a bookworm and devoured Tom Swift books in the library (Tom never "said" things, he "ejaculated") until I discovered Lester Chadwick's "Baseball Joe" series. I still have one dog-eared copy in my study.

On radio we loved "The Aldrich Family" ("Hen-*ry*! Hen-ry Aldrich!"... "Coming, Mother"). Bill Stern had a radio sports show of "strange and fantastic stories . . . some legend, some hearsay . . . but all so interesting." Glenn Miller's music was everywhere ("In the Mood," "Little Brown Jug"), Artie Shaw played "Frenesi," and Harry James, "Ciribiribin." The cheerful bellboy, "Johnny," sold cigarettes on the radio with his "Caaaaall for Philip Mooooooorris." An auctioneer's rapid chant sold Lucky Strikes, and the punch line, "Sold to American," became a figure of speech. So did another Luckies' radio slogan, "So round, so firm, so fully packed," usually repeated by older boys with a wink and a leer that I didn't understand.

Radio and World War II had not yet homogenized our speech, and people still talked differently. New Englanders said "ayeh," "Bahston," "pok ya caa in Hahvahd Yahd," "hoss," and "pust office," and drank "tonic" instead of Coke or soda, and "frappes" instead of milk shakes. New Yorkers really did say "New Yawk," Lawn-Guylan'," "Toi Daavenya" instead of Third Avenue, "dem Bums," and "yuzzle hafta" instead of "you'll have to." One Brooklyn fan, informing Dodger manager Burleigh Grimes that pitcher Waite Hoyt was injured, called: "Heh, Boily, Hert's hoit."

Ben Chapman had hit .340 in 1938, third highest in the league. But the Red Sox were so sure of their rookie in Minneapolis that over the winter they traded Chapman to Cleveland. Thus Ted Williams reported to the Sox in the spring, bearing a heavy sign around his neck as "best rookie of 1939"

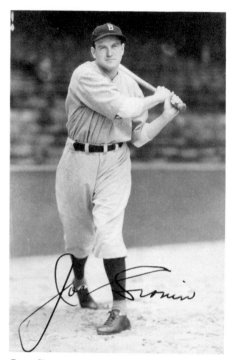

Joe Cronin *Author's Collection*

and "the second DiMaggio," at a salary of $4,500 a year (the Sox announced it at the time as $3,000).

Again Ted was lucky to have a manager, Cronin, who knew how to handle him. Joe, 32 in 1939, wore #4, possibly because he was batting clean-up the day uniform numbers were first assigned on the Red Sox—numbers were a relatively recent innovation. A shortstop, he was one of the last of the playing managers—the game has become much too complex to do that any more—and in 1933 as a 26-year old "boy wonder," had managed the Senators to the last pennant they ever won.

Joe married his boss, Clark Griffith's, daughter, and in 1935 his father-in-law sold him to Boston's new millionaire owner, Tom Yawkey, for a record quarter of a million dollars. In 1938 he hit .325 with 51 doubles off the Fenway Wall and brought the Red Sox in second to the Yankees. In '39 he would hit .308 and bring them in second again.

"Cronin was great for Ted," says Wagner, who also got promoted to Boston. "He was a delightful guy to play for. He and Bush both gave Ted room."

"I don't care if you don't make a single hit during spring training," Joe told the Kid. "All I want you to do is pay attention to business here. [Leo Durocher would later tell the young Willie Mays the same thing.] You've got it in you to be a hell of a player, so just don't get discouraged if things don't always go the way you want them to."

Comments Ted: "It was wonderful advice, even if I couldn't always manage to follow it."

In an exhibition game at Atlanta, fans warned Ted away from the wall on a long fly. The ball fell short of the fence, and Williams, in disgust, picked it up and heaved it over the fence. Cronin promptly pulled him off the field. One version of the story is that Cronin threatened to fine Williams $50 for every ball he threw over the wall. "OK," Ted supposedly countered, "if you give me $50 for every one I hit over."

"Right then and there," Joe said, "I talked to him as a brother. And from then on I told everybody on the club not to treat him like a clown."

Two more times Ted says he got in Joe's doghouse, "and each time it was my fault." He received a fine the first time, and was benched the second. "The fine was easier to take."

"Joe understood me better than anyone else," a mellower Williams later remembered. "He realized I didn't mean any harm with my pop-off tactics."

Cronin assigned Doc Cramer, an excellent outfielder, to teach the Kid a few pointers. While another player hit fungoes, Cramer watched Ted field. "He'd miss one, catch one, miss one," Doc remembered. "Ah, hell, Doc," Ted said, "they don't pay off on me catching these balls. They're gonna pay me to hit."

"Well," replied Cramer dryly, "I can see that."

The biggest stars on the Sox were Jimmie Foxx and Lefty Grove, the heroes of the Philadelphia A's 1929–31 dynasty, who had joined the Sox as part of Yawkey's campaign to buy a pennant.

Ted loved Jimmie, who was second only to Ruth as a home-run hitter—he had walloped 58 of them in 1932. Known as "Double-X," Jimmie wore a cheerful smile on his face and, on his back, a big #3, which stands for first base if you're scoring the game. (For decades all Boston first basemen wore #3 and all third basemen #5.)

In '38 Jimmie, aged 31, powered 50 home runs over the Fenway wall and drove 175 runners across the plate. That gave him 429 homers lifetime, third highest of all time, behind Ruth and Lou Gehrig. In 1939 he slugged 35 more with a .360 batting average. The next year he would hit another 36 to pass Gehrig and would remain in second place until 1966, when Willie Mays passed him.

Williams' eyes popped at Foxx' rippling biceps—Jimmie could wrap his hands around a man's ankles and lift him into the air—and Ted vowed to have muscles like that himself one day.

Jimmie's only weakness was alcohol, which ended his career at the age of 38. I met him a decade later when he was playing a pickup game on the Washington Monument grounds. He was down on his luck, living off a stipend from the Red Sox, his baseball earnings having gone to picking up

**Jimmie Foxx** *Author's Collection*

too many drink tabs for his friends. He would die in 1967, choking on a piece of meat in a restaurant.

In personality, Grove was the opposite of Foxx. Lefty was dour and temperamental, a hard loser.

Lefty didn't even get to the big leagues until he was 25, because there was no major league draft in those days and his minor league club, the Baltimore Orioles, refused to sell him. Otherwise, his 300 lifetime wins would have been considerably higher. The A's finally bought him for a record price, $100,600, or $600 more than the Yankees had paid for Babe Ruth.

Grove's fastball was compared to Walter Johnson's, and he led the league in strikeouts his first seven years in the

Lefty Grove and Lefty Gomez *Boston Red Sox*

league. Although his highest total was only 209, it was an age when hitters struck out about half as often as they do today.

Lefty also led the league in ERA nine times in the highest scoring era in baseball history. His best mark, 2.06, came in 1931, when the AL average was 4.38.

That year, 1931 he was 31–4 — and almost tore apart the dressing room after one of his four losses, 1–0.

Grove had come to Boston with Foxx in 1934 after 24 wins at Philadelphia As soon as he got to Boston he developed a sore arm. Here he was, a sore-armed 35 year-old with no more fast-ball on a second-division team—a left-hander in Fenway, the graveyard of left-handers—his career apparently at an end.

So, with the help of catcher Rick Ferrell, Grove learned a curve, won 20 games in 1935, and embarked on a second great career.

In 1938 Lefty posted a 14−4 record. In '39 he would be even better— 15−4, tops in winning percentage, and again tops in ERA.

The last time I saw Grove was at Cooperstown, sitting regally erect in the lobby of the O-Ta-Sa-Ga Hotel, puffing on a cigar. If he had come along 20 years earlier or later, when batting averages were much lower and strikeouts much higher, he would have posted numbers that would have confirmed what I believe he was, the best pitcher in the history of the game.

This was the club of aging super stars into which the 20-year-old Williams walked in 1939.

One key to the Red Sox' future was Doerr, who hit .318 in 1939 with 12 home runs—"warning-track power," he would smile deprecatingly years later at Cooperstown, when his coal-black hair had turned to white.

I still remember Bobby wearing uniform #1, with his thin lips, jutting jaw bones, his bat pulled back, head hunched forward, with the widest stance I've ever seen—his feet must have been four feet apart.

He's among the leaders in home runs by second basemen, and if he hadn't retired at the age of 33 with a bad back, he might have topped Rogers Hornsby's 307. He was especially tough on Bob Feller and Hal Newhouser, I remember. In fact, if it hadn't been for Doerr, Feller would have pitched five no-hitters, not three. Bobby broke up two of them, thanks to advice from Cronin to swing only at fastballs in his "hitting zone."

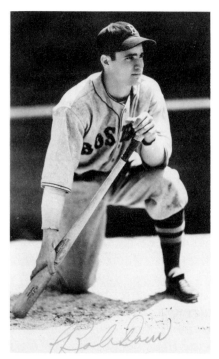

Bobby Doerr *Author's Collection*

Doerr was also the best clutch-hitter I ever saw. He topped even Williams as the most valuable hitter in the pennant-winning year of 1946. In the ill-fated World Series that year, after Enos Slaughter had put the Cards ahead with his famous dash, Bobby smacked a single to open the ninth and advanced to third, where he watched the Sox' last hope die at bat.

He was an ideal man to follow Williams, and in later years he batted clean-up for that very reason. Probably hundreds of the runs Ted scored were batted in by Bob, and without him kneeling on deck, Williams would have walked even more than he did.

But it was in the field that Doerr was at his best, setting records for errorless games and double plays. Yet I never saw

Bobby make a great catch. Great plays, yes; great catches, never. His rival and hunting buddy from Oregon, Joe "Flash" Gordon of the Yankees, was forever racing all over the infield after grounders, spearing some with sensational catches, letting other, easy two-hoppers bounce off his chest—he was always among the league leaders in errors. I never saw Doerr dive for a ball. As the old Negro league shortstop Willie Wells once told me, "If you ever saw me dive for a ball, you know I misjudged it." But if a grounder was hit through the box, there was Bobby, miraculously behind second, waiting to cut it off. A hard shot into the hole toward right, and Doerr magically appeared again right in front of the ball to throw the batter out. He had been there all the time. "It was a smaller league then," he says modestly; "it was easier to learn the hitters."

Bobby was also "a brilliant thinker on the field," Williams would say. "And he could spot what I was doing wrong when I got in a slump better than anyone else." He was also probably Ted's best friend.

Williams was what the players called a "loner." On a road trip, after the game Bob would say, "Come on, let's take a walk." At every town the two would walk miles through the streets. "What the hell," says Ted, "I hadn't traveled much, and I was excited to see Philadelphia, Cleveland, Detroit, St. Louis. I used to walk, walk, walk. Why Bobby Doerr—there's a beautiful guy, that Bobby Doerr—we'd go into a town and we'd start walking. Now you don't *dare* walk in some of these goddam towns. Jesus, some damn joke! It's a damn *joke*! We used to walk. Christ, we'd walk maybe two and a half miles, come on back; we'd walk four-five miles easy. Just walk, walk, walk."

Bob remembers their walks well. They talked fishing or stopped in for a cowboy movie. If one of the other players said, "Can I come too?" Ted would reply, "You guys go ahead." "He was that kind of fellow," Doerr says. "He liked to be by himself. Everybody understood it. He had so much pressure from the press. It made a fellow kind of crawl into a hole like."

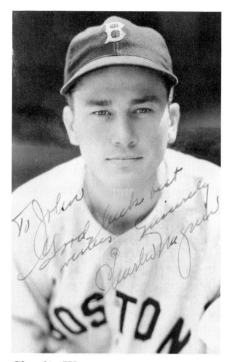

Charlie Wagner *Author's Collection*

Today Williams regrets being such a loner. "The thing you don't realize when you're playing is that, when it's all over, you kind of kick yourself in the ass that you didn't associate more with your teammates. But it wasn't a matter of you didn't like 'em, it was because you had other interests. I was a photo bug, and I wanted to learn how to tie flies, and I loved cowboy movies, and I liked to walk, and I liked to shop, and a lot of things like that. These other guys, they'd play cards."

Wagner and Williams roomed together again, and Charlie set about polishing the Kid's schoolboy image. Wagner wasn't called "Broadway Charlie" for wearing blue jeans. "I'm an old dress-hog," he admits with a grin. "The ballplayers looked better back then. You should look the part; people are looking at you constantly. I don't approve of the dress they're wearing today. No class."

And of course Ted was notorious for hating neckties ("They get in your soup"). In an age when all little boys—and adults too—had to wear a coat and tie to church or to a restaurant, I admired Ted as much for his emancipating sartorial style as for his *non-pareil* batting style—he and I must have suffered death by hanging in previous lifetimes. Williams may some day no longer be "the last of the .400 hitters," but he can never be preempted as "the first of the non-necktie wearers." Thus it was with a sense of deep disillusionment that I heard Wagner reveal that Ted actually did wear a necktie once or twice. "I've tied many a tie for him when he had to wear one." Even without a tie, however, Williams was a good dresser. "He had nice taste. And he's a good-looking man."

Ted made it a point to get back to the hotel early each night. "I don't think he ever stayed out past 12 when I roomed with him," Wagner says. Ted would talk about the next day's game and who the opposing pitcher would be. "You know what that guy's gonna do?" he would ask rhetorically. "He's gonna come inside on me." Says Wagner: "He was always psyched up for the next game."

And Ted was always swinging bats in front of the mirror. "He woke me up any number of times swinging that damn bat in the room." Williams "was a perfectionist in everything, didn't want to be second in anything. He was baseball, baseball, baseball."

(Tommy Holmes of the Braves once asked Williams, "If you had it to do all over again, what would you do different?" Ted's reply: "I'd practice twice as hard.")

The players were different back then. None of them wore mustaches, long hair, eye-black, batting gloves or helmets, form-fitting double-knits or names on their backs. They wore baggy, hot flannels with belts and buttons down the front. On their feet were steel spikes—many an infielder or catcher has been bloodied by them. Gloves were lumpy old leathers half the size of today's huge claws. Before each game the players had "pepper" games in front of the stands, one man tapping balls to four or five others a few feet in front of him; the "fielders" did tricks, throwing the ball around their shoulders, between their legs etc, to the amusement of the fans. While on deck, they swung two or three lead-weighted bats in the on-deck circle instead of using the modern "donut." There was no such thing as nautilus equipment or organized weight training.

The average player probably made $5,000-$10,000 a year, supplemented by cigarette and beer endorsements, plus barnstorming in October against Negro teams or white semi-pros. In the regular season the teams played one or two doubleheaders a week. With almost all games in the afternoon, there was plenty of time in the evening to drink or chase women. Owners put detectives on their trails and conducted bed checks. Many players were alcoholics, but none took other drugs. Most chewed tobacco, and spitting was an art. Chewing gum was considered sissy, and they would have guffawed at today's blow driers. Bench jockeying and invective were raised to a high level of excellence; it has almost disappeared today and would be considered poor sportsmanship.

In probably the biggest difference of all, the strike zone back then was from the arm pits to the knees, not, as today, from the thigh to the shoe tops. One wonders how Williams, a high-ball hitter, would have fared today. He might not have lasted one week.

Three decades later Williams would illustrate his classic book, *The Science of Hitting*, with a color photo of himself facing the pitcher and ready to stride into a pitch. Above home plate is the strike zone, from his shoulders to his knees, and filling the space are 77 colored baseballs, each labeled a different batting average. Those right down the middle belt-high are labeled .400; the low outside corner is labeled .230.

Today the umpires have ripped out the top half of Ted's strike zone and thrown it away. Only pitches below the belt are called strikes now—some umps even call strikes around the ankles. The rule book still says a ball from the belt to the letters is a strike, but the umpires say it's a ball.

This is probably the single most revolutionary change in the way the game is played since Williams' rookie season— more revolutionary than Astroturf, the DH, or the split-finger fastball. The umps, who are paid to enforce the rules, are themselves the number-one violators of the rule. Like a policeman double-parked in front of a fire hydrant, today's umpires believe the rules are for other people to obey, not for them.

That means that if Williams were playing with today's umpires, he would not get those juicy high pitches marked .380, .350, and .320 on his graphic. Instead he'd be seeing balls marked .300, .275, and .250—or even lower than that and not even on Ted's famous chart.

Most men are naturally high ball hitters, and so was Williams. "I was a *son* of a bitch of a high fastball hitter!" he says.

That's why "I always tried to keep the ball down on Ted," Cleveland pitcher Mel Harder said. "If you got it too high, he'd get under it and drive it quite a distance." If you kept the ball low, Harder said, he would hit either a sinker to the outfield or top it and drive a grounder to the infield. Other pitchers agreed that Williams hit low pitches with overspin, causing them to bend down in front of the outfielders, but he got under high pitches, imparting an underspin that made them sail over the fielders' heads and over the fences. (Yankee outfielder Tommy Henrich said he never caught a line drive by Williams. They were either low liners that sank in front of him or high liners that soared over him.)

If Williams were playing today, would he become a line-drive singles hitter? Would he even be able to hit .300?

By the same token, if Jim Palmer, a great high-ball pitcher, were a rookie today, he'd walk the first eight men he faced and be back in the minors the next day.

What the umpires have done in the last decade is to change baseball from a high-ball game into a low-ball game. They have banished from the major leagues all those athletes—I believe the majority—who naturally throw, or hit, high pitches and have replaced them with athletes who can successfully throw or hit low balls.

The Hall of Fame is essentially a pantheon of high-ball hitters and pitchers. Cooperstown would be a far different place if the old-timers had to play with the strike zone in use in the last ten years. Many a minor league failure, who couldn't hit the high ball, would probably be enshrined there, and many a plaque now on the wall belonging to a slugger who couldn't hit low balls would be missing, its owner virtually unknown to the baseball world.

The smaller strike zone should make it twice as hard to register a strikeout, thus today's inflationary strikeout totals are even more difficult to understand or excuse. Williams, who hardly ever struck out, would have whiffed even less. And his already astronomical base on balls totals might be twice as high. Would he have violated his own rule of never going outside the strike zone in order to slam the rare and tempting high pitch that got away from the hurler?

Many factors have been blamed for the death of the .400 hitter in the last half-century—night ball, jet lag, integration, bigger gloves, higher mounds, relief pitching etc., etc. But if Commissioner Fay Vincent is really interested in bringing the .400 hitter back to baseball, he might demand that the umpires enforce the legal strike zone—the same one that Babe Ruth and Ty Cobb enjoyed.

The second most revolutionary change in the game since 1939 is the emphasis on relief pitching. For a century, every team had four starters, who were the four best pitchers on the staff. Those not good enough to start were relegated to the bull pen for mop-up assignments if the starter got knocked out. The starter was expected to pitch nine innings. Some, like Lefty Grove and Bob Feller, regularly pitched relief between starts as well. In 1938 Buck Newsom had led the American league in complete games with 31 and in innings pitched with 330. In 1990 the league-leading totals were 11 and 237. To put in so much work, the old-timers had to pace themselves, bearing down only when they had to.

Today the best pitcher on the staff is often the closer, such as Dennis Eckersley. And starters are told to "throw as hard as you can as long as you can," which usually means six innings. Like a marathoner who is expected to cross the finish line without any kick left, today's starters are expected to end the sixth inning without a pitch left in their arms. If they can go seven innings, it means they weren't pitching hard enough in the first six.

Williams' first big league game came in New York on opening day, April 21, in front of 30,000 fans. It was not only the first major league contest he ever played in, it was the first one he had ever *seen*. Ted played rightfield and hit sixth in the line-up. The pitcher was the Yankees' great Red Ruffing, winningest pitcher in the league (Red had been 21–7 in '38 and would be 21–7 again in '39). "Nervous?" grinned Yankee second baseman Joe Gordon, who knew Ted from the Coast.

"Nervous as hell," Ted admitted.

In his first at bat, Williams fanned on three pitches, the last one a slow curve, as Ruffing presumably figured "the second DiMaggio" would be over-eager. Ted was fuming when Sox pitcher Jack Wilson sneered, "What do you think of the major leagues now, Bush?"

"Screw you," Ted snapped. "I *know* I can hit this guy." The next time up Ted lifted a 400-foot drive to the right-centerfield wall for a double.

The third time, Ruffing pulled the string, getting Williams on another slow curve strikeout. Finally, Ted popped to Gordon, as the Red Sox lost 2–0.

Also that day the dying Lou Gehrig muffed an easy play at first, hit into two double plays, and lined out to Williams in right. It's the only time the two future Hall of Famers ever played together.

The next day, April 22, Williams got his first look at Fenway Park, which would be his home for 21 years. It was a different field then from what it is today. First of all, there was no familiar Green Monster in left. The wall was there, but it was not green, it was covered with advertising signs for Lifebuoy soap and Calvert whiskey. The stands were single-decked. Centerfield was not roped off to give the hitters a better look at the pitch; instead, customers lounged out there in white shirts all summer. Most important, from Ted's point of view, was rightfield. A tough park for a left-hander even now, Fenway was even tougher in 1939. The rightfield foul line was 332 feet away, compared to the present 301 feet. And the bullpen was not there yet, so one had to hit the ball 402 feet, into the present rightfield stands, for a home run, compared to a 380-foot drive into the bullpen today. In the game that afternoon Philadelphia held Ted to one single in five at bats.

Ted did better the next day, Saturday, with a double and single in four trips. He scored one run and knocked in another as the Sox won 4–2.

Finally, on Sunday Williams ripped his first major league home run against Philadelphia's right-hander Luther "Bud" Thomas, who went on to a 7–1 record for the year. Thomas

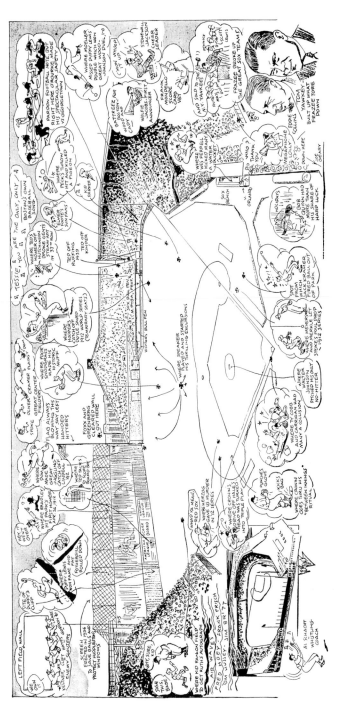

Fenway Park *Boston Globe*

was a dairy farmer in southern Virginia when I asked him about the game. He remembered the game and even the pitch—a change-up. "I got the ball inside on him. He pulled it hard."

The ball streaked on a line and thudded 430 feet away in the space between the grandstand and bleachers. Only half a dozen balls had ever been hit into that area before, one of them by Gehrig. One reporter said it was going as fast when it landed as it had when it left the bat.

After that, Thomas said, "Mr Mack (A's manager) told us to make him hit the ball to the opposite field, don't let him pull it."

In his next time up Williams faced Cotton Pippen, the man who had struck him out on three called strikes three years earlier in his first professional game. A 28-year-old rookie, Pippen would be 4–12 that year. This time Ted rifled Pippen's pitch high off the left-centerfield wall, missing another home run by inches. Then he lined a "wicked" single to right.

Lefty Eddie Smith (10–11 on the year) came in and served up another single. Finally Roy "Tarzan" Parmelee (1–6) got him on a long drive into the wind to left. It "nearly drove Bob Johnson through the left-field scoreboard," Gerry Moore reported in the Boston *Globe*.

Incidentally the kid also ran into short right-center to stab a Texas leaguer for the best defensive play of the game.

"His every move was the signal for an ovation," the *Herald*'s Burt Whitman wrote. With the game already lost, the fans stayed in their seats just to see Williams' last at bat, and as soon as Johnson made the catch, they rushed for the exits. Whitman hadn't seen them do that since Babe Ruth retired.

The next morning Wheaties was ready with an ad depicting Ted hitting and eating breakfast.

## WATCH THIS BOY WILLIAMS

it said.

Ted got his chance to face Ruffing again on Memorial Day in Boston before a turn-away crowd of 35,000 — the last ticket was snatched up at 9:15 that morning. "Red gave me that little extra (effort)," Ted would recall, "and I gave him that little extra. Oh boy, did I hit it! I never hit one harder."

The ball landed 20 rows up in the same sector as his first homer, about 500 feet unimpeded, Whitman estimated. He called it "deeper than anything we ever saw Babe Ruth hit that way." Moore called it the longest *ever* hit in "Yawkey Yard" and hailed "the gangling, intensely popular rookie . . . the incomparable Titanic Ted."

Then in the second game, Williams hit another, making four times in his last five games he had conquered the 400-foot barrier in right.

In Detroit, Briggs (now Tiger) Stadium was sporting a new roof over the second deck in right field 94 feet above the field and 318 feet from home. As Ted stepped in against right-hander Bob Harris (4–13), Boston pitcher Jim Bagby tried to wave Hank Greenberg, the Tiger first baseman, to play deeper and save himself a possible crippling injury. Greenberg ignored him, and Williams unloaded one far over Hank's head into the stands. "I hope that guy is still pitching the next time I come up," Ted told catcher Rudy York as he crossed home plate. "I'll knock it clear over the roof."

The next time up the count ran to 3–0. "You're not hitting, are you, Kid?" York asked.

"Yes, I am," Ted answered. A fat "cripple" came in, and Ted smashed it into the upper deck, foul. "I'm still hitting," he warned York, then blasted the next pitch over the new roof, the first man ever to do it. In fact, it wouldn't be done again for

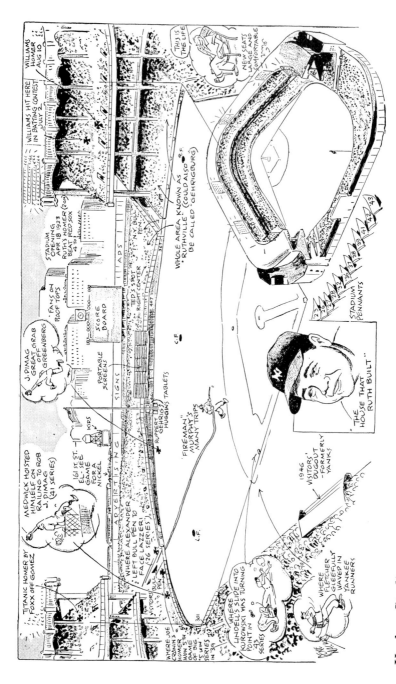

Yankee Stadium *Boston Globe*

18 years, until Mickey Mantle in 1957. As Ted rounded first, Greenberg was still gaping at the spot where the ball had disappeared. As Ted passed third, Billy Rogell asked, "What the hell you been eating, Kid?"

As he touched home, York welcomed him: "You weren't kidding, Kid, were you?"

Did Ted tip his cap? It isn't reported, but he says he tipped it a lot that wonderful rookie year.

In Yankee Stadium later that year, Tommy Henrich caught Ted eyeing the rightfield roof, about 22 feet higher than Detroit's and about 50 feet deeper. Not even Babe Ruth had ever reached it.

"Forget it, Ted," Tom said, reading the Kid's mind, "it's too far." In batting practice that day, Henrich said, Williams pumped one deep into the third deck, though still shy of the roof.

Eight years later, fan Peter Salmon wrote in *Baseball Digest,* he saw Williams drill one to the facing. Mantle, of course, has done it at least once—home run historian Mark Gallagher says Mickey even cleared the roof in batting practice—and Frank Howard may have cleared the left-field roof, though he literally hit it out of sight on a foggy night.

But trouble was brewing for Williams. Ted had a temper, and it soon got him into trouble with the writers.

"A sports writer in Boston, Bill Cunningham, started all that," Boston pitcher Eldon Auker says. An ex-football star from Dartmouth, for 20 years Bill had been the dean of the Boston press corps, with a host of loyal readers. "He was also a pretty heavy drinker. Ted despised the ground Cunningham walked on. Here was a young kid, his father an alcoholic, his brother an alcoholic. Ted was dedicated to being successful. It was quite a gap between a high school star and the dean of the sports staff."

Cunningham was in his cups one day when he approached Ted for an interview. "I'd rather wait until you sober up," the kid replied. "Bill Cunningham could be the nicest guy in the world," he recalled years later. "A hell of a football player, hell of a writer, hell of a reputation, out of Dartmouth, all the rest of it. And he didn't mean shit to me."

That was the opening shot in a war which would continue for years. "One of them had to give," says Auker. "Neither one would, because they were both proud. It was a complete stalemate. We watched it all the time; all year long it went on. It was a constant feud."

Other writers joined in. "They had a couple of vicious son of a bitches on the Hearst papers in Boston, Austen Lake and ('Colonel' Dave) Egan," Ted says bitterly. "They'd write one beautiful article, that you were absolutely the greatest thing in baseball, and then they'd write ten that would tear you down. Jesus Christ!"

Ted almost slugged Hy Hurwitz of the *Globe*. Melville Webb of the *Globe* was another foe: "A grouchy kind of a guy, a real grump." Eight years later Webb would get his ultimate revenge on Ted, the Triple Crown winner, by leaving him off his MVP ballot entirely, thus throwing the election to DiMaggio by a single point, though Ted outhit Joe by 12 homers and almost 30 points.

Williams made enemies among the New York press too. Dick Young, Bill Corum, and Dan Daniel were on his "list," along with Joe Williams of the *Daily Telegram*: "Fake, big talker, pompous. First day I immediately disliked him. And I wasn't diplomatic enough to smart it."

Williams did have friends in the press box too. In Boston they included Arthur Sampson of the *Herald*, Edd Rumill of the *Christian Science Monitor*, and Burt Whitman of the *Globe*. New York writers in his corner were Grantland Rice, Frank Graham, Red Smith, and Arthur Daley. Daley, of the *Times*, considered Ted "the most fascinating personality in sports."

"Only a few writers were unfriendly," Wagner says. "He gave them hell all the time. They gave him hell. He was his own man, he wanted to do what he wanted to do. No one was going to shake his tree."

The fans took their cues from the writers, especially those sitting in the left-field stands at Fenway, who were almost on top of the left fielder, which was Ted's position after 1939. "It was like a menagerie of rabid fans," Auker said, "and Cunningham was feeding them the kind of stuff they wanted. Anything Ted would do wrong, Cunningham would magnify it."

The atmosphere in a park was different then than it is now. Except for Sundays, crowds were small, sometimes 5,000–6,000 people or less, compared to over 25,000 on an average week night nowadays. There was less crowd "buzz," and voices carried better. Several stentorian fans were famous, such as Hilda Chester in Brooklyn. Boston had plenty, too.

And Ted acknowledges that he had "the best pair of rabbit ears ever developed." He heard every insult. "He got all steamed up," says pitcher Eldon Auker, who came to the Sox in the Chapman deal. "He had a temper. A very competitive spirit and a very competitive temper. When these guys would get on him and he'd read these stories, he'd just swim upstream. When he turned around and thumbed his nose, you could understand why. He didn't want to hurt the fans or the game itself. It was a very personal thing for him. He was trying to make a living, and here was a guy trying to make it tough for him to make a living. When you're doing your best and wake up one morning and read things you never dreamed of, and then have a thousand people yelling at you and calling you a dirty bum, it wasn't easy." One day he tried to skull a loud-mouthed fan with a foul ball but mis-timed his swing and had to settle for a double down the line instead.

Williams feels the Red Sox management should have protected him, a 20-year old rookie, from what he contemptuously called "the knights of the keyboard." "Cronin had to put me in my place a few times, and he was absolutely right. I guess I needed a kick in the pants now and then."

The fault did not lie entirely with the writers. Bernie Kamenske, who covered the Red Sox for the Associate Press in the 1950s, made the mistake of going into the clubhouse when Williams was in a bad mood. According to Kamenske, Ted roared, "Get that kike out of here!" while grabbing a bench and wielding it like a bat.

"He has the foulest mouth and the kindest heart of anyone I've ever known," Williams' companion, Louise Kaufman, says gently. He can be nasty to a friend trying to do a kindness for him, then turn around and give his heart to a beggar on the highway, she says.

"He was a very soft-hearted guy," says Auker. "He was like Babe Ruth with kids, visited hospitals. Later he worked his heart out on the Jimmy Fund (for children with cancer). He was the instrumental individual in building that up. In any city he went to, whenever he was asked to visit the underprivileged, he never refused. This was the side of him you don't read about."

Ted says modestly that his role in the Jimmy Fund has been exaggerated. But he did attend the first fund-raising dinner, along with a young comedian "and a couple of wrestlers." Ted got interested and got the Red Sox interested, and it became his favorite charity.

Ted's image in the press was "moody" and that's how most fans knew him, Buddy Blattner said. Actually, Williams was a "very, very likeable outgoing guy" in the right setting, such as having a beer in Boston's Kenmore Hotel bar. Even a simple beer was hard to enjoy, though, as a parade of fans kept stopping for autographs. Ted was gracious, Buddy says, even though at times the fans became "a little bit boisterous."

The Boston writers themselves once took a poll to name the Red Sox player they deemed least cooperative, least friendly, most temperamental, most generous, and most helpful. Williams finished first in every category.

Ted himself considered Grove the most temperamental Red Socker. He threw tantrums and punched lockers after a losing game. But, Ted noted, Lefty always hit the lockers with his right hand. "He was a careful tantrum thrower." There is a lesson there. Grove directed his temper at the other players, Williams at the writers. The writers forgave Lefty but pilloried Ted.

Jim Thorpe, the great Indian athlete, later came to Ted to try to help. "Cripe, try to ease up on these guys," Thorpe advised. "Don't get on 'em." "Dear old Jim Thorpe," Ted, older and mellower, muses, "a hell of a nice man." Today Williams admits objectively that "I deserved some of what I got. I was lackadaisical in the outfield."

In later years pitcher Steve Carlton refused to say anything at all to the press, and justified it by reminding the writers what had happened to Williams. If he could talk to Carlton, Ted says he would say, "My God, you gotta just switch it a little bit. You're deserving of every good thing they can say about you. Don't let 'em worry you; give 'em a little 'hello' line."

It's too bad Ted didn't play in New York, with its short right-field fence and its rah-rah press corps, Auker said. If he had, some believe, he might have been deified as a new Ruth. Gehrig had retired. DiMaggio had no color at all. New York writers did their best to make Joe's very lack of personality into a virtue, writing such things as "he had ice water in his veins," which, translated, meant DiMaggio never smiled or showed any emotion or said anything quotable.

The original New York demigod, Babe Ruth enjoys the image, preserved by historians, as a loveable back-slapper. But he had a darker side as well. Leafing through old newspapers one day, I came across this headline in 1922:

**Ruth Throws Dirt in Umpire's Face and Invades Grandstand**
**Home Run Champ Puts**
**On Storm When Official**
**Calls Him Out at Second**

That same year Ruth had been involved in a fist fight on the bench with Yankee first baseman Wally Pipp. Later he demanded manager Miller Huggins' job and once held Hug by his heels over the rear platform of a moving train. Even at his worst, Williams' conduct was positively Chesterfieldian when compared to the Babe's.

Ruth "couldn't say three sentences with a little class to them," Ted observes. Yet—here Williams reaches for a book to quote—Ruth was "baseball's most important player and most enduring personality."

Cronin took the Kid to dinner one evening and imparted another nugget of fatherly advice: "Ted, you're a great ball player, and you're with a great team. But you'll never be as famous in Boston as you would be in New York. Just remember that, and you'll understand a lot of things."

Williams thinks if Jimmie Foxx—"what a sweet, lovable guy he was" —had played in New York, he might have challenged the Ruth legend. "I never regretted I didn't play in New York. *But* for sure—for sure—the thing of it is, you do get the recognition there that you don't get any other place. Ty Cobb always felt like he'd been neglected just a little bit. He was a great player in Detroit. But"—Ted pauses, tilts his head and clicks his tongue—"Detroit ain't New York."

New York writers wouldn't say anything bad about a Yankee. Boston was very different. "The New York players couldn't do one thing wrong. But Boston was seeking every fucking little thing they could try, to keep things stirred up. Because they had 15 little towns around Boston, and they all had a sports writer, and they were all trying to get their names in the paper."

But the Ted Williams whom one read about in the newspapers was not the Ted Williams whom the other players, both in Boston and around the league, knew. I have never heard, or heard of, another player who had a harsh word for Williams, except for Harlond Clift, the St. Louis Browns' third baseman. "I didn't like him, no one liked him," Clift says firmly. "He wasn't a ballplayers' ballplayer." Just what the core of the problem may have been, Clift doesn't say.

There was one other class of players who didn't approve of Ted: the Red Sox pitchers, who objected to his giving free batting tips to opposing hitters. "He was a hell of a nice guy," insists Ken Keltner, the Cleveland third baseman. "He helped everybody as far as hitting. If we were doing something wrong, he'd let us know the next day."

The Kid was "one of the hardest working players on the club," Auker says. "He was young, very dedicated to the game—I never saw a man so dedicated. Always asking questions about the opposing pitchers. He'd watch a pitcher for a while, then say, 'Look, you know he started the last seven hitters off with a curve.' No one else had noticed it. But he was watching every move the man was making.

"All the boys liked him on the club. He was 100 percent a team man. He wanted to win the ball game. He'd get his hits, but he wanted to win the game."

Auker insists that Ted was "one of the nicest persons I ever met in baseball. A young boy, full of life. Didn't realize how much ability he had. A pure, clean-living young kid." The older guys called him "the Kid," a name hung on him by Johnny Orlando, the clubhouse man.

Was he as temperamental as they said? I asked Doc Cramer. "No, Teddy was a good boy" Doc replied. "He was all right. Had a little trouble with the sport writers, but I guess everybody did. He believed in his own ability, he knew what he could do. I liked Teddy a lot. He turned out to be a good ballplayer all around."

Ted was a good roommate, says Wagner. "I truly enjoyed living with him. He was a hell of a guy. A delightful guy. I don't think he ever talks about himself in the first person: 'Jeez, didn't we have a great day! Jeez, that was a fun day!' Even to this day he never talks about 'I.' That's why it's so nice to be around him; he never 'I's' himself." Adds Charley: "I don't think Ted ever talked about another ball player badly in our room. Never. Ever. If he doesn't like a guy, he doesn't speak of him."

Williams is proud of the fact that he was never involved in a baseball fight and never thrown out of a game.

Did the fans ride him? Some did. But I think most of them liked the guy. After all, he was the one most of them had paid to see.

Having grown up in New Jersey, well inside the Yankee propaganda orbit, I too got my information and impressions of Williams initially from the New York media—and from all the other kids who were arrogant partisans of the Yankees. Of course, at that age, being outnumbered and out-shouted only made me redouble my zealous allegiance to my beleaguered—nay, persecuted—hero. Still, I couldn't help believing all the reports that Williams was a temperamental tantrum-thrower who regularly ate writers for breakfast and chewed them up and spit them out, because that was what everyone, who presumably knew better than I, said he was.

In the meantime I have gotten to know Williams more personally, and my perception of him as a person has changed. Our first meeting was in April 1957, when I wanted to write an article about how much the war years had cost him. Surprisingly, no one had done that yet. So when the Red Sox were in town, I timorously phoned his hotel and, miraculously, was put through to his room. (I remember once reaching DiMaggio in similar circumstances and being bawled out royally for my pains.) I screwed up my courage, told Ted what I wanted, asked for 15 minutes of his time, and then waited for the blast. There was a pause. "OK, come on up," he said, and we spent a delightful two hours talking. He poured the charm on me. When the phone rang, he poured the charm on the callers too. He could banter man-talk with the men (to manager Mike Higgins: "This is Ted. . . . your left fielder.") One caller must have been female, for he switched to a seductive bedroom purr, while I pictured the poor girl on the other end melting with excitement.

(Ted, his 1942 teammate, Tony Lupien, laughs, "had a million women chasing him with mattresses strapped to their backs.")

On the other hand, some 30 years later, I was sitting in a restaurant with him and Ms. Kaufman, chatting amiably, when something set him off—neither she nor I could think what it could have been. But in a second he raised his voice angrily at us, while diners swung their heads around to watch. At that time he probably weighed almost 300 pounds and could easily have smashed each of us with one hand. She calmed him down, however, and the meal resumed as though a squall had passed.

Some people who know Williams intimately have similar stories of a dual personality. These same people add, however, that he has mellowed greatly in recent years, and that Dr. Jeckyl is slowly winning over Mr. Hyde. I wondered if he may still be working out the last vestiges of anger left over from an apparently unhappy childhood, anger which would have been much stronger half a century ago.

Probably both sides are right, those who see Williams as a boorish, foul-mouthed ogre and those who see him as a charming and giving guy. Which side you fall on may depend on which mood he was in when you first formed your impression of him—or which writer you happen to read, or believe, the most.

Players on the other clubs tried not to get him angry, saying, "Let him sleep, don't wake him up." In 1939 Auker saw Brownie right-hander Buck Newsom (20–11 that year) strike Williams out then laugh into his glove. Of course the Boston players made sure Ted saw it. "I thought he was going to go out and get him with a bat," Auker says. In his next time up, Williams whaled a home run off Newsom. "Laugh that off!" he yelled as he circled the bases.

Ted smiled when I repeated the story to him. "Naw, Buck Newsom was a good guy," he insisted. "Hell, nothing wrong with Newsom. He threw blooper pitches at me. Couldn't get 'em over. But I would let him think I was a little mad at him. Because if he got you out, he'd like to tell the world that it was the greatest thing could happen."

Williams' own version of the Auker story: Watching Newsom warm up, he decided that Buck wasn't going to be hard to hit. But facing him in a game was different. Newsom had a funny windmill windup (they don't use that any more): "arms, legs and butt all going in different directions. I nearly laughed myself to death." He also forgot to watch the ball. Ted has a theory that "style is harder to hit than stuff." It was a dark day in St. Louis, and before he knew it, Newsom had struck him out three times. Finally, Ted says, Buck got cocky, threw a "lousy curve ball," and Ted tagged it to win the game.

Williams can't help grinning. "Tell a funny story about Buck Newsom: He threw DiMaggio two curves one day; DiMaggio got two doubles. Hit 'em off low curve balls. They asked Newsom if DiMaggio had a weakness. He said, 'Yeah, a weakness for doubles.' "

After his first tour around the circuit, Ted told himself, "I don't see any blinding fastballs or exploding curves." He knew he could hit big league pitching.

By the All Star game, according to researcher Paul Doherty, Williams was hitting .306 with 12 home runs and 67 RBIs, the last number topping the league. Yet he was not picked to play in the Classic. Joe DiMaggio, hitting .420 with 38 RBI, opened at center, Doc Cramer (.331) was in right, and New York's George Selkirk (.304, 51 RBI) in left. Then, as now, reputation counted for more than performance.

The Red Sox played the first Hall of Fame game in Cooperstown that summer, baseball's supposed centennial and the first year the shrine was open, though elections had been taking place since 1936. The Kid stole away by himself into the Hall, where a writer found him wandering among the trophies. We can only imagine the thoughts that filled the rookie's head.

But Williams wasn't satisfied with his performance that year. He says he was swinging at too many high balls, and the word went around the league that that was his weakness. Marvin Breuer, who had pitched against Ted in 1937 and '38, joined the Yankees in '39 and helped spread the stories. Ted "could be pretty discouraging to pitch to, because he had such a good eye for balls and strikes," Breuer sighed many years later. "You could pitch him high and inside for a few years." When he first saw Ted in '37, he "had a pretty good 'hole' (that is, a blind spot in his swing). The next year it got smaller, the next year smaller than that. It kept getting smaller and smaller until you couldn't pitch him there at all any more."

But the pitchers were slow to appreciate that fact. They kept pitching him high, and, says Doherty, Williams averaged .345 over the second half of the season with 19 more home runs to finish at .327 and 31.

One of Williams' home runs came off lefty Thornton Lee (12-13). Twenty-one years later he would hit another, #517 of his career, off Thornton's son, Don (8–7). As Ted trotted around the bases, Don says, he grinned, "One off your old man, one off you. I'm gonna retire."

The Kid was still testy, though, and at one point snapped that he'd rather be a fireman in San Diego than a ballplayer in Boston. But Doherty, perhaps the nation's #1 authority on Williams' career, says Ted followed that with a perfect 6-for-6 in a double-header August 13, and the fireman talk was forgotten.

DiMaggio, meanwhile, went into September with a strong shot at hitting .400. At 24 years old, Joe already had three solid years in the major leagues, hitting .323, .346, and .324. In his sophomore year, 1937, he had walloped 46 home runs, a remarkable total for a right-hander in cavernous Yankee Stadium. It could have been 60 in a friendlier park such as Fenway or Detroit. Joe had played in three World Series already but had never hit a World Series home run at home—and never would.

DiMaggio came up two years after Ruth had played his last game as a Yankee. Gehrig had taken over as team leader

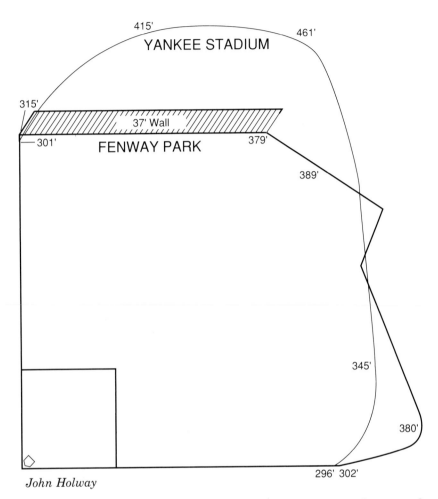

YANKEE STADIUM

415'    461'

315'

37' Wall

301'    FENWAY PARK    379'

389'

345'

380'

296' 302'

*John Holway*

in '36 and '37, hitting .354 and .351. But in '38, at the age of 35, Lou faltered, batting only .295, foreshadowing the disease that would take his life. In '39 Lou played only eight games before calling it quits.

The responsibility of team leader fell on DiMaggio. Like Lou, Joe had none of the Babe's panache, but, also like Lou, he quietly played his own steady game on the field. By September 1939 the Yanks were 12 games ahead of the second-place Red Sox, and the race was as good as over. The only thing left to see was whether Joe could maintain his .400 average.

DiMaggio was entering the three top years of a hitter's life, ages 24 through 26 —the three years, incidentally, that Williams was destined to miss.

Joe was batting .405 on the morning of September 1, the day the Nazi armies crossed the Polish frontier to mark the start of World War II.

### BRITISH, FRENCH ULTIMATUMS

the *Times* headline screamed.

### FDR WILL KEEP U.S. OUT OF WAR

That day, in huge Municipal Stadium, Cleveland Joe drove "a rousing belt" off Bob Feller (24−9) to the vast reaches of right field, good for a two-run triple. Then he singled for two more runs in the third. In the eighth he tripled against Harry Eisenstadt (6−7) for two more RBIs to win the game 11−8. DiMaggio had gotten 27 hits in his last 53 at bats (.509) to raise his average to .408. for the year.

The next day at Boston Joe went 2-for-5 with another home run against right-hander Denny Galehouse (9−10). (Ted went 3-for-5.)

On Sunday DiMaggio got three hits in four tries, one a homer, against Wagner (3−1) and Auker (9−10) to climb to .410 −Ted himself hit two homers, #23 and 24 for the year.

Meanwhile, Germany shelled Warsaw, Roosevelt appealed for neutrality, the State Department banned American travel to Europe, and Finland all but canceled the 1940 Olympics.

DiMaggio soon learned how hard it is to keep the average over .400. As Williams would himself discover two years later, "When you're up that high, Jesus, does it come down fast!" In a double-header in Philadelphia, Joe got only one hit in eight at bats to fall to .404. Two days later in New York he recovered with two hits, one of them home run #26 off Lefty Grove (15–4). The next day he went 2-for-3, including another homer, to pull himself up to .407.

On September 9 Joe, fighting a cold, went 3-for-4 against Joe Haynes (8–12 with Washington) and climbed to .409. Then disaster struck.

It was either the cold, or an eye-twitch associated with it, but DiMaggio went hitless in his next 13 at bats before singling off Feller, of all people. His average had now dropped to .397. There followed a 2-for-11 drought while Joe's average plunged to .388.

There was a second powerful enemy working against DiMaggio—Yankee Stadium. Pete Palmer's statistics in *Total Baseball* show that Joe was a .400-hitter that year when he was free of the Stadium's notorious "Death Valley." He hit .413 on the road but only .350 at home.

DiMaggio never made an excuse and never asked to be taken out of the line-up, which he could have done, since the '39 Yankees, possibly the most powerful team of all time, certainly since the '27 Yanks, had the pennant sewed up and could have spared him if he had requested it. Why he didn't is a mystery. Another mystery is the ho-hum attitude of the New York press, who noted Joe's fall only in occasional footnotes.

Meanwhile, Williams was finishing the season strong. In spite of the 400-foot target in Boston, Ted hit 31 homers, third best in baseball, topped only by Foxx (35) and Greenberg (33), both of whom hit against friendlier home targets. Williams hit 14 at home and 17 on the road, connecting in every park.

His final one came in New York on the last day of the season against Steve Sundra, a rookie right-hander with a perfect 11–0 record. The homer helped sink Sundra for his only loss of the year. It also put Williams one ahead of the slumping DiMaggio, who had faced an intimidating home park of his own and had come to bat 100 times less than Williams did.

Left-handers cut down on Williams' power: He hit only five home runs against them that year. One was a grand slam in Cleveland against Eisenstadt, one of two slams Ted hit that season and one of 17 he would hit in his career, tying him for third place with Foxx behind Lou Gehrig, 23, and Willie Mc-Covey, 18.

Fenway's fences cut down on Williams' homers, but, as Doherty points out, they did give him plenty of room for doubles, and he slugged 44 of them, second highest in the league.

Batting clean-up behind Cramer (.311), Vosmik (.276) and Foxx (.360), the Kid did something no rookie had ever done before—or since: He led the league in RBI—in fact, he led both leagues—with 145. DiMaggio was next with 126. With sluggers like Cronin (.308), Jim Tabor (.289) and Doerr (.318) hitting behind him, Ted scored 131 runs, second best in the league. In all, he contributed 245 total runs to the Boston attack (runs plus RBI, minus HR), which made him far and away the biggest run producer in the majors. DiMag, who was voted MVP, was a distant second with 204.

And Ted's hits won games. Boston won 89 games, and Williams provided the margin of victory in 29 of them, more than any other hitter in the league. Foxx was next with 28. I call these GWAB, Games Won At Bat, and dabble with them as time permits. DiMaggio won 18 games for New York to rank fourth on the Yankees behind Red Rolfe and Bill Dickey with 21 apiece. (Pitcher Red Ruffing topped them all with 21 victories on the mound and three more at bat, for a total of 24.)

New York, which won the pennant by 17 games, would have won with or without Joe. In fact, Joe hurt his leg in May and missed 30 games. With young Charley Keller replacing him, the Yankees won 23 of the 30 for a .767 average. With Joe in the line-up, the team was much less formidable— 71–46 for .609.

The Red Sox, who finished in second place, 3½ games ahead of Cleveland, would surely have been in the second division without their rookie sensation. Williams missed three games, and Boston lost two of the three. The writers voted Ted to fourth-place in the MVP poll, behind DiMaggio, Foxx, and Feller:

|  | Votes | Runs Produced | GWAB |
|---|---|---|---|
| DiMaggio | 280 | 204 | 18 |
| Foxx | 170 | 200 | 28 |
| Feller | 155 | — | 25* |
| Williams | 126 | 245 | 29 |

(*24 pitching victories plus one save)

It would have been unprecedented to give the award to a rookie, although 36 years later the writers did give it to a freshman, Fred Lynn (who produced only 187 runs).

Although Williams finished only fourth in the AL MVP vote, *The Sporting News* named him to its all-star outfield, along with DiMaggio and Joe Medwick of the NL.

Pitchers faced a dilemma. Should they pitch to Williams and run the risk of having him knock in one or two runs? Or walk him and risk having someone knock *him* in? They resolved it in favor of the latter 107 times; Ted was second in the league in drawing walks. DiMag walked half as often.

It's a subject Williams feels warmly about. "God, it burns me," he says. "This isn't jealousy either—this is not jealousy. But you know, I hear on the radio all the time, and Yastrzemski gets up to the plate with men on base all the time, and he *never* gets walked. They *always* pitch to him with men on third base. My God almighty. Jesus! You can bet your rear end I *never* got a chance to do that. They would not pitch to me. They would much prefer to have me at first and take a chance on a double play with the guy behind me. Jesus Christ. I never got that opportunity to drive in runs in that situation."

As Allie Reynolds, the ace of Casey Stengel's 1949 champion Yankees told me, "If there are men in scoring position, then I'm over-matched. I've got to walk him."

That October Ted attended the Yankee-Reds World Series, the first Series he'd ever seen. He was more excited than the players and couldn't eat all day. "The tension actually made me sick."

The Boston writers picked Williams the team's most valuable player, even ahead of Foxx. That meant that Wagner had to tie a black bow tie for him to attend the dinner and receive his award. It was Ted's first necktie since high school graduation.

The Red Sox rewarded him with a raise to $10,000. They gleefully rubbed their hands, and ordered workmen to build two new bullpens in front of the right-field stands, cutting 20 feet off the home run distances there; Ted's new targets would be 304 feet at the line and 383 down the power alley. Writer Jerry D Lewis hailed him as "the player most likely to crack Babe Ruth's venerable record" of 60 home runs. (The "venerable" record was then only 12 years old.)

Williams feels the new, shorter fence may have set up false hopes in the fans and may have been responsible for the trouble he experienced the following year.

# 1940

◆

The news from overseas was grim. German Field Marshall Erwin Rommel threw the British army back in North Africa. Hitler invaded Denmark, Norway, Belgium, Luxembourg, the Netherlands, and France, and took all six of them within three months. The year was summed up in my memory, and that of millions of others, by *Life* magazine's "crying Frenchman," the full-page photo of a Parisian biting back tears as he watched the Nazi army goose-stepping beneath the Arc de Triomphe. Italy attacked Greece; Yugoslavia was subdued, though guerrillas fought on. Winston Churchill called on Britons for "blood, toil, tears and sweat." England rescued its army at Dunkirk ("this was their finest hour"). The German air force unleashed the Battle of Britain in the sky, as daring Spitfire fighter pilots rose to oppose them. ("Never have so many owed so much to so few").

The U.S. Congress voted to send 50 over-age destroyers to Britain. In November FDR won a third term, over Wendell Willkie, with the promise that he would never send American boys to fight in foreign wars.

We sang "The Last Time I Saw Paris," but we were still pretty much isolated from the war. "You Are My Sunshine" and "Beat Me Daddy, Eight to the Bar" by the Andrews Sisters were more popular, plus the song that is still #1 on my all-time hit parade, Hoagie Carmichael's "Stardust."

We listened to the "Quiz Kids" on the radio, "Truth or Consequences" (the $64 question), Jack Benny, Fibber McGee and Molly, "Captain Midnight," and "The Lone Ranger," and sent in Ovaltine lids for Little Orphan Annie magic decoder rings. Sunday nights at the supper table we tuned in Gene Autrey's "Melody Ranch" which opened with Gene singing "Back in the Saddle Again." A new rival to Gene was already galloping across the screens, Roy Rogers. And although it didn't make an impression on me, Harry James broke away from Benny Goodman and formed his own band with a new singer named Frank Sinatra.

W. C. Fields had a big year at the movies with two hits, *The Bank Dick* and *My Little Chickadee* with Mae West ("Come up and see me some time.")

My allowance was 25 cents a week and covered a round-trip on the bus (ten cents) and a ticket to the Saturday matinee (ten cents). For that you could see two cowboy movies, a Three Stooges or Our Gang short, seven cartoons, coming attractions, a news reel ("Time . . . marches on!"), and a serial. The last always ended with the hero plunging through a trap door or falling into a bubbling volcano, followed by the words dreaded by every ten-year old boy in America: "Continued next week." I could stay and see everything all over again if I wanted to, which I frequently did.

The nickel left over went into the collection plate on Sunday.

Back then I seemed to be continually getting my tonsils and adenoids out. They clamped a mask over your face and knocked you out with ether, which had a revolting smell. Recuperating at home, I listened to "The Goldbergs" and "Mary Margaret McBride." Saturday mornings was "Let's Pretend," in which kids dramatized fairy tale classics. Dr. Vander Veer made house calls and took my temperature with a mercury thermometer, which, when broken, yielded little balls of quicksilver you could hold in your hands.

People didn't use funeral homes, the casket was brought into the living room, and a wreath on the door marked the doleful occasion.

We went to the World's Fair, where Chrysler stole the show with the Land of Tomorrow. For the first time we saw TV and heard our own (shocking) voices on tape.

That year I had my first kiss, stolen from Lois Donahue, who lived across the street.

I also saw my first big-league game. I had been the last kid chosen in my grade-school playground league and was promptly assigned to right field, where I would do the least damage. Despite our handicap, my team won the flag and were rewarded with free passes to see the Yankees play the Detroit Tigers. We sat way out in the left-field mezzanine, from whence the players looked like pin-striped ants. Bobo Newsom, who would lead the Tigers to the pennant, pitched, and Charley Keller of the Yanks hit a home run, inside the park.

Later that summer I got my first look at Williams. My father had been given a pair of three-dollar box seat tickets to Yankee Stadium right over the Red Sox dugout. As we hustled into the stadium, the game had already begun. Hurrying through the ramp on the first base side, suddenly I saw, framed in the exit, Jimmie Foxx menacingly waving his bat not 100 feet away. We were so close, I could see his biceps flexing and his cheek bulging with tobacco. I could have fainted. Lefty Grove was pitching, and at the end of each inning, he walked directly toward me, stopped at the top of the dugout steps, surveyed the crowd for a moment, spat, and disappeared. Moments like that come rarely in one lifetime, and can never be forgotten.

And Williams? To be honest, I don't even remember him! Foxx and Grove were the established stars, while Ted was still the Kid. He'd had one good year, but his reputation was far from made yet. To an impressionable boy, the big names were the veterans—Foxx, who had hit almost 500 home runs in his career, and Grove, who was bearing down on his 300th victory.

Ted still thought he could pitch and used to warm up by pitching to imaginary batters. "He was a great pantomimist," Cronin said. "He'd say, 'I got one ball and two strikes on this guy, now watch me throw him a curve ball low and on the outside.' He'd throw the curve, then jump up and down like a kid, shouting, "Did you see him miss that one?"

Finally, one day in August the Sox were taking a beating from the Tigers, the eventual pennant winners, and Cronin looked down the bench at Ted. "You've been popping off about your pitching so much, I'm gonna put you in." (As Williams recalled it, Joe muttered something about, "Who should I pitch next?" and Ted piped up, "I'll pitch.")

He ran out to hurl the last two innings. He gave a single to Frank Croucher (.105), and when the pitcher bunted, Ted got Croucher with a good peg to second.

In the ninth, MVP Hank Greenberg (.340, 41 homers) singled. So did Pinky Higgins (.271). Pitching low, Ted got the next man on a double play, but Greenberg scored. Next up was Rudy York (.316, 33 homers), who had already hit a homer, double and two singles that day. Williams struck him out on three pitches. "I gave him a real good sidearm curve," he wrote. "It broke about a foot, right over the plate, and he took it." York always claimed Ted quick-pitched him.

The fans left the park happy, Cronin said. They were all talking about Williams' pitching and had already forgotten the lopsided loss. "What a loss it was to pitching," Ted always said, "my not following up on my pitching career."

In the outfield, Williams was still considered sub-par. It was a bad rap, insist the players who saw him.

"I was a poor fielder when I came up," he admits, "but nobody bothered to teach me." Doherty points out that Ted made 19 errors his first year as a right fielder. After switching to left in 1940, his errors were sharply reduced. Perhaps it was more experience, perhaps the smaller area in left field in Boston, or perhaps it was the coming of Dom DiMaggio in center field in 1940 (although Doc Cramer had been an excellent center fielder too).

At any rate, "I think I'm a pretty good fielder now," Williams would declare later. "Writers don't want to recognize this. Once they give you a reputation, it sticks to you. I could make a good catch, but I was lackadaisical. If I hurt myself in the MVP votes, it was because I didn't concentrate on my fielding or realize the importance of making a good play out there. Hitting was the paramount thing in my thinking all the time. Anything else wasn't of any interest to me, because I had one thing in mind: Jesus, hit that ball."

Of course with deers like Cramer and Dom DiMaggio (and later Jimmy Piersall) next to him in center field, Williams didn't have to cover very much ground. And Cronin told him not to try any spectacular catches against the wall and jeopardize his career. Williams had missed two games in late 1939 from just such an accident, and he may have permanently damaged his picture swing in 1950 crashing into the wall in the All Star game.

"Ted was a great outfielder," insists Auker. "No one ever mentions that, but he was long-legged, he broke with the ball and covered a lot of ground. Had an excellent arm, a very good arm, a strong arm."

Doerr agrees. "Ted got a bad rap in the outfield," he says. "He was a big gangly guy, had a big lope. People would say he's not hustling. Some little guy [going the same speed] would look like he was running a mile a minute." Bob remembers sprinting with Ted in the outfield before a game. "Come on," Ted said, "I'll race you." "By golly," Doerr whistles, "you had to really go to stay with him when he really let out."

Williams also learned to play hits off the wall at Fenway like Willie Hoppe playing a bank shot in billiards. Doerr says Williams would go out every day and have guys hit balls off the wall at every angle. "I guess Yaz would be the only other guy who played the wall that well."

The ulimate expert, Dom DiMaggio concurs. Williams "knew as much about the left-field wall at Fenway as he did about hitting," Dom writes in *Real Grass, Real Heroes.* "He covered a lot of territory, had a strong arm, and always threw to the right base. . . . We never bumped into each other in all our years of playing together. . . . But Ted never got the credit he deserved as an outfielder."

Williams made the greatest outfield catch I've seen in half a century. It came in September 1947 in Yankee Stadium on a special "day" for Joe DiMaggio. Joe drove a long one toward the bullpen in left-center, a drive identical to the one he would pole in the World Series a month later for the celebrated catch by the Dodgers' Al Gionfriddo. Williams began chasing the ball like a newborn colt, legs and sleeves flapping every which way. At the last instant his long skinny arm reached up like those extension poles with grips on the end that grocers used to use to reach the highest shelves back before supermarkets. The ball hit the glove and Ted hit the railing at the same time, and he folded himself over it like a wet dish towel. For an instant he didn't move, and when he finally unwound himself, he was holding the ball aloft.

The partisan New York crowd roared. They were still cheering when he came in after the inning. They gave him another ovation when he came to bat and cheered when he trotted back to the field. For three innings they were still buzzing.

Yet the catch went unreported in some New York papers and appeared only low in the story, on the jump page, in others. Ted had been thrown out at home in a close play in the tenth, and this was the play the writers had chosen to feature high in their accounts. In those pre-TV days our main source of news about the games was the press, but if I hadn't seen the catch with my own eyes, I wouldn't have found out about it from the newspapers or the history books.

But in 1940 trouble was brewing again. The writers were riding Ted—according to Bill Cunningham—for "sassing" some Braves fans at an exhibition, for showing up at a testimonial in a sweat shirt, and for "being unable to get out of his own or the ball's way in the field" etc. Bill says Ted replied with "one of the most powerful hymns of hate ever delivered against an entire city." In an interview with Austen Lake, Williams said he was underpaid and wanted to be traded. "And you can put that in quotes."

By the end of April, Paul Doherty reports, Ted was hitting .380 but went 0-for-4 in a game against the A's. In Fenway Park the left-field stands run right along the foul line, within a few feet of the left fielder. Some fans out there loved to give Williams the "Bronx cheer," which approximated the sounds of flatulence. In New York Williams told a writer he had noticed his uncle, a fireman, sitting happily in the stands. "They sit around in the sun all day, draw $150 a month, and retire in 20 years on a pension. What a breeze!" That's what he wanted to be, Ted said, a fireman.

His critics loved it! Players today don't "bench jockey," but the old-timers raised the insult and the needle to a high art form. Opposing jockeys made loud fire siren sounds whenever Ted came to bat. New York's Lefty Gomez blew a fireman's whistle. White Sox manager Jimmy Dykes brought a fire hose to the park and wore a red fireman's hat in the dugout. Ted later insisted that he took it all in good fun. "I get a great kick out of Dykes. He's really funny. It's the boos I don't like." (My own memory of Dykes is yelling at the top of his voice six inches from the umpire's face while kicking dirt over home plate. Of course he got rejected to the merriment of the fans.)

If Williams remembered the fire hats as a joke, he didn't seem to regard them that way at the time. Once he pouted that he'd rather play in Brooklyn, where the fans would really appreciate him. One can only imagine Williams in Ebbetts Field with its 296-foot fence. He would have smashed every home-run record in the book there!

Next came the "pigeon incident." In the old days pigeons fluttered among the girders under the grandstand roofs, and the old joke was, "Thirty thousand people in this park, and that bird had to hit me." So Williams and Red Sox owner Tom Yawkey came to the park with rifles one morning and began picking them off. When Hy Hurwitz reported it, there was quite an uproar. (In his report, Hurwitz had forgotten to mention Yawkey's participation, so Williams took the heat alone.)

The fans razzed Williams' words while hailing his hitting. He decided this was hypocrisy and stopped tipping his cap when they applauded. He never tipped it again, no matter how much they cheered.

"The pressure the guy had was unbelievable," Doerr said. "I don't think I could have taken it. Colonel Egan (the columnist), every night he had a blast on Ted. Every night ten or 15 reporters came around Ted. I thought, 'My God, how can you stand it?' Once in a while you'd hear him give one guy a blast." If there was one good thing to come out of the newspaper ordeal Ted was being put through, Doerr thought, it was that he was taking the heat off the rest of the players.

Then too, Bob adds, Ted "had a lot of pressure from home. His brother was always in trouble, and his mother was always writing for money." The other players would wonder, "What the heck's the matter with him today?" while Williams tore the letters up, muttering "Damn!" to himself. The mail from home "disturbed him about as much as anything," Doerr says.

All the while the writers were riding Ted in print. "But he just got tougher." The more they rode him, "it seemed like he got better."

That year, Williams' average improved to .344, third best in the league, behind DiMaggio (.352) and Luke Appling (.348). "I tightened up on my strike zone," Ted recalled. In '39 he had been swinging at balls an inch above his shoulders; now he let those go by.

In spite of the new bullpen at Fenway, dubbed "Williamsburg," Ted's home runs dropped off to 23. He hit 14 on the road but, strangely, only nine into the new, shorter target at home. His batting average, Bill James points out, was remarkably consistent: .340 at home, .348 on the road. Again Williams homered in every city, and again the lefties stopped him; only four of his 23 homers came at their expense. But he hit 14 triples, an excellent total for a guy who was supposed to be slow on his feet. He also got two base hits on bunts. But he was third in slugging average and edged DiMag out of third place in total bases. He was tops in runs scored, though his RBIs fell to 113.

The Red Sox finished in a fourth-place tie, eight games behind the champion Tigers, who nipped Cleveland by one game and the Yankees by two. Without Williams Boston would surely have finished in the second division. He supplied 224 runs (runs plus RBI, minus home runs), more than anyone but Detroit's Hank Greenberg, the MVP. Yet Ted came in no better than a tie for 14th in the MVP vote! Not counting pitchers, the writers' vote broke down as follows:

**Hank Greenberg** *Author's Collection*

| Rank | Name | Team | Runs Produced |
|------|------|------|---------------|
| 1. | Hank Greenberg | Detroit | 238 |
| 3. | Joe DiMaggio | New York | 195* |
| 5. | Lou Boudreau | Cleveland | 189 |
| 6. | Jimmie Foxx | Boston | 189 |
| 8. | Rudy York | Detroit | 206 |
| 9. | Rip Radcliff | St. Louis | 157 |
| 10. | Luke Appling | Chicago | 175 |
| 11. | Roy Weatherly | Cleveland | 137 |
| 12. | Dick Bartell | Detroit | 122 |
| 13. | Joe Kuhel | Chicago | 178 |
| 14. | Ted Williams | Boston | 224 |

*(\*batting champ)*

One should give credit for fielding points, which would have benefited shortstops Boudreau, Bartell, and possibly Appling, and first baseman Kuhel, plus perhaps center fielders DiMaggio and Weatherly. Still, one is also forced to conclude that the writers of 1940 seemed blatantly biased in their voting. Yet Williams never complained.

Two years later Williams won the Triple Crown, leading in batting, home runs, RBI's, runs, total bases, slugging average, and walks. That year he finished second to Yankee second baseman Joe Gordon, who led in two categories, most errors and most times striking out. Ted says the writers were punishing him for not being in military uniform. But, then, neither was Gordon—nor, for that matter, Joe DiMaggio, who nevertheless escaped criticism.

In October 1940 Williams left Boston for Minneapolis to see his girl friend and do some hunting. He had just turned 22 and I, 11. We didn't know it yet, but he was about to have one of the greatest seasons ever enjoyed by a batter in the annals of baseball.

# 5

## *The Winter of '41*

The Nazis were massing 150,000 troops on the Greek border. Phillies pitcher Hugh Mulcahey (known as "Losing pitcher Mulcahey from a familiar line in the box scores) posed for photographers packing his bags to enter the army, the first major leaguer caught in the draft. Mayors Fiorello LaGuardia in New York and James Curley in Boston were running for reelection.

Commentators Raymond Gram Swing, H. V. Kaltenborn, Gabriel Heatter, Elmer Davis, Lowell Thomas, Drew Pearson, and Cal Tinney brought us the news on radio.

In the movies we saw *Dumbo*, *I Wanted Wings* with starlet Veronica Lake, wearing her satin blonde hair over one eye, Abbott and Costello in *Buck Privates* and the brand new "Looney Tunes" ("Eh, what's up, Doc?") The big bands—Glenn Miller, Tommy Dorsey, Guy Lombardo, Xavier Cugat, Phil Spitalny's All-Girl orchestra—were playing "The Last Time I Saw Paris," "Deep in the Heart of Texas," and "Bewitched, Bothered and Bewildered." Rudy Vallee crooned, opera star Jan Peerce sang "Bluebird of Happiness," Kate Smith, who made obesity popular before Roseanne Barr, sang "When the Moon Comes Over the Mountain," and the Andrews Sisters belted out "Boogie Woogie Bugle Boy From Company C."

We listened to "Can You Top This?" a comedy show, "Inner Sanctum" with its creaking door hinge, and "Truth or Consequences," a game show.

As they did twice every winter, black men carried sacks of coal from a truck into the bin next to our basement furnace. And twice a day my father shoveled the coal into our furnace. Our cleaning lady was the only black I knew; our neighborhood, and thus our school, was as segregated as if we had lived in Alabama.

Milk was delivered by horse-drawn wagons to the kitchen door. The cream rose to the top, and you could pour it off into your coffee or homogenize the bottle by shaking it. On winter mornings the frozen milk pushed the bottle cap up an inch above the bottle rim. We warmed our clothes each morning on the hot-water radiators and took fishy-tasting cod liver oil for colds.

We bought "punch-out" books of cowboys or soldiers that we could dress in different uniforms. I was as proud of my pearl-handled cowboy guns and holster as I was of my fielder's glove. (We kept all five fingers inside the glove, incidentally.) We played roller skate hockey with skates that clamped onto the soles of your street shoes and were tightened by keys kept on strings around your neck. We made "scooters," out of odd wood, nailing skates to the bottoms, sort of early versions of skate boards.

We read "big little books," which were about 2" × 2" × 1", with a comic strip panel on one page and text on the facing page. They cost ten cents each, and I had rows and rows of them on my bookshelf. We also read comic books—Captain Marvel ("Shazam"), Superman, Batman etc etc—to the dismay of our parents. And we read the "funny papers" or newspaper comic strips—Jiggs and Maggie, the Katzenjammer Kids, Popeye, Prince Valiant, Li'l Abner (with Daisy Mae and Mammy Yoakum), Dick Tracy, Gasoline Alley (Skeezix was just a kid then, and Uncle Walt still had all his hair), and Blondie (Alexander was named Baby Dumpling, and his sister, Cookie, hadn't been born yet).

We listened to "Jack Armstrong, the All-American Boy," and best of all, "The Lone Ranger" with the rollicking theme from "Flight of the Bumblebee" ("From out of the West come the thundering hooves of the great horse, Silver. . . . The Lone Ranger rides again!")

We collected bubble gum cards. Some had baseball players, some had war scenes, and some had G-men (government men) gunning down John Dillinger, Baby Face Nelson, Machine Gun Kelly, or Pretty Boy Floyd. Lines traced the bullets from the muzzle straight to the bad guy's forehead and out the other side.

I wrote to movie cowboys—William Boyd, Wild Bill Elliott, Johnny Mack Brown, George O'Brien—for autographed
pictures to put on my wall. (I didn't ask Gene Autrey, because
he was a singer, not, in my mind, a real cowboy.)

Later I added baseball players. Besides Ted Williams, I
had Tris Speaker, Honus Wagner, Tinker and Evers (but not
Chance, who had died)—enough treasure to put my grandchildren through medical school. When I got older, I waylaid
players for autographs after the game. Sometimes they scrib-
bled as they walked, sometimes they brushed you aside
gruffly. Today they take a bus instead of walking, so you can't
do that any more.

Records were 78 rpm and broke when you dropped them.
They were easily scratched, making the needle jump the
track, jump the track, jump the track. Needles had to be
changed every few records, and the Victrola had to be wound
up every third record or so, or else sopranos would slowly
become altos, then baritones, then basses.

Women got permanent waves or made their own curls
with hot irons, holding the waves in place with bobby pins;
these were highly prized by superstitious ball players, who
regarded each pin found as worth one hit. Any female under
40 with any sex appeal at all was a "girl." A "woman" was my
third grade teacher, Miss Cunningham, who wore pince nez-
glasses and pulled her hair back tight in a bun—I still don't
know why girls today would rather be called women. When
women put on weight, they laced corsets around their waists.
Older girls wore silk stockings, which were always developing
runs. They wore only one-piece swim suits. (Boys and men
modestly wore tops to their swimming trunks too, with belts
around the waist.) We stood when a lady entered the room,
pulled out her chair, and opened her door. Females always
wore hats to church. Only a daring few smoked. None used
biological verbs or scatological nouns, and it still shocks me to
hear them do it today. Every girl wore lipstick, usually a
bright red. Later I discovered that when you necked, or

"smooched," it got all over her face and yours, not to mention your collar. Many an errant husband was trapped that way.

In February the snow lay on the ground in Minnesota in dirty clumps as the teams began arriving in Florida to open spring training.

The Boston Braves announced that they had signed a rookie left-hander named Warren Spahn to bolster manager Casey Stengel's weak pitching staff. Casey needed all the help he could get. The Braves finished next to last in '40 and would finish there again in '41. Casey was once hit by a taxi and knocked out of uniform for a few weeks, whereupon the Boston writers voted the taxi driver the team's MVP. Spahn and Stengel would meet again 24 years later on the last-place Mets, prompting Spahn to observe that he played with Casey both before and after he was a genius.

At the Red Sox camp, one man was missing. Ted Williams hadn't been heard from in a month. He had spent the winter hunting around Minneapolis, where his fiancee Doris Soule lived. The Sox had no other news of him, no contract, nothing. He was a holdout.

On March 3 Red Sox manager Joe Cronin dashed into the clubhouse from infield practice to take a long-distance call from general manager Eddie Collins in Boston. Williams had just mailed in his contract for $17,500 (Ted now says it was actually $20,000.) Cronin hung up and motioned to the writers to come get the news.

Joe DiMaggio meanwhile was ending his own holdout. As two-time American league batting champ, he had demanded $40,000, just half of Babe Ruth's top salary, but finally settled for $35,000, just twice Williams' pay. Highest paid player in the game was 1940 MVP Hank Greenberg of Detroit.

Of course, it was a different world then. The average worker took home about $1,250 a year. A room clerk made $40 a month, less than $500 a year, plus room and board. A farm-hand made about the same. Typists pulled down $70 a month, $840 a year. A barber could make $4 a day, almost $1,000 a year, plus tips. A good salesman could live like a king on $250 a month—$3,000 a year.

Money went further then. A Havana cigar cost five cents. Bread was eight cents a loaf, a bar of Lux soap was nine. Milk was ten cents a quart, coffee 14 cents a pound. Peter Pan peanut butter ("Sho' keeps perfect"), 16 cents a jar. A rib roast cost 25 cents a pound, turkey 29 cents, and eggs 35 cents a dozen.

A bleacher seat at Yankee Stadium cost 50 cents, a dollar for grandstand.

Silk stockings cost 89 cents a pair. A man could buy a necktie for 59 cents, a shirt for $1.25, a pair of Thom McAnn shoes for $3.50, a gabardine raincoat for $6.95, and a suit for $17.50—five dollars extra for a second pair of pants.

A new Buick cost $795. A Chrysler with "fluid drive," the first automatic transmission, was more. You could get a 1940 Packard for $800, a 1938 LaSalle for $450, and a '32 Ford for only $49. A gallon of gas cost 17 cents, a penny extra for "ethyl."

You could buy a six-room house in the suburbs for $4,500, $31 a month, or a five-room house on the beach for $2,540. A dining room suite was $79.95, a washing machine with hand wringer $45, a push-yourself lawn mower $3.49. For as little as $5.00 you could buy a 14-karat wedding ring (only 50 cents a month), propose to the girl of your dreams, and move in.

Williams wouldn't starve on $17,500. It was about 20 times as much as the average secretary took home. Still, today Jose Canseco, at about $5 million, makes as much as 250 secretaries.

Ted made the long drive to Florida in three days, arriving March 7. He suited up as flashbulbs popped and trotted out to the batting cage. Three days later he held up his hands for the writers: Both mitts were red and swollen from batting.

On March 14 Ted started his first game against the Cincinnati Reds. He drilled two 450-foot fly balls but couldn't get a hit. Still, he was exhilarated. He had put on weight, mainly in his shoulders and upper arms, and was happy about it. It was going to take "some pitching" to stop him, he said.

On March 19 the Newark Bears, the Yankees' top farm club, arrived. Williams tripled his first time up. In the third, he smacked a single, and with rookie Al Flair at bat, the hit-and-run sign was flashed. Ted dug for second, but Flair missed the pitch, and the Newark catcher fired the ball. Ted started to slide, but his spikes caught in the clay and he fell, wincing in pain, and hobbled off the field. Trainer Win Green announced that Ted had suffered a slightly sprained ankle but should be ready to play again "in a few days."

That proved to be optimistic. Williams would sit out the rest of the month, giving the foot hot and cold water treatments. While the Sox set sail for Havana, Williams stayed in Florida and read the papers or limped to the movies, perhaps to see Edward G. Robinson in *The Sea Wolf* or Jimmy Cagney and Gloria DeHaviland in *The Strawberry Blonde*.

# 6

## The Spring of '41

As the weather grew warmer, my school yard became littered with little holes dug with heels, or with circles drawn in
the dirt, a sign that boys were playing marbles again. Marbles
was big then—Dodger rookie Pee Wee Reese had been the
state champ in Kentucky. You bought a bag at the five-and-
dime store (you could buy a lot of things for ten cents or less
then), but I was a lousy player and was always "losing my
marbles" to the other kids. Nobody plays marbles any more,
although 45 years later I saw Himalayan kids playing the
exact same games we used to play.

We also played the centuries-old game of one o' cat, with
one base and two boys at bat and two in the field. The batter
hit fungoes, and the fielders tried to put him out at base or
home, or, if a fly was caught, to roll the ball to the bat at home
to complete the out. We used a ball until we literally "knocked
the cover off it," then covered it with black electrician's tape,
which made it hard to find in the tall grass. Most of our time
seemed to be spent kicking in the outfield weeds, while the
batter ran laughing to first and home. Kids don't play that any
more either; Little League ensures there are always enough
guys for two full teams. (Girls weren't allowed to play—
women's lib was still far in the future.)

Girls played jacks with little rubber balls, and we all
played kick-the-can, a form of hide-and-seek—if you could
kick the can before "it" could find you, all the others captured
were free. Both these games have also disappeared today.

With warmer weather, windows and doors were open, so
that when we walked home from school for lunch, we could
hear "The Romance of Helen Trent" from house to house on
the way home and "Our Gal Sunday" on the way back.

Evenings too were planned around radio: Monday was
Edgar Bergen and Charlie McCarthy. Tuesday was Orson
Welles and comedian Bob Burns, who played an Arkansas
instrument called a "bazooka." Wednesday was "Amos and
Andy" doing black dialect (Ah's ree-gusted!"), "The Lone

Ranger," and "Blondie" ("Uh-uh-uh-uh, don't touch that dial").
Thursday was "Duffy's Tavern" ("where the elite meet to eat")
and Major Bowes' Amateur Hour.    Friday, singer Ginny Simms.
And Saturday was "The Green Hornet" and "Your Hit Parade."

The last one played "Chattanooga Choo-choo," "Blues in
the Night," "I Don't Want to Walk Without You," and "I Don't
Want to Set the World on Fire."

After the Red Sox returned to the States, Williams joined
them April 1 and did "some fancy hitting" in batting practice.
The ankle was a little stiff, but he was anxious to hit. He
pinch-hit in a game that afternoon and slashed a hard foul,
then tapped a weak dribbler to the box.

At Fort Benning, Georgia the next day Ted didn't play in
spite of the pleas of the GIs ringing the field. On the 4th at
Birmingham, he slugged some mighty practice drives over the
fence, but his instep was still sore.

On the 5th doctors finally got a look at the x-rays.

### ANKLE BROKEN, WILLIAMS
### LOST TO RED SOX FOR MONTH

the *Herald* proclaimed.

"That's bunk!" Ted exploded, according to the papers though
personally I doubt if he said "bunk." "I'll be back in a couple of
weeks—at least I hope so."

The Birmingham doctors insisted that "it's just a tiny bit
of bone loose." Perhaps a bandage would do the trick and Ted
could be playing again in a week. But Cronin was taking no
chances; he put Ted on the next train north, where club phy-
sician Tommy Richards could examine him.

Williams arrived in Boston April 8 "jovial and sunny." "If
he keeps it up, he may be one of the most popular players
ever," the *Herald* said.

Even Boston's number-one Williams baiter, Dave Egan, offered a hand of reconciliation. He wrote in the *Record* that Williams "has a brilliant career spread out ahead of him ... However wrong and however mistaken he may have been in 1940, this is 1941 and he is entitled to start from scratch."

The foot only hurt when he ran, Ted assured everyone. Eddie Collins said Williams would be ready for opening day in a week; he might even play in the city series against the Braves. But by April 12 it was clear that Williams would miss the series. He was on the sidelines as the punchless Sox lost to the Braves (or Bees, as they were also called) 10–3.

Meanwhile a poll of writers picked the Yankees or Indians to finish first, the Red Sox fifth.

Still without an OK from Richards, Ted took batting practice April 14 and powered several drives into "Williamsburg," the *Globe*'s name for the new bullpen. Cronin shook his head. "Look at the Kid faking he can run," he said. "He wants to play in the opener tomorrow in the worst way."

Meanwhile the Yanks were opening the season officially at Washington, where President Roosevelt as usual threw out the first ball. DiMaggio's triple batted in the year's first run.

---

*Wednesday,*
*April 15*

---◆---

The Nazis opened a drive toward the Suez Canal, and Boston opened its season against the Senators at Fenway. In batting practice Williams pumped four balls into the bullpen or over it. "I never wanted to play all 154 games more in my life," he said. He'd be ready to pinch-hit: "There's nothing wrong with my eyes." But Doc Richards vetoed the idea "unless absolutely necessary."

In the ninth, with the Sox losing 6–4, Cronin decided it was absolutely necessary. Most of the 17,000 fans were already filing out, dusk was falling, and catcher Frankie Pytlak was at bat, when Joe looked down the bench and jerked his head at Ted. Williams pulled three bats from the rack and sauntered into the on-deck circle as the fans cheered and hurriedly resumed their seats. Ted swung the bats, knelt, sucked in his breath and began squeezing one of the bats as if he were going to throttle it. He squeezed so hard, the squeal of his hands could be heard in the pitcher's box, a sound that didn't do anything for the pitcher's confidence. Ted had kept his eyes glued on the pitcher, Sid Hudson, the whole time—Ted is "the only man I could never stare down," Yankee pitcher Vic Raschi would say. Hudson, unnerved, may have lost his concentration, and Pytlak hit him for a double. Then Williams stood and tossed two bats away, while the crowd gave him the best ovation of the day.

Handsome Sid Hudson had been the rookie sensation of 1940, winning 17 games with a last-place team. His first pitch was in the dirt, and Pytlak scampered to third. Hudson elected to pitch to the crippled Williams, a bad decision, because Ted sent the next pitch on a line into rightfield. Though he limped off the field for a pinch-runner, his hit "fired up the Red Sox," the *Globe* reported, and they went on to score two more runs for victory.

### TED WILLIAMS SPARKS RED SOX

the *Globe*'s page-one headline read.

## Wednesday,
## April 16

◆

Londoners suffered under the heaviest air raids of the war thus far.

In Boston the Sox were losing 6–4 again when Williams went up to pinch-hit against the Venezuelan right-hander, Alex Carresquel (6–2). Ted couldn't get a hit, though the Sox won in the 12th. Doc Richards told Ted to forget about playing regularly for at least a week.

Thursday the Yugoslav army surrendered to the Nazis.

In Boston the weather turned cold and the game was canceled. Williams had a choice of movies, *Blondie Goes Latin* or *Ziegfield Girl* with Jimmy Stewart, Hedy Lamarr, and Judy Garland. Ted probably ignored Tallulah Bankhead's opening on the stage of the Boston Playhouse. Radio offered Kate Smith, the nation's favorite singer. He also probably passed up the talk show, "Information Please," with critic Clifton Fadiman and columnist Franklin P. Adams, the man who had authored the poem, "Tinker to Evers to Chance."

## Friday,
## April 18

◆

The Nazis raised their flag atop Mount Olympus in Greece.

The Sox arrived in Philadelphia to play the Athletics. In the eighth Williams pinch-hit against Jack Knott, a big right-hander with an over-hand fastball (11−9 the year before), and again drilled a sharp single to right. The Sox won in the ninth on Doerr's home run 3−2.

With two hits in three at bats, Ted was doing all right for a guy with a broken foot. Actually, he says, he thinks the injury helped him.

"I had it taped the whole damn year," he says. "But the big thing was, it *might* have put more restrictions on my swing." To favor the ankle, he tightened up on his swing slightly, didn't swing with all his might. "And it *might* have—I don't know, but it might have helped." It was the right ankle, that is, the front foot for a left-handed hitter, and forced him to put more weight on his rear foot. He disagrees with Charley Lau's "new theories of hitting," such as hit off the front foot. "It's so wrong, but still these modern hitters will listen to that, at least some of 'em will listen to it."

Then too, because he couldn't run, he spent more time in the batting cage, "and I had a chance to have more good batting practice that year probably than any time in my career. That year we got a pitcher from Cleveland, who in 1939 and '40 was tough as hell for me. Name was Joe Dobson. Had a real good curve ball, and a *good* overhand fastball. And he liked to pitch all the time, pitch to me. We'd have a game. He'd be bearing down as hard as he could to me, and I'd be bearin' down against him. I was just young and really comin', and boy, it was the greatest thing that ever happened to me."

Dobson officially won 12 games for the Red Sox that year—and unofficially many more, thanks to the help he gave to Williams.

Ted didn't play on April 19th as the Red Sox won 7−2, their fourth win in a row.

Joe Dobson *Author's Collection*

---

## Sunday,
## April 20

◆

The temperature stood at 90 degrees in Washington's Griffith Stadium, the biggest field in the majors with a left-field foul pole 406 feet away. Right field had a 30-foot high wall, but unlike Boston's, which was at right angles to the foul line, this one started at 328 feet and angled back at an obtuse angle. In deep center the wall was about 440 feet from home. (In the late '50s the Senators would put a bullpen out there to

Dom DiMaggio *Author's Collection*

help the hitters a little. Roger Maris hit one of his 61 homers into it.)

Williams, who calls himself a warm-weather hitter, came up to pinch-hit in the seventh with the bases loaded against the Senators' big right-hander, Arnold "Red" Anderson, a fast-ball pitcher who, teammate Mickey Vernon said, wasn't very fast. Williams fouled out, though the Sox won 14–8, thanks mostly to little Dom DiMaggio, who hit three doubles and stole third base twice.

Dom was playing his second year as the Sox center fielder and lead-off man. He was the third of the DiMaggio boys, after Vince and Joe, to make the majors. Four inches shorter than Joe and some 30 pounds lighter, he didn't have Joe's power, but he had more speed and a better arm and was probably a better outfielder. In fact, later on, in the pennant-winning

year of 1946, Boston fans would sing, to the tune of "Maryland, My Maryland":
"He's better than his brother Joe —
Do-mi-nic DiMaggio."

Dom, the story went, was a waiter in Joe's Italian and seafood restaurant back on Fisherman's Wharf in San Francisco, and we all pictured him in a white apron, balancing big trays of spaghetti on one hand. Dom peered at the pitcher through thick-rimmed glasses, a great rarity among players in those days. The glasses gave him a donnish look, hence the nickname, "the Little Professor." He had a smiling face, tight black waves in his hair, which he parted in the middle, and Joe's prominent nose.

Dom also took Joe's wide-spread, high-bat, right-handed stance at the plate, a red #7 on his back (blue on his gray road uniform). I remember his mannerism of tugging his sleeves up as he waited for the pitch, first one sleeve, then the other. He was a sharp singles hitter, who had batted .301 as a rookie. He was an excellent table-setter for Williams and always among the leaders in runs scored. Many of Williams' RBIs were Dom.

Boston fans knew all the tales about Dom's miraculous catches, such as climbing the wire fence in Detroit to one-hand a high drive by Greenberg. He had one of the two strongest arms I remember seeing—Clemente had the other. The phrase, "he threw a rope" was invented for Dom. He almost won the 1946 World Series with a base clearing, game-tying double in the eighth, pulled a charley horse, and limped off the field. The Cardinals' Enos Slaughter, who scored an inning later on a hit to center, always said he would never have tried it with Dom in the outfield. In fact, Dom told me, "I think I might possibly have had a shot at him at third."

Dom once led the league in steals with the laughably low total of 15. But stealing second—or even hitting a double— hurt the team instead of helping, for it "took the bat out of" Williams' hands and almost guaranteed he would draw a walk. (Significantly, in the year Dom led in steals, 1950, Williams was out for half a season with injuries.) If the Little Professor hadn't missed three years in World War II, he would have run up stats similar to Richie Ashburn's and, I think, would be a deserving candidate for the Hall of Fame. In fact, I still think he is.

---

*Monday,*
*April 21*

---◆---

Washington right-hander Steve Sundra (9–13) was beating Dobson 6–3 in the eighth when Williams pinch-hit and grounded out. Foxx followed with a triple to ignite a two-run rally, but the Sox fell one run short and lost 6–5.

Williams had swung on the first pitch—something, he would later write in *The Science of Hitting* that you should never do. As he told me, "Get yourself a little familiar with his delivery, whether he's a little sneaky: 'Jesus Christ, this guy's fast,' or, 'Goddam, *that* ball broke like hell!' " Take the pitch, Ted says, "rather than making the out and saying, 'Goddam, that ball broke more than I thought it did.' You get freshened up." He admits that, "Hell, yes, they're going to lay it [the first pitch] in there. Why shouldn't they?" But he feels one strike is a small price for the information he gets.

Actually, Williams preached taking the first pitch only the first time he sees a pitcher that day, just as a reminder of exactly how his curve breaks or how his fastball hops. Still, Williams seemed to violate the rule often in '41.

Another of Williams' rules that has apparently changed with the years is the one on wrist action. In September Ted

Ted Williams *Author's Collection*

would be photographed by *Life* magazine showing his wrists "well broken" as soon as he connects with the ball. If they were firm, *Life* wrote, all his power would be lost. That winter I wrote to Ted, asking how I could become a great hitter, and I still have his type-written reply in a scrapbook. Live clean, he advised, get plenty of sleep, and put plenty of snap in your wrists. As late as 1954, in a *Saturday Evening Post* interview, Ted still said he was snapping his wrists.

But 20 years later he would write that you do not snap your wrists at contact, you hit with stiff wrists, somewhat like hitting a telephone pole with an axe. In one of our interviews he gave me a simple pencil test to illustrate why: Holding the pencil like a bat, he snapped his wrist. "Where does the pencil go?" he asked. Up in the air, is the obvious answer, which anyone can confirm by trying it himself.

The *Life* writer also reported, presumably with Williams' approval, that he "keeps his body out of the swing and puts all his drive into his forearms." This from the future author of the "hips before hands" theory that rotating the hips generates the power, the arms merely follow.

I once asked Tony Lupien, Ted's teammate on the '42 Sox, to explain the contradiction. Tony laughed. "Ted's a natural," he said, "he doesn't know what he's doing himself, he just does it."

---

*Tuesday,*
*April 22*

---

Pete Fox, who was playing left field in Ted's absence, was out with an ulcerated tooth, and Williams, "though still limping perceptibly," begged for a chance to play. Cronin nodded gratefully, and thus Ted took the field to start his first game of the season. It was a "spectacular" return, the *Globe* wrote. Right-hander Walter Masterson (4–3) was pitching for the Senators and yielded two quick singles before Ted stepped up. Williams drilled the first pitch down the right-field line for one run, and Foxx knocked in two more. An inning later Masterson walked the bases loaded with two out, and Ted, first-ball hitting again, lashed another single to knock in two more runs. He ended with 2-for-4 for the day, giving him 4-for-9 for the year.

He was a liability defensively however, letting several balls fall safe that a healthy man would have caught, and Boston lost 12–5.

As the Red Sox caught the train to New York, King Paul fled Greece and Boston's Cardinal O'Connell urged the United

States to stay out of the war. The cardinal was echoing the feelings of many Americans, including Colonel Charles Lindbergh, who addressed a huge America First rally on the same theme.

---

## *Wednesday, April 23*

---

◆

---

Williams didn't play in the first game in New York, an unfortunate break, because the pitcher was Lefty Gomez (15–5), Ted's favorite cousin that year. Gomez and Wagner dueled for nine innings 2–2. When the Sox put a man in scoring position, Gomez motioned to his rookie shortstop, Phil Rizzuto, who obediently trotted over. "Is your mother here today, kid?" Lefty asked.

"Yes sir, Mr. Gomez," Phil answered respectfully.

"Well, stay here and talk to me a minute," Lefty said. "She'll think you're giving advice to the great Lefty Gomez."

Beaming, Rizzuto went back to his position, and Gomez pitched out of the jam. (Why Cronin didn't insert Williams to hit is a mystery.) In the 11th little Phil smacked the first home run of his life to win the game. He said later he had promised it to his mom.

## *Thursday,*
## *April 24*

◆

Ted pinch-hit against another lefty, Marius Russo, the Brooklyn-born sinker baller who had beaten the Red Sox five times the previous year on his way to a 14–8 record. Ted couldn't get a hit.

Joe DiMaggio did even worse; he went 0-for-3, and his average fell to .090. The Yanks won, however, to take first place.

Ted missed the next two games in Boston, won by the Sox, and featuring Foxx's 501st home run. Jimmie was only the second man to reach 500, surpassed only by Babe Ruth's 714. Mel Ott would join the 500-club in 1945, and Ted himself would be the fourth to top 500, in 1960.

On the 28th the Sox embarked on their first western swing. Parks out there generally had bigger left fields than Fenway. Could Williams patrol them without damage to his team? But Pete Fox' tooth still hurt, and Cronin left Pete home, confident that Williams could do the job. The Sox needed him badly. With him on the bench, their outfield was hitting just .276.

◆

Their first stop was Detroit against Johnny Gorsica, who was 9–11 in 1941. "I had a sinker, a side-arm sinker, and a screw ball," John says. I just showed him the change-up, just to get his timing off. He'd guess with you. If he knew what was coming, it was 'Skinny, bar the door'—if he knew what was coming, he'd hit anybody. We tried to keep the ball away from him, make him pull the outside sinker. Ordinarily he'd hit it into the ground, but once in a while he lost it."

In the sixth Ted "lost it"—"an old-fashioned Williamsonian four-bagger" 440 feet into the upper stands for his first homer of the year. "I never saw him hit a freak home run," Gorsica winced. "His were *hit!*"

In the eighth Williams went to the opposite field with a drive that might have been a homer in Fenway. It almost went for a triple in Detroit but for an excellent cut-off by center fielder Barney McCoskey, who held Ted to two bases. Williams' two hits in three at bats raised his average to .458.

Ted also proved he could field his position. He galloped in for "a classy catch" of a sinking liner and made a "desperate dash" into short left for an out. He showed no sign of a limp.

The Sox lost, however, 5–3, as Lefty Grove, going for win #294, was batted out early.

◆

Williams got only one hit in five tries against Buck Newsom, a 20-game winner the year before, and Floyd Giebel, the unknown rookie who had upset the great Feller the autumn before to knock Cleveland out of the pennant.

Newsom was one of the great characters of the game, the Dizzy Dean of the American League. Buck was christened Louis back in South Carolina, but most people called him Bobo, because that's what he called most people. Traded from the lowly Browns to the mighty Tigers in 1940, Bobo received $35,000, topping even Bob Feller as the highest-paid pitcher in the game. He strode into owner Walter O. Briggs' office to sign the contract, telling Briggs' son, "Step aside, little Bo, big Bobo wants to talk to me." After pitching the Tigers to their first pennant since 1909, plus two more victories in the World Series, Newsom bought a car with neon lights that spelled "Bobo" and a horn that played "Tiger Rag."

However, Bobo would run into bad luck in 1941, losing 20 games as the Tigers fell to fifth. They also lost a dispute with Commissioner Kenesaw Mountain Landis, who ruled 90 of their farm players free agents. Bald-headed general manager Rube Zeller cut Bobo's salary to $12,500. "Hell, Curly," Newsom said, "you just lost 90 players, and I don't see *you* takin' no cut."

In the game, Williams drove in a run with a ground ball to the mound, and his long fly sent Dom from second to third, whence he scored on Foxx' fly. Under the rules of 1930, when Terry hit .401, that would have counted as a sacrifice fly and no time at bat. In '41, however, it was just an out. Ted's average fell to .389.

**109**

## Thursday,
## May 1

◆

Orson Welles' masterpiece, *Citizen Kane*, opened in New York.

In Detroit the Sox smashed 20 hits against curve-balling Tommy Bridges (9–12), fast-balling Dizzy Trout (9–9) and rookie Hal White (no decisions that year). But only one of the hits was by Ted, a first inning single to drive in Dominic with the first run. "I think Bridges threw me a spitter," Ted said. "That ball sure did a lot of tricks. But I rammed it for a hit."

In the third, with a man on third, Williams drew a walk.

He came to bat four more times and smashed three balls labeled home run, but the wind blew them out of the stands and into the hands of the outfielders. Williams' average dropped to .348.

## Friday,
## May 2

◆

Iraq appealed for Nazi aid in its fight against Britain, and Roosevelt asked Congress for $3.5 million in new taxes.

The Red Sox arrived in Cleveland's cozy League Park. The Indians were co-favorites with the Yankees to win the

**110**

pennant after just missing it on the final day the year before amid charges of "cry babies" for their clubhouse revolt against manager Ossie Vitt.

In batting practice, the *Globe*'s Melville Webb reported, Ted "elicited countless ohs and ahs from the girls" with some "ferocious flies" over the chummy (290') rightfield wall.

But against right-hander veteran Mel Harder, he had a tougher time. Harder, 31, had only a 5−4 record that year. But even today, when the Hall of Fame is bulging with unworthies, room might be made for Mel. His 223 wins for the Indians, who never won a pennant while he was with them, are more victories than 12 pitchers already in the Hall who played for better clubs. And if Harder's pitching didn't qualify him, his record as a coach alone would. He handled the Cleveland staff in the halcyon days of 1947−60, when they boasted no less than 12 20-game winners in 14 years—Feller, Bob Lemon, Early Wynn, Gene Bearden, Herb Score, and Mike Garcia. Harder converted Lemon from an infielder and probably single-handedly transformed Wynn into a Hall of Famer.

Harder kept the ball down to Williams, trying to induce grounders. "You couldn't just throw strikes. You had to hit the corners and out-think him a little."

The strategy worked. Against Mel and reliever Joe Heving (5−2) that day Williams couldn't get the ball out of the infield in three attempts, and his average plummeted to .308, the lowest it would be all year.

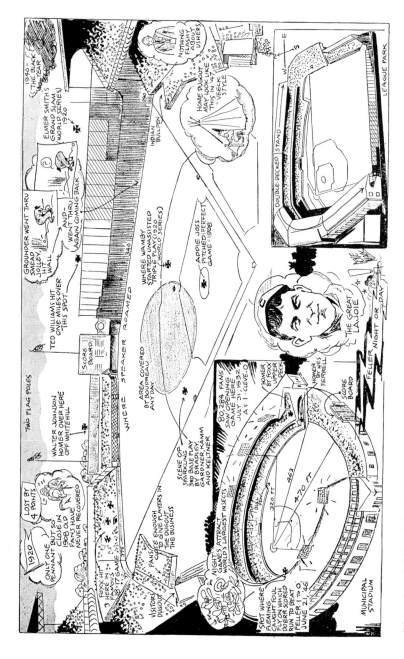

Cleveland Municipal Stadium *Boston Globe*

## Saturday,
## May 3

The teams moved to cavernous Municipal Stadium on the shores of Lake Erie. In 1948 Indians owner Bill Veeck would build a low wire fence to cut down the horrendous distances to the power alleys (435 feet) and dead center (450). But in '41 the spacious outfield was a graveyard for long-ball hitters like Williams.

His opponent would be lefty Al Milnar (12–19 with the fifth-place Indians that year). Burt Whitman of the *Herald* thought Williams wasn't keeping his eye on the ball. But Ted complained that Milnar had an unorthodox motion that made it hard to follow the ball. He throws "stiff-like," Williams said, with a funny wrist-snap. ("Styles can beat styles," Ted told me. "I think Joe Louis was the greatest heavyweight; he beat every son of a bitch. *But* I really do kind of think Muhammad Ali might have beaten him, even though Louis was more devastating than Ali was.") In addition, Milnar threw the new-fangled pitch called the slider. Now a staple of most pitchers' repertoires, the slider is thrown like a football forward pass, with the palm toward the pitcher, so that the ball spins like a curve but without as much break, sort of a fast curve. Ted indicts it as one of the chief reasons no one hits .400 any more.

"Back in '41 I had a good slider," Milnar says, "and I had pretty good luck with Williams. But he was tough to get out. Throw and pray," he laughs.

After the praying was over, Ted had walked twice and managed just one single in three official trips. The Red Sox lost 4-2, their fourth defeat in five games on the road trip, then caught the sleeper for St. Louis.

**113**

In Louisville Whirlaway galloped to victory in the Kentucky Derby, the first leg on jockey Eddie Arcaro's two Triple Crowns.

---

### *Sunday,*
### *May 4*

---

◆

---

As the weather got warmer, my mother saved money by whipping up batches of moonshine root beer in the kitchen sink. Some people had refrigerators with big coils on top, but we still had an ice box (I sometimes still inadvertently say ice box instead of refrigerator). The ice man carried large cakes of ice with tongs from his wagon and put them in the ice compartment once or twice a week.

Some families had the new electric vacuum cleaners, but we had a carpet sweeper. My mother patched our clothes on a Singer sewing machine which she operated with a foot treadle. She did her laundry with a tin-ribbed washboard. Later she got a washing machine that swished the clothes back and forth. She wrang them out and put them through a hand-cranked ringer (the source of the joke about Grandmother's painful misfortune), then hung them out to dry on a clothesline in the back yard, hanging them with wooden clothes pins.

After Williams' 1-for-6 slump at Cleveland, he must have looked forward to Sportsman's Park. Except for the unfortunate 1946 World Series, he always hit well there. The Brownies were usually deep in the second division, and their pitching was not among the league's best. In Ted's first two years there, he hit six home runs over the friendly pavilion screen only 310 feet away—even closer than Fenway's notorious left-field wall. St. Louis had been a favorite target for Babe Ruth and Johnny Mize and would a few years later beckon Stan Musial as well.

Right-hander Bob Harris (12–14) started for the Browns against Grove, who was gunning for his 295th win. Ted got two singles in five at bats, plus a walk. He scored one run, knocked in two, set up two more, and even stole a base (he would steal only one more that year and only 24 in his entire career). In all, he was in on nine of Boston's 11 runs in an 11–4 victory.

Brownie shortstop Johnny Berardino committed two errors. He's young and has a lot to learn, the *Post-Dispatch* wrote. "Rooters will be calling for his scalp if he has many more days such as this." Eventually Johnny decided that baseball was not his true *metier*, dropped the second "r" from his name, took up acting, and 40 years later starred as Dr. Steve Hardy in the hit TV soap opera, "General Hospital." He was also parodied in Dustin Hoffman's hit film, *Tootsie*.

It rained the next two days, but while the other players lolled in their hotel rooms, Ted went to the park anyway with Shellenback, his old San Diego mentor, to try to hit a few balls.

Back at the hotel the rain was getting on Ted's nerves. He kept swinging his bat in front of the mirror, hit the bedstead, collapsed the bed, and spilled the terrified Wagner out onto the floor.

Meanwhile, in Detroit, Hank Greenberg hit two homers against the Yankees, his only two of the year, then hung up his Tiger uniform and reported to the Army, trading his $50,000 salary for a buck private's pay of $21 a month. Hank was 30. There were many who feared he might have played his last major league game. (Discharged in December, Hank immediately reenlisted after Pearl Harbor, went on to become a captain in the air corps and flew the hump in the China-Burma-India theater. In all, he sacrificed four and a half years of his career to his country.)

On the train to Chicago, Webb of the *Globe* spotted Williams playing checkers with coach Tom Daley. Ted "is a much mellowed man this spring," Webb wrote in wonder.

---

### Wednesday,
### May 7

---

Comiskey Park was a tough home run park then. "There was a big opening in centerfield, just like a funnel (of wind) coming in," Williams remembers. "Jesus, you couldn't hit it out. When conditions were tough, it was a tough park. But when conditions were right, the ball would really go in Comiskey."

Wagner, who was having his problems staying on the roster, started against handsome Johnny Rigney, sometimes nicknamed "Adonis," a hard-throwing right-hander who would marry the boss' daughter, Grace Comiskey. Rigney was making his first start of the season after being hit by a strep throat in spring training. He also held a low draft number and, still a bachelor at that time, faced an early call-up.

Rig (13–13) had one of the league's better fastballs, which looked even faster after his change-up, which he considered one of his best pitches. He knew he couldn't overpower Williams. "He was so damn quick with his wrists, he could get that bat around in a hurry." John tried to keep his fastball in tight on Ted, hoping he'd pull it foul.

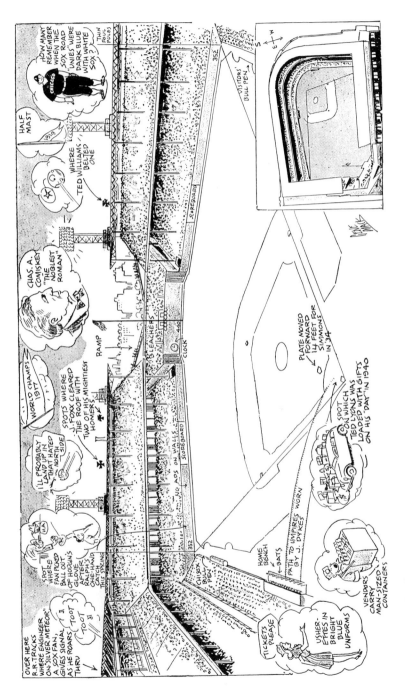

**Comiskey Park** *Boston Globe*

The game that day was one of the finest in Williams' career. In the first, with a man on second, he drilled a hit well out of reach of the second baseman to drive in the game's first run.

In the third he walloped a fastball far into the upper right-field stands. Burt Whitman of the *Herald* estimated it at 500 feet and pronounced it the longest hit in that sector since Ruth.

In the field Ted also made a good catch of Luke Appling's line drive.

After the homer, Rigney pitched dazzling ball. In the eighth, with the score tied 3–3, Williams came up with Spence on second again, but this time Johnny wisely decided to walk him and pitch to Foxx, whom he then struck out.

The teams battled into the 11th, when Rigney decided to try his change-up on Williams. Ted timed it just right and unloaded an awesome wallop even farther than the first one, over the roof above the second tier to win the game 4–3. He says it's probably the longest home run he ever hit, though not the hardest. It also moved the Red Sox into third place and raised Ted's average to .368. The next day Whitman reported that Rigney had tipped his hand just before he threw. Ted read the pitch and tagged it.

Thursday's and Friday's games were rained out, and Williams asked permission to fly back to Boston, but Cronin vetoed that idea as too dangerous. Ted would take the train with the rest of the team, sticking safely to Mother Earth. (Oddly, five years earlier the Red Sox had been the first team to fly.) While the train rattled eastward, German bombers swarmed over London, and the Royal Air Force shot down 49 of them, earning Churchill's famous accolade, "Never have so many owed so much to so few."

In Boston Saturday's game against the Yanks was also rained out, and the players had their choice of entertainment. They could listen to the Preakness, won by Whirlaway, or catch a couple of new movies—Gary Cooper and Barbara Stanwyck in *Meet John Doe* or Bette Davis in *The Great Lie*. It is possible that a few of them may have ended up at the Latin Quarter that night to see fan dancer Sally Rand in action.

---

### *Sunday, May 11*

◆

---

Some 39,000 fans clamored for tickets to the Yankee game, and 5,000 had to be turned away. The New York pitcher was Spurgeon "Spud" Chandler, a right-handed sinker-baller from Georgia who would be 10–4 that year. Williams would call him one of the toughest pitchers he ever faced—a herky-jerky hurler with a quick curve that was hard to pull.

"Williams was the only hitter I was a defensive pitcher against," Chandler told me. "Any of the others, I'd go right after them. But Williams, I was always behind him 2–0, 3–1." Williams always looked for a fastball and would take the curve, at least until there were two strikes. "I'd set him up for a fastball and never give it to him." Chandler said.

"There really was no way to pitch to Williams," Yankee catcher Bill Dickey admitted. "He had the best eye of any batter I ever saw. We tried to pitch him down—fastballs, change-ups, sliders, curves—all down. Tried not to give him any strike three inches above the knees. Once in a while brush him back with a high fastball inside, but he never would swing at it."

That day however, the Yankee strategy apparently wasn't working. Ted went 3-for-6, as the Sox pounded Chandler for a 13-5 victory, knocking New York out of second and moving into that spot themselves. Ted left the park hitting .386.

In other news, the colorful and loquacious Dizzy Dean retired.

That night the German Luftwaffe pounded London's Westminster Abbey and Parliament. Newscaster Edward R. Murrow described the havoc via shortwave that crackled and faded on its static-riddled trip across the Atlantic, ending with his familiar signature, "Good night . . . and good luck."

But the big story, one of the most startling of the war, came from a farm field in Scotland, where the Nazis' number-three man, Rudolph Hess, parachuted out of his fighter plane and was arrested by a surprised Scot farmer with a pitchfork. In school the next day I remember debating it, as were people all over the world. Why had Hess done it? Was he defecting? Did he carry a secret message from Hitler? The answers remained a mystery for almost half a century, which Hess spent as a lonely war-criminal prisoner. Today, if anything, the mystery is even deeper, amid reports that the old man who died in prison was not Hess at all, and that he may indeed have been murdered.

---

*Monday,*
*May 12*

───────────◆───────────

Grove went after his 297th victory against his old rival, Lefty Gomez, a battle between the two greatest left-handers of the 1930s. Gomez had "a moving fastball," his catcher, Bill Dickey, said. He was the Yanks' biggest winner in 1941, with a 15−5 record. But Foxx smashed a 500-foot homer against him, and Williams got one hit in three at bats, as Grove won the game 8−4.

"I helped get Ted in the Hall of Fame," Gomez grinned years later. What was the secret of pitching to him? "I don't believe there's any secret when a guy hits .400. You'd try to keep him from pulling the ball. They'd say, 'Why don't he bunt?' I'd be tickled to death if the guy bunted against me. At least you know where he'd stop: at first base."

---

### Tuesday, May 13

---◆---

Ted was living by himself at the Kenmore hotel near the park. His morning routine was to rise about 9:00, do some exercises from his stack of physical culture magazines, breakfast in the dining room on a double order of cereal and ham and eggs, then call the garage to bring around his car. Tuning the radio to swing music, he drove around town or parked by the Charles River to watch the ducks—hunting was his favorite winter pastime. At last he put the car in gear and drove to the park, arriving promptly at noon.

The western teams began their invasion, beginning with Chicago, and Wagner opened against Rigney again. Johnny pitched another strong game. In the first, he struck out Williams with a man on first. He gave up a homer to Foxx but also whiffed Jimmie three times, making six times in two games.

In the ninth, Johnny held a 3−1 lead on a three-hitter when Ted, 0-for-3 for the day, lined a pitch just inside the right-field foul pole. Rigney won the game 3−2, but Williams had now slugged three homers off him in two games.

After a game Ted almost always had a date, writer Cleveland Amory reported. In Boston, he called the girl; on the road, they usually called him. "I see plenty of girls," he told one writer, but he wasn't much on "this crazy jitterbugging." Ted hadn't learned to dance, was too nervous for cards, and didn't drink or smoke, so presumably his dates had to enjoy popcorn at a western. He had two rules: one, she was not expected to talk baseball, and two, she had to get him home by midnight.

---

### *Wednesday,*
### *May 14*

---
◆
---

The Red Sox faced bespectacled Bill Dietrich (5−8). In the first, with a runner on third, Dietrich took the dare and pitched to Williams, who slapped a grounder back to the box. Bill threw him out, though the run scored. In the third, with a man on second and no one out, Dietrich again pitched to Ted, and again he got him, this time on a fly to left.

In the seventh Williams came up with the bases loaded and Boston losing 7−6. Reliever Pete Appleton (0−3), a 37-year-old right-hander, reared back and blew a third strike past him, only Ted's second strikeout of the year. Although Cronin, then batting .408, followed with a grand slam to win the game, Ted had a disastrous day, going 0-for-5. His average shriveled to .339.

Down in New York, meanwhile, Joe DiMaggio was also having a hard time against Cleveland. On Tuesday Feller had shut him out 0-for-3, and on Wednesday he had to face Harder, whom he called "the twirler I least want to see." Joe claimed that his lifetime average against Mel was .210. If everyone got him out as easily as Harder, Joe said, he'd be back in the minors. "Harder nips the corners. He gives me large chunks of nothing to hit." Harder was not a thrower, he was a *pitcher*, Joe declared.

"I always had pretty good luck with Joe," Mel admits modestly. "He was always thinking just the opposite of what I was pitching. I was a sinker-ball pitcher and a curve-ball pitcher. Joe liked the ball out over the plate; he didn't like it in on him. I'd waste my curve ball outside of the plate a little, six inches or so, and throw my sinker ball in on him, and that was the way I got him out."

For the second day in a row, Joe was hitless. He'd knocked in only one run in his last 12 games, and his batting average was just .291. The Yanks had lost four in a row, were 14–14 on the season and in fourth place behind Cleveland, Boston, and Chicago.

Harder didn't know it then—in fact, he wouldn't know it until many years later, when I pointed it out to him—but he had just gone down in trivia annals as the last man to shut DiMaggio out before Joe began his 56-game hitting streak.

## Thursday,
## May 15

First-place Cleveland arrived at Fenway, and Ted collected one hit in three at bats against Al Milnar.

DiMaggio meanwhile, faced Chicago's lefty, bespectacled Ed Smith (13–17 with the third-place White Sox). In the first Joe unleashed a bad throw trying to catch a runner at third, hitting him on the shoulder. But he singled Rizzuto home in the bottom of the inning to make up for it. It was Joe's only hit in four tries as the Yanks lost 13–1, their fifth loss in a row. Nobody realized it yet of course, but the clock of history had just been set ticking. It was the first hit in Joe's now famous streak. "I started him off," Smith says proudly.

## Friday,
## May 16

Williams faced his former Red Sox teammate, hare-lipped Jim Bagby (9–15). Jim said he fed Ted screwballs, which broke away from the left-handed Williams. Bagby got one up too high, however, and Ted walloped it for a single. It was his only hit in four trips, however, and his average fell to .333. More than 40 years later Bagby even remembered the score. "We won it 9–2 (actually 9–3). At the end of the year I can tell you every game I lost, how I lost it, who hit it, and what he hit. If you don't have a good memory in athletics, you're out of luck."

DiMaggio, meanwhile, faced the veteran lefty, Thornton Lee (22–11), perhaps the best pitcher in the league that year, with a league-leading 2.37 ERA. Lee, 85, recovering from brain surgery when I talked to him in 1990, said he tried to keep the ball down and away from DiMaggio and take a little off it. "Belt-high, you were in his power." Joe slugged him for two hits, a triple and a homer, as the Yankees won 6–5.

---

### Saturday,
### May 17

---◆---

DiMaggio continued his streak with a single in three tries against Rigney.

Williams faced the great Bob Feller, "undoubtedly the premier pitcher of my era"—in fact, probably one of the top three or four of all time. Fans can argue endlessly which was faster—Walter Johnson, Lefty Grove, Feller, Sandy Koufax, or Nolan Ryan. There were no radar guns in Feller's day, but Bob's hard one once out-raced a motorcycle going 97 miles an hour.

In addition, like the young Ryan, Feller was wild enough to throw terror into the hearts of the hitters. He added to the effect by half-turning his back before he delivered to the quaking batter. "Man, he'd blind you," whistles Negro leaguer Othello "Chico" Renfroe. "He'd take that left foot and raise it up

Bob Feller *Author's Collection*

and twist that body around—man, can you imagine him having that delivery when he was *wild?*"

Who was the toughest pitcher in the league? "Feller," answers Doerr without a pause. "He held his stuff for nine innings, and he had as good a curve as anybody."

Only 22 years old in 1941, Feller, the dimple-chinned Iowa farm boy, had been in the major leagues since he was 16. In his first game, an exhibition against the Cardinals, shortstop Leo Durocher had to be dragged away from the water cooler and up to the plate. Leo was only half-joking—Bobby struck out 16 men that day.

Since then, his victory totals—5, 9, 17, 24, 27, 25—added up to 107. At that age Christy Mathewson had won 63, Walter

Johnson 57, and Cy Young and Warren Spahn had yet to win their first victories.

Feller had already hurled the first of his three no-hitters. In all, he would also throw 12 one-hitters. And that's in spite of three and a half years in the Navy. With a little luck—a bang-bang play at first, a fly misjudged by a rookie, a popup falling between infielders etc—Bob could have had ten no-hitters in all.

Feller would lose the biggest years of a pitcher's life to World War II— ages 23 through 26 —which is why today's fans have hardly heard of him. As it was, Bob won 266 games and struck out 2,581 men, but the war cost him, by his own conservative estimate, 100 victories and 1,000 strikeouts. Without a war, Feller would probably have smashed Walter Johnson's strikeout mark (3,508) before either Steve Carlton or Nolan Ryan did. And he would have been within striking distance of 400 wins. "I might have stayed around a few more years and gone for it," he says.

In 1941 Feller had a 25–13 record with 260 strikeouts. Players didn't strike out as much then—the average American league team whiffed only 3.6 times per nine innings, compared to 5.4 now. Thus, pitching under today's conditions, Feller might have struck out 400 men instead of 260. In 1946 he would whiff 348, which translates to about 440 in today's league.

"Feller had a real good curve ball, along with his terrific fastball," Mel Harder says. But Jimmie Foxx claimed he hit Feller by waiting for his curve. Bob couldn't get his fastballs over, Jimmie figured, so he never swung at them.

"A hitter like Williams, a fastball don't mean too much," Harder said. "Once he got the timing on a man, he thought he had him." Then, too, Williams was hard to strike out—he whiffed only 27 times all year in 1941.

Bob said he pitched Ted the classic way—"breaking stuff down and away." But "nobody had his number. I never could get him out consistently. He hit me more times than I got him out. He was the best hitter I ever pitched to."

How did Williams do against Feller that day?

In their first head-to-head clash in 1941, Ted ripped Bob for two doubles and a single in five at bats. Williams always did hit "stuff" pitchers well, he says.

Ted was now batting .353.

---

### *Tuesday,*
### *May 20*

---◆---

Detroit was next to arrive in Boston for three games. On Sunday and Monday Williams could get only two hits in eight at bats, one in each game, against Newsom, Al Benton, and Johnny Gorsica (9–11).

On Tuesday Hal Newhouser (9–11), a wild young left-hander, defied the other pitchers' "book" that said to pitch Williams outside. "I took him inside, because I wanted him to pull." Newhouser says. "He was left-handed, and I was left-handed. I figured he'd have to get the bat moving a little faster inside than out over the plate. So I let the ball carry inside. He was a good breaking-ball hitter. I don't want to get beat on a breaking ball. You might hang it, even though I had a good breaking ball, so I'd just show him the breaking ball, not for a

Hal Newhouser *Author's Collection*

strike, and keep him off guard that way. I'd overpower him with a fastball inside and keep it down and make him pull."

Newhouser was wild and he was fiery, Williams writes. If you got a hit off him, he'd give the batter a "rotten stare . . . like you'd taken his blood." He just didn't think batters should get a hit off him.

Newhouser held Williams to one single in three at bats to leave him hitting .342. The Red Sox beat Prince Hal 4–2, snapping a five-game losing streak.

In New York DiMaggio was having his problems against the Brownies. On Sunday he had gotten three hits, but all of them were questionable. One glanced off the injured Harlond Clift's glove at third, one "squirted out" of Chet Laabs' glove in deep right "for what was called a two-base hit," wrote Rud Rennie of the *Herald-Trib*, and the third was awarded Joe when the catcher tipped his bat on a pop-up. (Under the crazy scoring rules, Joe got a hit but not an at bat.)

Now on Tuesday he faced under-hander Eldon Auker, the Browns' biggest winner that year at 14–15. Eldon's curves broke up and his fastball broke down. "He really didn't like my underhand pitch," Auker says. "I was the only one using it in the league, and I was a bit different. Joe got hits off me, lots of them. I didn't scare him any. But overall I was fairly successful with Joe." DiMag came up five times against Auker that day and managed only one single, his sixth game in a row with at least one hit.

---

## *Wednesday, May 21*

---

DiMaggio extended his streak with two hits against Detroit's Schoolboy Rowe (8–6). Strangely, when Joe came up in the ninth with men on second and third and the Yanks losing by one run, reliever Al Benton, the Tigers' ace at 15–6, refused to walk him. He brazenly pitched to DiMaggio and got him on a ground ball, though the Yanks went on to tie the game anyway and won it in the tenth.

The Brownies moved to Boston, meanwhile, led by Roy Cullenbine, who was tops in the league with .409. Williams exploded with 4-for-5 as the Sox blasted temperamental Johnny Allen (2–5) by a score of 8–6.

The next day, Thursday, against rookie Bob Muncrief (13–9), Ted got two more hits in four at bats to raise his average to .375.

Nazi paratroopers descended over British-held Crete. One of them was ex-heavyweight champ Max Schmeling.

---

### *Saturday,*
### *May 24*

---◆---

Germany's battle ship Bismarck blasted the British Hood out of the water.

Williams and DiMaggio, each with eight-game hitting streaks going, met Friday in Yankee Stadium to open a three-game series. Ted got one hit in three times up and knocked in three runs.

Joe went 1-for-5 and drove in two as the two teams tied it 9–9.

On Saturday Ted got two more hits off his "cousin" Lefty Gomez and two other pitchers.

Joe and Ted *Associated Press Photo*

For the second time in four games, Joe came up in the ninth with New York behind and with runners on second and third and first base open. Lefty Earl Johnson (4–5) was on the mound, the Sox were leading 6–3, and Joe was 0-for-3 in the box score. Boston Manager Joe Cronin faced a decision: pitch to DiMag, or walk him and pitch to Joe Gordon (.276 that year)? One would suppose Cronin would put DiMaggio on, and if he did, Joe's mini nine-game streak would be over. Cronin trotted to the mound from shortstop. "Don't walk him, you can get him," he told Johnson with a slap on the pitcher's rump. Johnson turned to the plate and fired, and DiMaggio whipped a single to drive in a run, as the Yanks went on to win 7–6.

## Sunday,
## May 25

American sailors were called out of the stands at Yankee Stadium as the navy went on alert following the Hood disaster. On the field both DiMaggio and Williams extended their streaks to 11.

DiMaggio got a double in four tries against "Old Man Moses," Lefty Grove, who was seeking his 296th win.

Williams faced Marius Russo, the Yankees' most effective pitcher that year with 3.09 ERA (14–10). Ted walloped four hits in five at bats against him and his successors to help Grove win 10–3 and push Ted up to .404, tops in the league. First baseman Johnny Sturm practically played right field, Cronin chortled, "but Ted kept lining those drives right through him." Williams also made a fine catch off New York's Henrich.

Since their streaks began, Ted had collected 21 hits in 43 at bats; Joe, 15 in 44. Williams was now at .400 for the first time since April 29.

Jimmy Halperin *Jimmy Halperin*

---

### Monday,
### May 26

---

◆

---

It is one of the great myths of baseball history that Joe DiMaggio hit in 56 straight games. He may have hit in 56 straight *American League* games, but he didn't hit in 56 straight *baseball* games. His streak was stopped after 11 games by a sore-arm Class-B pitcher who never won another game in Organized Baseball (he didn't win that game either).

His name was Jimmy Halperin.

Sunday night the Yanks boarded an overnight Pullman to Norfolk, Virginia for an exhibition with their farm team, the Norfolk Tars.

In the Atlantic, the German battleship *Bismarck* sank Britain's *Hood*, the largest battleship afloat, with a loss of 1300 lives. King George of Greece fled his capital ahead of Nazi paratroopers. In Poland, the German army began to mass on the Russian frontier.

On the lighter side, Tony Pastor's orchestra was playing at Norfolk's Granby Theater, along with films of the Louis-Buddy Baer fight. Movie fans could also see Alice Faye, Ceasar Romero, and comedian Jack Oakie in *The Great American Broadcast,* Marlene Dietrich in *The Flame of New Orleans,* William Powell and Myrna Loy in *Love Crazy,* or James Stewart and Hedy Lamarr in *Come Live With Me.*

The Tars had arrived home at six Monday morning after an all-night bus trip from Asheville, North Carolina and snatched a few hours sleep before pulling themselves out of bed to get to the park. Not only was it a challenge to be facing DiMaggio, Keller, Henrich, and Rizzuto, but Yankee general manager George Weiss would be on hand to give them all a look-over for possible promotion up the ladder to every player's dream, a chance with the Yankees.

Among the awe-struck farmhands who watched the Yankees take batting practice was a 23-year old left-hander named Jimmy Halperin. At 6'2" and 190 pounds, he had dropped out of Georgetown University two years earlier because "I had my heart set on a baseball career." He pitched that summer in Easton, Maryland in the Yankees' chain, where his record was 6–15 with a 5.30 ERA. In Akron, Ohio in 1940 he pitched the club to the pennant with a 13–6 record to earn a promotion to Norfolk in '41.

"But I hurt my arm in spring training," Halperin told me from his home in South Amboy, New Jersey, where he was an insurance salesman. "I started forcing myself so I wouldn't be shipped out. I pushed myself a little too hard. Instead of getting better, it got worse."

"Halperin had a pretty good arm," recalled Tars manager Eddie Sawyer, who would later become famous as skipper of the 1950 NL champion Philadelphia Whiz Kids. "The only problem was, he was a little wild." Jim pitched three games for the Tars, lost two of them and won none. In 18 innings he gave up 15 hits, 14 walks, and 11 runs. When the Yankees arrived, Weiss wanted to take one more look at him before deciding whether he had anything left in his arm or whether to cut him loose.

Was Jim nervous? "No, that wasn't the case," he said. "I didn't even know I was going to pitch" until just before game time, when Sawyer put the ball in his hand and said, "You're it." "If I'd known the night before, I might have been nervous."

Halperin had four pitches—fastball, curve, sidearm curve, and change-up. "But I wasn't throwing good fast pitching that day."

Yankee rookie Johnny Sturm (.239 that year) led off and walked. But Jim kept the ball low to third baseman Jerry Priddy, another rookie (.213), who slapped a grounder for a fast double play. The dangerous Henrich (.277) struck out swinging.

The first Tars batter, Tony Sams, about to be drafted into the army, teed off on New York pitcher Norman "Red" Branch (5–1) with a long drive to the fence in left-center. "The ball was labeled a sure double or triple," Tom Ferguson of the Norfolk *Virginia-Pilot* wrote, "but DiMaggio stabbed the ball like a football player pulling down a pass."

Joe was the first man up in the second. He "fouled off one or two," Halperin said, then walked on a 3–2 count. After George Selkirk (.220) and Joe Gordon (.276) went out, catcher Bill Dickey (.284) doubled DiMaggio home. Rizzuto (.307), himself a recent Norfolk graduate, made the final out.

The Tars tied it on two singles and a double play. Rookie third baseman Jersey Joe Buzas whaled a long drive to center. "I thought it was going to be in there," Buzas recalled years later behind the hot dog counter at the Reading PA ball park, where he was general manager in the Phils organization. "I was running like hell, but DiMaggio made a spectacular catch off me, over his head."

In the third the Yanks went ahead on Sturm's triple and Priddy's single, but DiMaggio ended the inning by lifting a high foul to Buzas at third.

Halperin settled down to shut the Yankees out in the fourth and fifth. He hadn't pitched in a week, one scribe wrote, but "the lefty did a swell job. His slow curves had the Yanks lifting high ones to all fields."

DiMaggio strode to bat for the third time in the sixth, and he too hit the ball in the air, where the center fielder pulled it down. Joe turned and trotted back to the dugout to sit out the rest of the afternoon. Officially he had gone 0-for-2 in the box score.

Could Halperin go on and complete the miracle, whip the Yankees, and win a trip to the major leagues? The idea must have danced through his head. But in the seventh Frankie Crosetti (.223) and Buddy Rosar (.287) singled and Rizzuto doubled to break the game open. Branch sacrificed, Sturm walked, Priddy scored Rizzuto with a fly, Henrich and Frenchie Bordagaray (.260) singled, and the score was 6–2 before Selkirk popped up to end the rally.

Halperin walked dejectedly to the showers. He had given 11 hits and walked two (Branch gave ten hits and also walked two). Weiss slowly shook his head. That night Jim caught a bus for Augusta, the next stop on the road down. He never won another game in professional ball.

Later, amid all the adulation poured on DiMaggio, Halperin remained the forgotten man. A wire service recalled his feat of shutting out DiMaggio back in May, but almost no newspapers ran the story, and most historians still studiously ignore it.

Halperin and DiMaggio had not spoken that afternoon in Norfolk, nor did they ever meet again. "He probably wouldn't even remember me," Jim shrugs. "The man deserved everything he got. I'd like to have seen him go all the way."

Halperin spent three years in the army, but when he came out, the arm was still bothering him. Today it would probably be diagnosed as a bad rotator cuff, but 40 years ago doctors didn't know anything about such things. "I wanted the Yankees to sign me, send me to a doctor, or do something," Halperin says. Instead "I got my release."

As for his big moment of glory, "it was just a lucky day. It was nothing spectacular. But it was a thrill after it was over."

---

*Tuesday,*
*May 27*

---

The Yanks moved to Washington, and DiMaggio burst back to life with three singles and a home run off five Senator pitchers.

The Red Sox played two games against the A's in Boston. Williams slammed a homer, his sixth, against Bump Hadley (4−6) in the first game.

Phil Marchildon of Penetanguishene, Ontario (10−15) whipped the Sox 11−1 in game two. "Boy, he was a tough son of a bitch," Williams says. "He had a damn fork ball."

Marchildon also had a baffling slider, which was still a rarity in those days. Some hitters called it a "nickel curve." Phil recalls that Ted came up to him one day and asked, "What is that ball you throw me inside high? I've never seen anything like it."

"What do you mean?" Marchildon asked.

"It comes up here, then all of a sudden breaks in on me," Williams answered.

"I don't know," Marchildon replied innocently, "but I hope it continues to get you out." In Boston that afternoon he held Ted to one single in four at bats.

In the North Atlantic, the British Navy cornered the Bismarck and revenged itself by sending her to the bottom.

---

***Wednesday,***
***May 28***

---◆---

Williams came back with three hits against the A's.

In Washington, meanwhile, the Yanks prepared to play the first night game in the city's history. Veteran Walter Johnson threw a strike over home plate, breaking an electron beam to turn the lights on to the oohs of the fans. In the game DiMaggio got one hit, a triple, against right-handers Sid Hudson (13–14) and Alex Carresquel (6–2).

Writer Dan Daniel discovered Joe's streak, which now stood at 13 games. For the next six weeks he would make it his proprietary property.

---

### Thursday, May 29

---

In Washington DiMaggio collected a single against righty Steve Sundra (9–13).

Up in Boston Ted slapped three more hits, including another homer, "a gigantic" blow over the bullpen against right-hander Jack Knott, at 13–11 the only winner on the A's last-place staff that year. Ted also made a nice catch in the field and left the game hitting .421.

◆

The Yankees arrived in Boston for a Memorial Day—we called it Decoration Day then—double-header. Some 60,000 New Englanders began lining up at 4:00 A.M. for tickets, though only about half of them actually stuffed themselves into the park. The others either listened by radio or joined the crowds at the beach or at the movies. Tyrone Power and Rita Hayworth were starring in a bullfighter movie, *Blood and Sand*, in the still novel technicolor process. The French classic, *Grand Illusion*, was in town. Boston that day catered to all tastes, from soprano Lily Pons at Symphony Hall to stripper Georgia Sothern at the Old Howard. Out in Indianapolis Maury Rose won the Indy 500, ending Wilbur Shaw's record string of three victories. And on Broadway "Tobacco Road" finally closed after a record-breaking seven years.

The Yanks and Red Sox split the two games. Williams got one hit in the first game against Atley Donald (9–5) and Breuer (9-7). He got two more in the second against a trio of pitchers before retiring to rest his ankle, which was giving him a little pain. His batting average had grown to .425.

But DiMaggio was having one of the worst days of his life. He woke up with a painfully sore neck and probably should not have played at all. In the first contest he dropped Cronin's easy fly, although he atoned with a fierce single to keep his streak alive.

In the second game, Joe kicked Williams' single away, then bobbled Pete Fox's single, picked it up and heaved it into the grandstand as Ted scored. That made four errors for the day—for the rest of the year he would make only five others.

**141**

Some of the partisan fans started hooting "Meatball Joe" whenever the ailing Yankee came up to bat.

Boston's lefty Mickey Harris (8–14 for the year) was working on a perfect game in the fifth when DiMag lifted a lazy fly to right field. Pete Fox circled under the ball, then suddenly appeared to lose it, and it plopped to the ground in front of him. Some reports indicate that Pete lost the ball in the sun, others that the wind played tricks on him. But the official scorer had no choice but to give DiMaggio a double. The hit was "windblown," wrote Jack Smith of the New York *Daily News*; "tainted," according to Gerry Moore of the *Globe*. If Fox had even gotten a glove on the ball, it would have been an error, and the streak would have been over. Joe was the only baserunner the Yanks would have until two outs in the ninth, when Jerry Priddy (.213) singled. The Sox won 13–0.

Joe's hitting streak now stood at 16 games; Ted's at 17.

---

*Sunday,*
*June 1*

---

◆

---

Both the Yanks and Red Sox began their western swings. New York, in third place, four games behind Cleveland, won a double-header from the Indians, as Joe got a single in each game, one of them off third baseman Ken Keltner's glove. The sweep knocked the Indians out of first.

Light-hitting Johnny Sturm (.239) hit one of his three homers for the year in the second game. It started the Yankees on a record-breaking skein: They would hit at least a homer a game for 25 straight games to pass the record of 18 set by

Detroit a year earlier. It was this, unnoticed, team streak, even more than DiMaggio's more famous individual streak, that would power the team into a lead they never gave up.

In Detroit, Ted walloped four hits in nine at bats in a double-header, including home run #8 as Boston won 7–6 and 6–5. Two of his outs were run-scoring flies; they helped the Red Sox win each game, but they hurt his batting average since each one counted as an at bat (they'd be sacrifice flies today).

In New York Mel Ott hit his 400th home run, a National league milestone.

And in the Atlantic, a Brazilian ship picked up a lifeboat of Americans who had been floating for 18 days since their ship, the Robin Moore, had been cold-bloodedly sunk by a German U-boat. They reported that three other lifeboats were still missing.

---

### Monday,
### June 2

---◆---

In a hospital in New York, Lou Gehrig passed away at the age of 37. Yankee manager Joe McCarthy and Lou's old roommate, Bill Dickey, immediately left the team to hurry east for the funeral as the down-hearted Yankees took the field against Feller, who was 7–5 at that time.

Joe hit Bob pretty well—back in 1938 he had knocked in seven runs in one game against the 19-year-old. Bobby was a fastball pitcher, and Joe a fastball hitter. Ruefully, Feller admitted that he didn't learn how to pitch to DiMag until Joe was almost ready to retire—fastballs at the fists. But in '41 Bobby hadn't found the formula yet; that day Joe slapped him for a double and single. For the first time the New York *Times*, in a footnote, took note of the streak, now at 19 games.

With one single in Detroit, Williams ran his own streak to 20 games, although no one had discovered it yet.

---

### *Wednesday, June 4*

---

◆

---

The Yankees and Red Sox switched cities, New York moving to Detroit and Boston to Cleveland. DiMaggio hit a homer on the third. Williams was rained out.

They were both rained out on the 4th.

One Cleveland writer, Henry Adams of the *Press*, sat down with Williams and came away impressed. "Tall Ted turned out to be an affable, slender gent who seemed all legs and arms," Adams wrote. "He talks volubly, and this is extremely refreshing. There are too many ballplayers whose conversational repertoire consists only of a few grunts with an occasional 'yes' or 'naw.' " ("That's one of my big problems," Ted grinned. "I'm always saying what I think.")

Williams was modest about his own hitting. He was using the same stance he always had, hitting in the same parks, and using the same bat. "I'm just lucky, but the way I feel, no one is going to stop me." He had praise for Cleveland's Jeff Heath, who was hitting in the .380s, and for his own teammates, Dom DiMaggio, "a helluva player," and Foxx, "the world's greatest hitter."

"That surprised us," Adams reported. "Tall Ted is supposed to be a cocky fellow who talks about Williams. He wasn't that way when we found him. Don't think, however, that he doesn't have confidence in himself. He does. Plenty."

Williams did not follow his mentor Hornsby's advice against going to the movies. But he did tell Adams that he "tries not to read too much, especially on trains." The rest of the Red Sox were bookworms, he admitted. That summer the best sellers were Churchill's *Blood, Sweat and Tears*, the patriotic poem "White Cliffs of Dover," and *Random Harvest* by James Hilton. But the number-one author for the Red Sox, Williams reported, was Zane Grey.

"In our book, Ted goes down as an 'all right guy.' He may pop off once in a while, but after all, he's only been out of San Diego high school four years."

Elsewhere in the *Press* a headline warned:

### U.S. DEFENSE
### HEADS STUDY
### NIGHT BASEBALL

"Dim outs" could be a more serious threat to the game than the draft, the story said.

Meanwhile, Hitler and Mussolini were meeting at the Brenner Pass in the Alps to chart their war moves. British bombers hit Beirut. The Nazis were mopping up in Crete after the British had fled. Germany was also completing its seizure of the Balkans, the source of horsehide for American baseballs. For the rest of the war, major league batting statistics would go into a tailspin.

The players were closely following the war news—it was their number-one topic of conversation. Could they finish out this year without being drafted? Would there even be a league next year? The future weighed on everyone's shoulders—

except Williams'. He says he hardly followed the headlines that year, he was so wrapped up in his hitting.

---

### *Thursday, June 5*

◆

---

DiMaggio kept his streak going with one hit, a triple, against Buck Newsom.

Williams got a homer and two singles against four Indians pitchers to help Joe Dobson win the game. Joe pitched a four-hitter and hit a homer himself for his son, who had suffered a brain concussion in an automobile accident.

On Friday DiMaggio had an off-day.

In Chicago Williams slammed a double and an upper deck homer against Johnny Rigney to raise his batting average to .442 and extend his hitting streak to 22 games. It was his second homer off Rig in two games. Rigney may have been worrying about his draft call, set for June 20. The Red Sox won 6–3.

---

### *Saturday, June 7*

◆

---

In St. Louis DiMaggio slapped three singles to run his streak to 22.

And in Chicago, Williams collected one single off the little round southpaw, Ed Smith, to make 23 games in a row. The Boston *Herald* finally noticed Williams' streak, reporting that it was the longest of the year in the Majors. In 23 games Ted had hit an even .500, driven in 24 runs, and scored 32 more. Six of his hits were homers.

That day he also made a circus catch off Luke Appling. After "stumbling and almost falling on his face," one writer wrote, Williams finally recovered to make a nice running catch. An inning later, he made "an even better one," whatever that meant. The Red Sox won 6–3.

---

### *Sunday, June 8*

---◆---

At Belmont, Whirlaway completed the Triple Crown.

In a double-header at St. Louis, DiMaggio blasted three home runs and a double to give him 4-for-8 on the day and run his streak to 24 games.

In Chicago two great future Hall of Famers squared off in the first game of a double-header: 41-year-old Lefty Grove and 40-year-old Ted Lyons.

Lyons was a powerful man, Williams says: "When he grabbed you, you stayed grabbed." Lyons had become the White Sox' "Sunday pitcher," who saved his ancient arm for just one game a week. It proved to be smart strategy; that year Lyons won 12 and lost 10, and the next year he would lead the league with a 2.10 ERA. Lyons thought he would have been even better in '43, but he decided to go into the Navy even though he was 42 years old.

The two navy officers, Lyons and Williams, would become close friends. Lyons is the only man to throw a home run to Babe Ruth in 1927 and pitch to Williams in '41, so one day in Honolulu Williams asked him suddenly, "Ted, do you think I'm as good a hitter as Babe Ruth?"

Lyons replied that it was too soon to tell, and Williams sulked until Lyons finally told him, "Look, Ted, you're different from the Babe. Babe would swing at balls up around his cap, you won't swing at one above your letters. You're two completely different hitters." Williams still wasn't satisfied, until Lyons finally relented with a laugh: "OK, you're as good a hitter as Babe Ruth," whereupon Williams' mood turned abruptly sunny again.

Actually, Lyons considered Williams more of a Ty Cobb, "as far as being an intelligent batter." And for his part, Williams thought Lyons excelled in "those little pitcher-batter thinking games" that Williams enjoyed with such relish. "And you can't guess with the son of a gun, because he'd usually out-think you." Lyons was "sneaky fast," Williams said, threw his curve to spots, and mixed in a knuckler.

"For the most part I didn't give Williams too many fastballs," Lyons said. "I tried to get him to hit curves; I'd waste the fastball, but when you get behind, you had to come in there. He didn't like that change of pace, he liked the fast stuff. A change bothers anybody." But Williams knew the pitchers. "He knew what they were going to throw; he was another Ty Cobb. If he'd been playing in Detroit or St. Louis, there's no telling what he'd have done."

That afternoon Lyons and Grove dueled for ten innings before Lyons finally won. Williams called it "the greatest exhibition of pitching I ever hope to see . . . . Two old-timers maneuvering, outwitting hitters, making their heads do what their arms used to do."

Ted was so transfixed, he forgot to hit. Lyons gave the red-hot Williams three walks and got him out the other two times to bring Ted's hitting streak to an end.

Though the bases on balls cost Williams his streak, the value of his walks was demonstrated once again. The second one came in the eighth inning with the bases loaded, forcing in one run and setting up one more to tie the game, which Dom DiMaggio won in the tenth with a single. It was win #297 for Grove.

In game two Thornton Lee walked Williams once and stopped him the other three times up. Again the walk was key. It came in the seventh inning with the score 0–0. Cronin followed with a double to the scoreboard, and the Red Sox went on to win. In the box score Ted's effort for the day was 0-for-5. His three walks didn't show up at all, yet they had helped move the Red Sox into second place and knock the White Sox out of first. Should Williams have swung on a wide pitch to try to get a hit and extend his streak? Or was he more valuable to his team to take the walks?

To compile a hitting streak, the first essential is to get four chances to hit every game. That year Williams walked 145 times in 143 games; DiMaggio walked 76 times in 139 games, or about once every other game. Thus Ted came to bat officially about three times a game on average; Joe about three and a half. If DiMaggio had received as many bases on balls as Williams that year, how long could he have kept his streak alive?

DiMaggio said he liked to hit aggressively "early in the count." Today batting coaches would instruct him to be more "selective." Would Joe have been a better batter if he had waited more often for the right pitch? Would he have helped his team more?

The other essential of a hit streak is to put the ball in play and not give away any outs on strikeouts. Both men were among the best of all time in this—that year Ted whiffed just 27 times, Joe 13.

Meanwhile, Ted told the Associated Press he was through feuding with the writers. He wants to be "a good guy" now, he said, admitting that his reputation as a "bad guy" is "partly deserved" and partly the fault of the park:

"When they moved right field 20 feet closer to the plate at Fenway Park, I really got in bad in Boston [wry smile]. Everybody thought I'd hit 80 home runs, and I guess I thought I would too. When I hit only 23, I got mad about it myself. And a few of the boys got sore at me. Boy, it got so I hated to go out and meet people. But when I did, a lot of them said, 'You're not as bad as we thought you were.' " (Those who know Williams know that he probably didn't say "boy." His favorite expletive is Jesus.)

"But that's all over now. I'm just trying to get along. It's a dream I've always had, the way I'm hitting now. Boy, I'm just busting the cover off that ball. I'm lucky, because a lot of my drives are going 'where they ain't.' But hell, it's only June. I may be down to .360 in another month."

In Chicago the Yankees entered their game in third place, four games behind the Indians. (Boston was in sixth, six games behind.) DiMaggio got a single in five times up, a high bouncer to third base, to run his streak to 25. James P. Dawson of the *Times* called it a "scratch single," Rennie of the *Trib* said it was a "hard grounder." Take your pick.

In St. Louis the Red Sox were rained out, but Williams headed straight for a theater for several hours of steady cowboy movies. "Boy, it was great, that bang, bang stuff," he told Carl T. Felker of *The Sporting News*.

Felker spent an afternoon with Williams in Boston publicity director Ed Doherty's hotel room as Ted strode restlessly about the room, pausing in front of the mirror to grit his teeth and take a few practice cuts with a rolled up newspaper. "Hitting is the biggest thing in my life," he said. "And the thing I like next best is hunting ducks in Minnesota."

Williams was aiming at Hugh Duffy's all-time record of .440. "If you don't have confidence in yourself, who will?" he asked. He fidgeted around the room, swinging the paper, or flopped in a chair, shaking his foot, while he talked incessantly.

Felker was charmed, as many others have been, by Williams' "unconcealed boyish delight in batting, and his quick, hearty laugh." He speaks his mind "without a moment's reflection to choose his words." He takes "a boy's pleasure in praise and quick, youthful resentment of criticism." But the feud with the writers was all forgotten now, Ted assured

Felker. "I found out that sports writers can hurt you, but you can't do anything to them. I'm getting along fine with them this season. Maybe it's because I haven't talked to them. I let my base hits do the talking."

Ted was also getting along fine with the fans, at least the kids. He gave autographs to the youngsters freely, "but not to grownups. The heck with the old fellows." He gets a lot of requests for talks to youth groups and had recently been invited to give out varsity letters at a Boston high school, Doherty said. Ted was a big, awkward hit, waving his arms and legs and almost knocking over the mike.

In the hotel lobby Williams was approached by a high school coach and two players from Moberly, Missouri. They asked him for some tips, which he promised to type up and leave in the coach's mailbox at the desk. His advice:

1. Practice swinging all the time.
2. Be relaxed at the plate.
3. Don't stride too far.
4. Always keep your eye on the ball.
5. Get that extra snap in your wrist.

Who were the toughest pitchers for him? Felker asked. Ted named Feller, lefty Ken Chase of Washington, Chicago's Pete Appleton, Detroit's Tommy Bridges, New York's Marius Russo, and Mel Harder of Cleveland as hurlers who "used to give me trouble." But, he said, laconically, "I've had better luck against them lately."

The draft wasn't worrying him. He had registered in Minneapolis but didn't even know what classification he was in. (It was 3-A, meaning he was the sole support of his mother.)

Williams, it turned out, was also proud of his fielding. "I haven't been charged with a single error in 43 games," he boasted.

Doherty corrected him. He'd made one error on May 28, when he hit a runner with a throw.

"Not me!" Ted protested. "Who the heck did I hit?"

Doherty told him. Williams smacked his forehead. "Do you mean to tell me they can give you an error if you hit a runner! What kind of scoring is *that*?"

---

### Thursday, June 12

---

After more rain-outs on the 10th and 11th, the Red Sox and Browns played two games on the 12th.

In game one Williams faced Bob Harris (12−14), plus Bob Muncrief in relief. Ted got only one single in five at bats; however his fly ball was deep enough to advance Dom from second to third to ignite a four-run inning. Neither then nor now was that considered a sacrifice fly, but in 1930, when Bill Terry hit .401, it would have been scored a SF and Ted would have saved one more at bat.

In game two knuckleballer Johnny Niggeling (7−9) struck Williams out with Lou Finney on third. Ted was so mad, he smashed his bat in two over home plate. Two innings later he came up with Finney on first, and this time he smashed Niggeling's pitch "a mile over the roof" with his new bat for home run #11.

The following day the game was called after four innings when a whistling tornado almost blew the roof off the park.

The Sox boarded their train for the longest hop in the majors, 28 hours back to Boston from St. Louis. Rookies slept in the upper bunks over the wheels, while stars like Williams were given lower berths in the quieter and smoother middle of the car. Today a team makes the trip in five hours or less by plane. But, old-timers like Dom say, today's players miss the bonding that came with the long train rides, when the men played cards, sang, chewed the fat, and got to know and like each other in a way that is rare nowadays.

---

### Sunday, June 15

---

In Fenway on Saturday Ed Smith of the White Sox beat Boston 5–2 in spite of Ted's two singles and a "wicked" double down the line to right.

In New York, Feller walked DiMaggio twice, but Joe got a double in two at bats to keep his streak alive.

Sunday Lyons faced Boston in the first game of a double-header. This time Ted whipped two singles in three at bats to help beat the White Sox 8–6.

In the second game he got two more hits in three tries off right-hander Buck Ross (3–9). One of his hits was homer #12, 20 rows into the grandstand and just inside the foul pole. Back then the foul pole was literally a pole, as thin as a flag pole, leading to heated disputes now and then. The present poles with yellow screens attached to help umpires judge fair and foul better had not come in yet.

DiMaggio, meanwhile, hit barely enough to keep his streak alive. Against Cleveland's Jim Bagby and Al Smith, he got only one hit, a home run off Bagby, which also kept the team's home run streak alive and beat Cleveland 3–2.

His streak had now reached 28 and was getting to be news. One wonders why the sudden interest in a subject that had hardly elicited any curiosity when other, earlier hitters had put streaks together. Willie Keeler's 44-game streak in 1896 was as unknown to Keeler as to everyone else until a historian uncovered it long after Wee Willie had died.

In 1911 Detroit's Ty Cobb had hit in 40 straight games without arousing much excitement. Larry Amman, perhaps the nation's number-one Cobb scholar, writes that no newspaper even mentioned Ty's streak until it was over, not even when he passed the new American League record of 29 set by Bill Bradley in 1902.

Only on three occasions did Ty keep the streak alive with the last time at bat—on May 19 (#3), June 17 (#27) and 22 (#32). On the 17th the only hit was an infield type. But "there was never any mention of a debatable scorer's call helping Cobb during the streak." The fact that no one even knew Ty was on a streak "renders moot" the question of a friendly scorer or umpire giving him some help, Amman says. Cobb was so detested anyway, that he probably got more close calls against him than for him.

Amman points out that Sam Crawford hit behind Ty throughout the streak, enjoying probably his best season ever with a personal high of .378. That's the major reason that Cobb received only one intentional walk in the 40 games. Since both men were left-handed, the Tigers saw a lot of left-handed pitching that season.

Cobb was finally stopped on the Fourth of July by Big Ed Walsh (27–18). Ironically, 24 years later Walsh's son, Ed Jr, would stop DiMaggio when he hit in 61 straight games at San Francisco in 1933.

In 1922, when the Browns' George Sisler hit in 41 straight games, breaking Cobb's "modern" record, the New York papers tucked the information in paragraph three of their stories.

That September the Browns and Yankees were in a pennant fight. Sisler tied Cobb with a hit off Yankee Bob Shawkey (20-12). The next day he singled off Waite Hoyt (19-12) to set a new "modern" record, a footnote which the *Times* reported in a box beside the game account.

But Sisler was ailing. One arm hung uselessly as he ran out infield hits. "It's aching terribly," he admitted.

On September 17 New York's Bullet Joe Bush (26-7) took the mound against the Browns, the same man who had started Sisler off on his streak six weeks earlier. Sisler grounded out twice, fouled out, and, on his last chance, slapped another ground ball to second for his final out. George lost his streak, and the Browns lost the game and the pennant. If they had won, they might have gone on to establish a dynasty—at that time the Cardinals hadn't won their first pennant yet. It is just possible that if the Browns had won that game, it might have been the Cards who had to move to Baltimore. Bush therefore might have stopped a streak, won a pennant, and destroyed a franchise, all in one day.

At any rate, the newspapers were so intent on the pennant race, they forgot to mention the end of Sisler's streak at all! And no one even thought to put in a phone call to Brooklyn to interview the dying Keeler, then 50 years old, probably because no one even knew of Keeler's feat, including Wee Willie, who would be dead within six months, still ignorant of what he had done. It is probable that news of Sisler's streak did not reach the papers in San Francisco. Even if it had, seven-year-old Giuseppe DiMaggio would have been too young to notice it.

In 1922 Rogers Hornsby of the Cardinals hit in 33 straight games, a "modern" National League record, but again no one paid any attention.

In 1938, when still a third St. Louis hitter, rookie first baseman George McQuinn of the Browns, passed Hornsby's total, his own teammate and best friend, Harlond Clift, didn't even know he had a streak going! McQuinn "never mentioned the streak to me," Clift says. Harlond does remember George as "a great guy" and a fine left-handed batter. "When he got two strikes, he'd go to left. He could hang out those little line drives. And he had power, that kid did. And he had a pretty good short porch in St. Louis."

(I remember George McQuinn as a neighbor in Alexandria, Virginia a few years later. I was selling war bonds for my high school and, unknowingly, rang his door bell. It was quite a surprise when a major league first baseman opened the door.)

Ironically, McQuinn had come up through the Yankee organization, and in 1937 played for the legendary Newark Bears, perhaps the greatest minor league club of all time. But, with Lou Gehrig hitting .351 and knocking in 159 runs, there was no room on the Yanks for McQuinn, and they dealt him to the lowly Browns. If he had come up to the Yankees, the events of the following year would have insured him a hero's mythic status. But, a thousand miles away in St. Louis, McQuinn's feat earned him only yawns from the Gotham editors.

In 1938 the Browns were, as usual, in seventh place, and, as McQuinn would say wistfully later, "There wasn't all that hullabaloo back in those days, especially with the Browns. The newspaper men never bothered me, never interviewed me until the day my streak ended."

George McQuinn *Author's Collection*

McQuinn had reached 34 games when he was scheduled to play in Philadelphia before arriving in New York, where the editors had at last waked up to the story. They sent a photographer down to Philadelphia to shoot some pictures to use when George arrived in the big city the following day. But Big Buck Ross (9–16), whom McQuinn usually hit without difficulty, shut him down 0-for-4. The editors canceled the picture coverage.

"I should have bunted like Pete Rose did," George said, "or made a deal with the third baseman to play back deep. The A's weren't going anywhere, and we weren't either. But I never bunted during the streak." McQuinn did get a raise at the end of the season, but for his average, .324, not for the streak.

During all the publicity over DiMaggio's streak, did McQuinn ever ask why no one remembered his? "No way," says Clift firmly. "He was a perfect gentleman."

## Monday,
## June 16

When DiMaggio's 1941 streak reached 28 games, New York papers were already talking about it. The Yankee record was 29, held jointly by Roger Peckinpaugh and Earl Combs. Both men would be in uniform for game #29, Combs as a Yankee coach and Peck as manager of the visiting Indians. Against Al Milnar, Joe got a double in five at bats, and the Yankees, who swept three games from the front-running Indians, were now just one game behind.

## Tuesday,
## June 17

All the papers were covering DiMaggio's streak now, blocking Williams' .424 average out of the headlines, as the White Sox moved into Yankee Stadium for a two-game series. For the first game, Chicago manager Jimmy Dykes started Johnny Rigney, who had given Joe trouble twice since the streak began. In game three he held Joe to a single in three at bats, and on June 10 in Chicago DiMag managed only one single in five tries against him.

DiMaggio was a good fastball hitter, Lyons said, and "Rigney was strictly a good fastball pitcher, but he could strike out those high fastball hitters." Compared to Williams, who

**159**

wouldn't swing at many bad balls, "DiMaggio was a very aggressive guy, he'd hit balls outside, a little high."

Rigney kept the ball inside, and again he had DiMaggio under control. Three times Joe came up; three times he went down. Joe was now 2-for-11 against John for the year.

In the ninth Joe topped a ground ball that bounded to Hall of Fame shortstop Luke Appling, hitting Luke on the shoulder and bouncing into left field. A hit or an error?

The streak was either dead or still alive, depending on what official scorer Dan Daniel of the New York *Telegraph* ruled. The Yankee players sprang off the bench to the dugout steps and craned their necks toward the press box.

Daniel, in the opinion of Washington *Post* sports editor Shirley Povich, "was a perfect ass." He was pompously positive that he knew more about baseball than any man alive, yet he was always getting scooped. When other papers broke big stories, Daniel's second-day lead would read: "The news of . . . came as no surprise to this reporter."

Years later Daniel would vow that "I never want to become involved again in a similar streak." The press box, in the mezzanine, was exposed to the fans below, who were in the habit of shouting up, "Heh, Mac, who do you write for? Say sumpin' nice about the Yankees, you creep." Daniel muttered, "When I tell you the life of the scorer was in jeopardy, I am not exaggerating. DiMaggio supporters waited for me after a game, day or night. They forced me to cut off telephone service at home."

Now, with the fingers of the reporters poised over their typewriters, Daniel slowly and dramatically held up one finger. A hit. It was a lucky hit, Louis Effrat of the *Times* wrote. "It was a legitimate hit," Yankee pitcher Marv Breuer insisted years later, "a lucky hit but a legitimate one."

Wrote Daniel the next morning: Joe had "a very narrow escape from a very ignominious stoppage."

The Yankees beat their bats on the concrete steps and hugged each other. But most of the fans were in the dark. In those days there were no "Hit" and "Error" signs on most scoreboards: It was feared that a player would be too embarrassed to have his miscue displayed for everyone to see. Many a pitcher has been working on a no-hitter while no one in the stands was sure just what the status was. Sometimes the pitcher wasn't sure either. Even for this historic occasion, no one thought to break with tradition and inform the cash customers.

Up in Boston the Red Sox split a Bunker Hill Day doubleheader with Detroit. Ted's 13th home run off reliever Bud Thomas (1–3) put the Sox ahead to stay in game one. The wind cost him a second homer on a shot into the extreme rightfield corner. In the second game, Ted walked three times to raise his average to .424.

The United States, meanwhile, closed all Nazi consulates in the country, and Britain opened its campaign against the Nazi panzer army under General Rommel in Libya.

---

### Wednesday,
### June 18

———————————◆———————————

Veteran Schoolboy Rowe (8–6) stopped Williams cold at Boston, Ted couldn't even get the ball out of the infield as his average fell to .417.

In New York, for the second day in a row, DiMaggio was again saved by Daniel on a bouncing ball to Appling. Against Thornton Lee, Joe was walked intentionally in the first and hit into a DP in the third.

In the fifth he sent another bounding grounder to Appling. "It was labeled 'easy out'," wrote Louis Effrat of the *Herald Tribune*, But the ball "suddenly took a bad hop and hit Luke on the shoulder." Appling bobbled it, picked it up, but didn't even make the throw. Again, Daniel called it a hit.

"Appling picked it up and dropped it," says a long-time New York baseball historian, who requests anonymity because he is a friend of Joe. "I marked it an error on my scorecard. I left the Stadium thinking the streak was over until I got home that night and found out it had been scored a hit. If the record hadn't been on the line, I don't think he'd have called it a hit."

Effrat called it a "lucky" hit. Arthur Daly of the *Times* labeled it a "scratch hit" but "legitimate." Joe Williams of the *World-Telegram* called it "a lucky fluke" and added that the official scorer was "perspiring tensely under the strain . . . taking DiMaggio's streak harder than Joe is." Daniel himself wrote the following morning that the hit was "flukey."

It's a good thing Daniel gave it to him, for in DiMaggio's last at bat, he sent a long drive to right that Taffy Wright leaped and caught at the grandstand wall.

Would Daniel have called either of Joe's grounders a hit under other conditions? Would a Chicago or Detroit or Philadelphia scorer have called them hits? We'll never know. But if either one of the two calls had gone the other way, DiMaggio's 56-game streak would suddenly have become two short streaks, and no one would remember them today.

One wonders why, 50 years later, baseball still employs hometown writers as official scorers—imagine the howl if hometown umpires were allowed to call the game on the field. Even the most conscientious scorer is prey to normal emotion, and if a close call does go the home team's way, eyebrows will be raised, whether justified or not.

I asked Appling about both plays at a Hall of Fame weekend in Cooperstown. "It wasn't me," Luke replied. "It was (third baseman) Dario Lodigiani." But there is no doubt at all that Appling, and not Lodigiani, was at shortstop both days and handled both plays. How can one explain the contradiction? I have interviewed hundreds of ball players about games many years in the past. My experience is that great plays remain indelibly in their memories, while failures tend quickly to fade. One can only blame this familiar trick of memory for the discrepancy.

DiMaggio, all the Yankees, Appling, and Daniel all share a common motive for defending the hit call. Only the pitchers, Rigney and Lee, would lobby to change it, and they are clearly outvoted.

That night in the Polo Grounds DiMaggio joined 50,000 other fans to watch light-heavyweight champ Billy Conn, vastly outweighed and a long shot underdog, almost score the biggest miracle in boxing annals. Conn danced around Joe Louis for 12 rounds and had the title safely won, when he got careless in the 13th and danced in range of Louis's dynamite right hand. Louis saved his title with one devastating uppercut. We talked about that fight for weeks afterward, if not for years.

And on the Polish-Russian border, the massed German divisions were getting little sleep while Berlin dispatched a final ultimatum to Moscow.

## *Friday,*
## *June 20*

---◆---

On Thursday DiMaggio erupted for three hits against Chicago and on Friday for four more against Detroit's Newsom to run his streak to 33.

In Fenway, Williams faced Auker and the Browns. Auker's strange windup and underhand delivery bothered him, Ted said. Still, he went 2-for-3 against Auker and veteran Johnny Allen (5-5), as the Red Sox won 4–2. He doubled to the flagpole to knock in one run, then scored on Jim Tabor's single. The play at the plate was close, but Ted didn't slide. The ankle was flaring up, he explained afterwards. He was supposed to have it X-rayed, but he was afraid the doctors would tell him to sit out a few games.

By the seventh inning rain was falling hard, but, wrote the *Herald,* "Ted showed his contempt for such a little thing by whacking a wicked drive safely into right field, scoring DiMaggio."

# 7

## *The Summer of '41*

## *Saturday,*
## *June 21*

◆

Williams had a bad day against St. Louis, with two ground ball outs and one walk. He didn't play the last two innings, as the Brownies KO'd Grove in the second and went on to beat the Sox 13–9.

The same afternoon 250 miles away, I was standing with my nose pressed to the glass in the front car of the uptown subway hurtling toward Yankee Stadium, on my way with my father to see if Joe DiMaggio could make it 34 straight.

## WON'T YIELD SEAS, ROOSEVELT SAYS, BRANDING GERMANY AS AN OUTLAW; FINLAND ORDERS FULL MOBILIZATION

the *Herald-Tribune* cried.

### Helsinki Goes on a War Basis—Soviet Paper Defies 'the Enemy'

◆

### Reich Is Poised for Drive

◆

### Preparations From the Arctic To Ukraine Complete—Russia Due to Yield or Fight Soon

We barely glanced at the paper as we hurried out of the station and bought tickets to the third base mezzanine.

My memories of the game are four:

One, I remember the Yankees playing catch in front of their dugout before the game. Red Rolfe stood with his hands on his hips, flicking out his glove at the last second to catch the ball. I thought that was cool, although I didn't say "cool," I probably said "neat."

Two, I recall DiMaggio running in from center field after the first inning after skimming his glove onto the grass behind him, as was the custom then. (I never heard of a fielder tripping over a glove or a ball hitting it and taking a crazy bounce, but it must have happened sometimes.) Joe ran pumping his knees high, his fists together at his belt buckle. "See that?" the people around me nudged each other. "That's the way he always runs."

Three, I remember Joe standing at the plate, legs spread, big #5 facing us on his pin-striped back, hands at his ear, bat held straight up, waiting motionless as fastballer Dizzy Trout (9–9) kicked and pitched. "It must have been a fastball," Detroit catcher Birdie Tebbetts theorized years later. "Trout had a 94-mile-an-hour fastball, and we didn't curve DiMaggio too often." In my memory, Joe stroked a clean line drive into center field. Actually, I discovered in checking old newspapers, it was a handle-hit blooper over first base. Said the Detroit *Free-Press*: The ball "floated lazily just beyond Rudy York's reach." (How memories can fool us!)

It was Joe's only hit of the day, but it moved him past Hornsby's right-handed record of 33 games and pulled him even with McQuinn's 34. (What a contrast between the excitement over DiMag and the silence that had greeted McQuinn.) Only Cobb (40) and Sisler (41) remained ahead of DiMaggio now—Keeler's feat still had not been discovered. DiMaggio said later that for the first time he seriously thought about going for the record.

Four, I remember tiny Phil Rizzuto lifting the second home run of his life into the left-field stands. It tied Detroit's home run record of 18 straight games, though the Tigers won the game 7–2.

By next morning the news was out: Germany had invaded Russia.

---

### Sunday, June 22

---◆---

DiMaggio got two hits, one a homer, against Detroit's Newsom and Newhouser, to break the homer record.

Williams' slump continued; he collected only one single in six at bats against the Browns, as the Red Sox split the double header. Ted had now gone 1-for-10 against the lowly St. Louis pitching. Whether his foot was still bothering him or not, we don't know; the newspapers didn't discuss the injury at all.

---

### Monday, June 24

---◆---

The first-place Indians came to town, and the great Babe Ruth himself was in the Fenway stands. Williams doesn't remember that day specifically, but he does recall Ruth attending other games. There would be a commotion in the crowd, everyone would stand to look. "There's Babe Ruth!" would go from fan to fan like a modern wave. The Babe was only 45 years old then, only one year older than Nolan Ryan in 1991, and had been retired only six years, or just one year more than Tom Seaver now. So in 1941 Ruth was not a mythic figure from the mists of baseball prehistory. Except for the very youngest kids, like me, most of the people in the park had probably seen him play. His record-breaking 60-homer season had come only 14 years earlier.

Earlier that spring the Babe had told reporters that Ted has strong wrists with a fast swing and uncoiling of the hips. He also waits much longer on the pitch than Ruth had. "Yeah," Babe grunted, "he could do it, he could hit .400."

If Ted hoped to impress the great Ruth, they were both disappointed. Williams was the only Boston player to go hit-less in a 13−2 rout of three Cleveland pitchers. He got only two strikes to hit and beat both of them into the ground, one for a double play. He got walked three times. One was intentional, and, said the Boston *Post*, "the other two might as well have been."

But Ted did turn in the best fielding play of the day—"another one of his recent grand catches," as the *Herald* wrote. He "thundered over toward the left-field grandstand, crossed over his glove hand and made a backhanded clutch, just shy of the foul line."

In New York the Yankees whipped the Browns 9−1, but DiMaggio had another scare, this one against rookie Bob Muncrief, the Oklahoma right-hander with an excellent 13−9 record.

"They said I had one of the best curve balls in the league," Muncrief told me, "but I thought I won more with my fastball. They had to guard against my curve. Joe wouldn't swing at my curve ball until he had to." How did he pitch to Joe? "As the old saying goes, you just in-and-out, up-and-down," Bob shrugs. "You didn't fool him on pitches. You gave Joe the line in Yankee Stadium, it was so short (301'); you played him in left-center, deep." A fly down the line would be a home run, but fielders had a better chance of catching anything in the far reaches of "Death Valley" in left-center.

"Joe hit one 452 feet off me," Muncrief winces. "Roy Cullenbine caught it by the run-way in left-center in the corner where the bleachers begin. We doubled Henrich off first. Took three relays to get it back."

In DiMaggio's last at bat, the Yanks were leading 4–0, but Joe still didn't have a hit. Then, says Muncrief, "he hit a fastball on the 2–2 if I'm not mistaken, a line drive over the shortstop's head. Luke Sewell (the manager) eat me out, said, 'Why didn't you walk him? That's why I left you in.' He eat me out because I didn't walk him, break his streak. But I wouldn't have done that. I wanted to put him out, but I wouldn't have walked him. We had 9,000 people in the Stadium on a Monday. I knew they weren't there to see me. Joe was the one put them in there." To Sewell, Bob replied, "That wouldn't have been fair. It's him or me. Hell, he's the best ballplayer I ever saw."

---

*Tuesday,*
*June 25*

◆

Williams broke out of his slump with a "lordly" homer ten rows into the bleachers behind the bullpen against his old teammate, Jim Bagby. The blast tied the score, and the Sox and Lefty Grove went on to win 7–2 and knock the Indians out of first place. It was Grove's 298th victory.

The Yankees moved into the lead, beating St. Louis 7–5. DiMaggio contributed only one hit, but it was a three-run homer, which also kept the team's home run streak alive. His own streak had reached 37 games, only four short of Sisler's modern record.

Meanwhile, the German blitzkrieg was driving deep into Russia.

### U.S. TO GIVE REDS ALL POSSIBLE AID

the *Herald* headline said.

### U.S. to be World Oil Arsenal

***Thursday,***
***June 26***

◆

Bobby Feller beat the Red Sox 11–8 for his 16th win, tops in the majors, although Williams clipped him for three hits in five at bats.

However, Frank Gibbons of the Cleveland *Press* charged, Ted "was a lackadaisical fielder, and even worse on the bases." He played two balls "indifferently" in left field, "and was lucky to make it from first to second when Tabor hit one off the wall." Gibbons also discovered a new Williams "eccentricity." Every day for a week, he wrote, Ted took a different watch to the jeweler "just to watch him take them apart and put them back together again. . . . He likes to see what makes them tick."

DiMaggio meanwhile was giving Daniel another cardiac emergency.

New York's Marius Russo was working on a no-hitter, which was broken up, ironically, by McQuinn's home run. Then all attention turned to Joe, who hadn't gotten a hit yet against Auker.

In the sixth DiMaggio banged a ground ball to shortstop Johnny Berardino, who fumbled it as Joe crossed first base safely. It was clearly an error, but the Yankees went into their routine of rushing to the dugout steps and craning their necks to the press box. This time, however, Daniel wouldn't be intimidated. He signaled error—and "properly" so, the *Times* wrote, although Joe Gordon "waved his arms in disgust."

Daniel would later boast of giving Berardino the error. Writing in the third person, he said that Gordon "semaphored his disgust," but "the scorer was going to let Joe make his own hits the way Joe wanted to make them."

It looked as if DiMaggio might not get another chance. He was due to bat fourth in the eighth inning, and, with the Yankees ahead 4–1, there probably would not be a ninth.

Sturm led off the Yankee eighth with an out as the crowd groaned and Daniel sweated.

Then Rolfe walked as the New York fans stood and clapped and catcher Rick Ferrell, a future Hall of Famer, fumed. "Bill McGowan was umpire, and he walked the guy! Threw six strikes, and he still walked the guy."

Henrich was next up, then DiMag.

I asked Auker if he had considered walking Henrich to give DiMaggio another chance at bat. "I don't think so," Eldon replied. "I wasn't thinking about his streak, I was just thinking about the ball game. I never gave too much thought to records. I didn't know about the streak until after the game was over. I don't think I'd have walked him even if I had known it. When you're working like that, you're only thinking of getting the man out who's at the plate. All I was trying to do was get them out as they come up. I don't think any pitcher would walk anybody to pitch to DiMaggio if they're in their right minds."

Conventional strategy for the Yankees, with their heavy hitters coming up, was to hit away and pad the lead. But what if Henrich hit into a double play to end the game? Tom strolled back to the bench. "Mind if I bunt?" he asked McCarthy.

"Good idea," the manager nodded. In Keeler's day, or even Sisler's, when hitting streaks were either unknown or just curiosities, no manager would have bunted in such a situation. Who knows how many other potential streaks have been nipped in the bud because the teams didn't change strategy to protect them?

But if Henrich bunted, that would leave first base open. Would the Browns walk Joe? Maybe Tom shouldn't bunt after all.

Henrich says he never doubted that Auker would pitch to Joe. He bunted, as the New York crowd cheered and the Browns sneered. "In those days the Yankees didn't bunt," Muncrief said. "They were playing for the streak, not for the game."

If Sewell wanted to break up Joe's streak with a walk, this was the time to do it. On the bench Muncrief looked at the manager. "Now let's see you walk him," he thought. But Sewell didn't make a move.

Would Auker rather pitch to Joe, who was right-handed but on a hot streak, or walk him and pitch to Keller, who was a left-hander and was leading the league in homers? "I'd rather pitch to Joe than to Keller," Auker said. "I'd been having pretty good success with Joe. I'd gotten him out three times. And I didn't want him on base."

The first pitch was a curve. "Joe was a low-ball hitter," says Harlond Clift, the Brownie third baseman, "and I think that pitch was a little above the waist." DiMaggio rifled it straight to Clift, one of the best—and most unsung—third basemen of his generation.

Clift was wearing one of the old "pancake" gloves of that day, not one of the "peach baskets" or jai alai *cestas* that fielders use nowadays. Like many old-time infielders, he had cut a little hole in the palm, the better to feel the ball. And instead of a web between thumb and first finger, Clift says, "I made me a web with shoe laces. I think it was a little bit illegal—the umpires looked at it three or four times." When DiMaggio's shot streaked toward him, "I jumped up two or three inches and caught it in the webbing." The ball tore through the lacing "and just fell right down gently behind me," while Joe raced across first base, and Daniel flashed the hit sign. "It should have been an error," Clift says, "but I was glad (Joe) got it—it was good for baseball."

The Yankees pounded their bats on the dugout steps and "danced in delight," and Daniel recalled the moment as a bigger thrill than Babe Ruth's 60th homer. It must have bemused McQuinn—no one had danced when he had hit in his 34th game three years earlier.

The catcher, Ferrell, was disgusted with Auker. "I'd have done something if I was the pitcher," Rick said. "I wouldn't have laid one in there."

More than 40 years later, Ferrell, then an official with the Tigers, was also still disgusted with the Yankee strategy. "Joe's a good friend of mine," he said, "but that always stuck in my mind, the way they went about it."

If the odds against hitting in 56 straight games are one in a million, that may be true in the case of Willie Keeler, whose 44-game streak was entirely unself-conscious: It just happened, without trying to make it happen. But when all 18 players on the field, plus both managers, three umpires, and the official scorer all know there's a hitting streak on the line, the odds go down exponentially.

Up in Boston Williams was in the habit of getting telegraphic reports of other games from the scoreboard operator inside the left field wall. As soon as Ted heard the news, he shouted it to Dom in center.

Ignoring Russo's one-hit masterpiece, the *Times* the next morning went to the heart of the news:

### DIMAGGIO HAS CLOSE CALL

*Friday,*
*June 27*

◆

In Washington, Williams played his first night game of the year (an earlier one at Cleveland had been rained out) and right-hander Steve Sundra (9–13) held him to a single in three at bats as the Red Sox lost. Williams denies that he was less effective at night, arguing that he had played under lights most of the time in the minor leagues and had hit very well there.

In Philadelphia the Yankees also lost 7–6 and fell one game behind Cleveland again. DiMaggio slugged a homer and single and drew an intentional walk in the ninth with the winning run on base.

Since the streak began, Joe had lifted his average from .291 to .355, though he was still far behind Ted's .410. DiMaggio had also moved into the league home run lead.

***Saturday,***
***June 28***

With school out, our family piled into the car to drive to my grandmother's house in New Hampshire, a 300-mile trip that takes an afternoon now but took a long day back then. You drove on two-lane highways, slowed down through every city, stopped for interminable freight trains that crawled across the highway, followed trucks that chugged with maddening slowness around curves and up hills where you couldn't pass. Our car didn't have a radio. To combat boredom, we read Burma Shave signs or counted the freight cars, which often numbered 100 or more. Sometimes we broke the trip up by stopping mid-way at a "cabin," a primitive, un-air conditioned motel, usually with peeling paint, a hole in the screen door, and a pull chain on the toilet.

The trip could be dangerous. Cars had no side-view mirrors, safety belts, or turn signals. To turn, you rolled the window down and stuck out your hand. (In Iowa, drivers opened the door slightly, which meant, "Watch out. I'm going to turn one way or the other.") Highways had multiple mirrors on the crests of hills so you could see the traffic on the other side and decide if it was safe to pass that damn truck. But the mirrors often led to head-on collisions and were soon outlawed. We drove on retread tires, which were cheaper than new ones but were always blowing out, and at 65 miles an hour, that could be fatal. My father had to get out and change the tire at least once every trip, sometimes twice.

My grandmother's house had a black wood-burning stove, an outdoor privy, a well with a bucket on a pulley, a cistern to hold rainwater for baths, a jar of ginger on the side board, and horsehair sofas, which prickled your bottom when you sat on them. The beach had plentiful jellyfish and star fish, both of which are gone entirely now. On the radio two nonsense songs were big hits—"Free Ittoo Fitties" (Three Little Fishies) and the "Hut Sut" song (Hut sut ralson on the rillara and a brawla brawla suet). You never hear them any more, probably for a very good reason. You could also hear the Red Sox games sponsored by Narragansett beer.

If I had been listening that day, I would have heard Williams being held to one single by Washington right-hander Bill Zuber (6–4). Ted also let a single go through him, his third error in the last four games, as Boston lost 3–1.

In Philadelphia DiMag faced his old Pacific Coast League rival, Johnny Babich (2–7). Like DiMaggio, Babich had been signed by the Yankees but was traded away to the lowly Dodgers' organization and actually pitched against Joe during his 61-game streak in 1933. The legend is that John still held a grudge against the Yankees, and, indeed, in 1940 he whipped them five straight times to knock them out of the pennant. In '41 he reportedly threatened to walk DiMaggio every time up to stop his streak.

When I asked Babich about it, he scoffed. "Joe and I are the best of friends," he insisted.

So I went to Ed "Dutch" Doyle, one of Philadelphia's preeminent baseball historians. Now a retired school teacher and an active member of the Society for American Baseball Research, Doyle was selling scorecards in Shibe Park that afternoon. "No one in Philadelphia knew about it [the grudge]," Doyle writes. To confirm his memory, he went to the library and checked all four Philadelphia beat writers for a week before the game. Not one of them mentioned the subject. Doyle adds: "For those who are aware of Connie Mack, one should know that Mr. Mack would never deny anyone a record by denying him an opportunity for the record."

At the game, "Babich went right after Joe," Doyle reports. In their first face-off, DiMaggio popped up to short. In his second at bat, with the count 1−0 he drilled a hot grounder back through the pitcher's legs, as Babich skipped out of the way. "Sam Chapman fielded it leisurely in center field, and Joe, without breaking stride at first base, slid into second with a double," Doyle reports. (Legend says this happened in the first at bat after Babich had deliberately thrown three wide balls. This is not true.) Joe also popped to third, grounded to second, and singled to center.

Joe had now hit in 40 games, tying him with Cobb, and leaving him just one behind George Sisler.

For the first time that I know of, a writer, Don Basenfelder, pointed out that Sisler, at 41, was not the recordholder—Bill Dahlen had reached 42 in 1894 and Willie Keeler, 44 three years later. Sisler's was the so-called "modern" record.

The Yankees won the game and moved back into a tie for first.

That evening DiMaggio paid a visit to the hospital to visit a dying 11-year old named Tony Norelli. "You be listening on your radio tomorrow and hear me break that hitting record," Joe said. "That's a promise, kid." But Tony never heard if the promise was kept or not. He died that night.

## Sunday,
## June 29

———————————◆———————————

The temperature in Washington stood at 98 degrees, and the only cool spots in town were the movie theaters, which advertised the new air conditioning. The Columbia Theater was showing *Road to Zanzibar* with Bob Hope, Bing Crosby, and Dottie Lamour. *Million Dollar Baby* was playing at the Earle, starring Priscilla Lane and "Ronald Regan." (Marquees and movie ads used Regan and Reagan interchangeably, but no matter how they spelled it, we all pronounced it Reegan.)

### 4,000 NAZI AND SOVIET TANKS
### ARE LOCKED IN MIGHTY BATTLE

the Washington *Star* headline read as Joe and roommate Lefty Gomez lounged in their hotel room before leaving for the park.

### EARLY INDUCTION FACES MANY
### REGISTERING FOR DRAFT TODAY

Farther down the page Joe might have read that Texas Governor Lee "Pappy" O'Daniel had fallen behind in the ballot counting in his Senate race against young Congressman Lyndon Johnson.

Joe's reading taste ran more to Batman and Superman, Gomez said. The *Star* didn't offer those strips, but it did offer Tarzan, Little Orphan Annie, Moon Mullins, and Mutt and Jeff.

Some 31,000 Washingtonians braved the heat to crowd into the Senators' old ball park, which seated 28,000. One of them was Phil Eisenberg, a young government writer. "Let's see if Joe can break the record," a friend had suggested, so they joined the "mob" waiting in line for 75-cent bleacher tickets. During batting practice, fans swarmed over the field badgering Joe for autographs. "Everyone was rooting for DiMaggio," Eisenberg remembers. "Every time he came up, everyone stood up. There was a tremendous roar."

The knuckleballer Dutch Leonard was on the mound. Dutch deserves to be in the Hall of Fame. He won 191 games with perennially second-division teams, two more than Hall of Famer Lefty Gomez won with perennially championship teams. That year Dutch would win 18 with a seventh-place team behind him.

Leonard held Joe hitless for two at bats. Then, as he told me, "I got smart, and I forgot."

The sweat was pouring down everyone's face that day. Dutch wiped his forehead and thought to himself, "Well, I wonder if he can hit a spitball?" Gripping the ball with sweaty fingers, Leonard aimed a pitch at DiMaggio's knees. The ball darted down at the plate, and Joe dipped his knee to go down with it, lining it over shortstop for a clean base hit. ("It was!" laughs Senators catcher Jake Early—"it *was* a spitter!")

Between games an over-enthusiastic Italian fan grabbed DiMaggio's bat out of the bat rack and raced off with it. Joe used a 32-inch 36-ounce bat and had carefully sandpapered the handle to take off exactly ¾ of an ounce until the bat was just right. Now he was forced to play the second game with borrowed bats. On his first time up, he swung on a 2–0 pitch and lifted a fly ball to right. "If it had been my ball bat, it would have been in there," he muttered to Henrich.

The new bat "didn't quite balance right," Henrich says; "it was too heavy." Tom offered Joe his own bat, a Joe DiMaggio model, but Joe turned him down with thanks. However, after making two more outs, he agreed to accept the offer on his last at bat, against right-hander Arnold "Red" Anderson (4–6). Joe stroked a low line drive to left, and the modern record was his. The crowd was on its feet roaring, and in the dugout the Yankees tossed their caps in the air and danced a jig.

In the locker room later, teammates slapped Joe and mussed his hair, while he pulled thirstily on a bottle of beer. A photographer snapped his picture. "You shouldn't have done that," he protested, "I had a beer in my hand." A few minutes later he was sitting nude on a trunk, still dodging towels tossed by his teammates. "What about Keeler's record" of 44? someone asked.

"The hell with it," Joe shot back. (Burt Hawkins of the Washington *Star* delicately spelled it "h—l.") "I'm just going up there and take my cut."

"There wasn't any real hoop-de-doo" Henrich says. "Joe was made of ice water. He was going to do it, that's all."

---

### Tuesday,
### July 1

◆

---

After a day off on Monday, DiMaggio resumed the pursuit in a double-header against the Red Sox in New York.

The city was suffering in a sweltering heat wave that drove thousands of apartment and tenement dwellers to haul their mattresses out on the fire escape to sleep. The players soaked their sheets in ice water to try to keep cool. Electric fans whirred all over the city, and people held their papers down with paper weights, an almost unknown artifact today.

Six New Yorkers would die of the heat before the day was out. At game time, Yankee Stadium was covered in a bluish heat haze, Everett B. Morris of the *Herald-Tribune* wrote, and 52,000 fans, the largest crowd of the season there, sat in "steamy, perspiring proximity."

DiMaggio's woollen uniform was already drenched in sweat when he stepped in to bat with two men on against lefty Mickey Harris, who had almost stopped him after 15 games back on May 30. Joe fouled out to the right side.

In the third he hit a hard smash to Rawhide Jim Tabor at third. Tabor made a great play to nip Joe at first.

On Joe's third trip, "a pall settled over the stands," the *Times'* Arthur Daley wrote. Boston's 38 year-old reliever, Mike Ryba (7–3), gave Joe two screwballs for strikes, then threw three balls as the crowd booed. On the next pitch Joe hit a high bounder to third. This time Tabor's throw was over Lou Finney's head at first. A hit or an error? In the press box, necks craned toward Daniel, who smiled and held up one finger: hit. Wrote the *Herald-Tribune* dryly: "Only those near the press box cheered. Everyone else apparently figured it was an error all the way." In fact, one writer pointedly held his nose at the call.

But on his next time up, with the pressure off, Joe left no doubt. He rifled "a screaming single" to left, as the cheers were "deafening."

No Yankee hit a homer, however, bringing that streak to an end at 25 —the record still stands—but they did beat Harris 7–2. In fact, during the streak, the Yanks had won 17 out of 25 games and surged from third place to first, two games in front. DiMaggio is usually given exclusive credit for lifting the team into first, but it was the collective home-run streak that actually carried them into the lead.

In the second game, Joe quickly removed all suspense by singling sharply off lefty "Black Jack" Wilson (4–13) to tie Keeler, as thunder cracked, lightning flashed, and black clouds gathered. It's a good thing he got his hit early, for the storm broke in the fifth, washing out the rest of the game.

The Yanks swept the double-header. They were now three games ahead of Cleveland.

Williams got one hit off Russo in game one. He singled in game two against the mis-named Ernie "Tiny" Bonham, a 200-pounder. One of the first forkball pitchers, those pioneers of today's popular split-finger fastball, Bonham had a 9–6 record that year.

Ted was booed when he let two grounders get through him, and Dave Egan in the Boston *Record* wrote sardonically: "We shall not discuss the fielding ability of our Master Williams in this particular essay. Suffice it to say that he has escaped the disaster of being hit on the head by a fly ball—up till now, that is to say."

Dick McGann of the New York *Post* took a different tone. Williams' hitting had been overlooked amid all the publicity about DiMaggio, he wrote. Apprehensive about Ted's reputation for chewing up writers and spitting them out, McGann deferentially sidled up to him on the bench before the game but quickly found he needn't have worried as they fell into an affable conversation.

Another "knight of the keyboards," Jack Malaney, who had had his feuds with Williams, said Ted no longer baited writers and never squawked to umps. After a called strike, he might turn to tell the umpire, "Ain't I a dope. That was right in there." There were rumors that Williams was jealous of Foxx, but Malaney said that wasn't so. Ted also told him he plans to work out all winter to build up his arms until he's as strong as Jimmie.

In Russia the Germans were advancing relentlessly toward Moscow, as Stalin ordered the people to destroy everything in Hitler's path. In Washington Roosevelt said he hopes he can keep America out of the war, but George C. Marshall, the Army chief of staff, asked Congress to permit American troops to be used overseas, and the government began discussing plans to issue gas masks to citizens. In Texas, Lyndon Johnson found himself out-cheated and lost his bid for the Senate. And in New York *Sergeant York* opened on Broadway, and a historic first commercial TV program was broadcast.

---

## *Wednesday, July 2*

---
◆
---

This was supposed to be a match-up between the two great lefties, Grove and Gomez, but Grove begged off. He said it was the heat, though it may have been that he didn't want to be remembered as the guy who gave DiMaggio the record-breaking hit—but imagine if Grove had been the man to stop Joe; what a story that would have been! Anyway, the assignment went to the hot rookie, 29-year old Heber "Dick" Newsome, who would go on to win 19 games.

Before the game, umpire Tom Connolly stopped by DiMaggio's locker. "Boy, I hope ye do it," he said. "And if ye do, ye'll be breakin' the record of the foinest little fellow that ever walked and who never said a mean thing about anyone in his life. Good luck to ye."

Curiously, only 8,682 New Yorkers came out to watch history being made.

Williams singled in three trips against Gomez, giving him an even .400 average.

DiMaggio in the first hit a sharp liner to right. Boston's Stan Spence appeared to misjudge it, came in, then backed up, and finally made a leaping catch.

In the third Joe hit another hard one to Tabor, who made a "dazzling" backhand catch and threw him out.

In the fifth Newsome teased him with two wide curves as boos echoed through the Stadium. The next pitch was a fast-ball inside, Joe swung, and the ball flew into the upper deck—foul. Then Newsome threw a knuckler which didn't break enough, and DiMag "hit one where they ain't"—over Williams' head into the left-field stands. The ball veered close to the foul pole but stayed fair, while Ted chased it to the railing, then merely waved his glove, as the crowd went delirious.

Believe it or not, neither the *Times* nor the *Trib* thought the feat was page-one news, though the *Tribune* did find room on the first page for a two-column picture of sea lions at Rockefeller Plaza.

No one knew it then, but Joe *still* hadn't beaten Keeler. Willie's streak had come in the first 44 games of 1897, but he had also hit safely in the last game of 1896 — in fact, he had hit in all three Temple Cup (World Series) games that fall as well. So Keeler had really hit in 45 straight regular season games — 48 in all, counting the postseason contests.

Of course, it should be pointed out that in 1897 foul balls did not count as strikes. How many extra at bats did Wee Willie get as a result? He was adept at fouling off pitches he didn't like. He could even bunt them foul with two strikes, which is against the rules today.

## Thursday,
## July 3

The Yankees didn't play, but Williams walloped a home run and single off Chubby Dean (3–8) in Philadelphia to help Grove to his 299th win. Ted's homer, #16, came as heavy black clouds blanketed the sun. He hit it "high and far into the teeth of the wind," to put him one behind Keller for the lead.

Both teams were rained out in their big July 4 doubleheaders.

Up in New Hampshire, I was celebrating the holiday on the beach, watching naval rescue ships try vainly to raise the sunken sub, Nautilus, which had gone down with 33 men on board. That evening we set off firecrackers and cherry bombs—the latter, about as big as marbles, made a loud bang when you threw them against a rock. Many kids lost their fingers or their eyes with such toys, and eventually they were banned in most states.

## Saturday,
## July 5

In Boston, Ted got one hit, a double off Washington's Dutch Leonard. With Finney on second, he smacked a wicked foul into the far right-field corner, then drove a fly that clattered off the Calvert whiskey sign on the left-field wall. "That was a demonstration of Ted's power to the opposite field," Whitman noted.

Williams relayed the news to Dom that Joe had homered off the A's Phil Marchildon, who would soon be shooting down Nazi fighters as a gunner on a Royal Canadian Air Force bomber. Joe's streak was now 46 if you didn't count the Norfolk game.

---

***Sunday,
July 6***

---◆---

DiMaggio got his favorite bat back. Two Newark friends, Jerry Spatola and Jimmy Ceres, had answered his appeal for help and traced it to Lyndhurst, New Jersey, and a fan, who gave up the bat in return for free game passes. With his old bat back in his hands, Joe went wild against the A's, with four hits against Babich and two more against Jack Knott (13–11).

Gratefully, DiMaggio gave Henrich back the now historic bat. Whatever became of it? I asked Tom.

"I broke it over home plate one day when Sturm missed a hit-and-run sign," he said.

"Can I have the bat?" Yankee batboy Timmy Sullivan asked casually.

"Get outta here!" Henrich replied. "You know what bat this is, and so do I." He strolled over to Joe's locker. "You know what bat this is?" he asked. Joe nodded. "You want it?"

"Yeah."

Some time later Henrich discovered DiMaggio at his locker with his head in his hands. "What's the matter?" he inquired.

Joe showed him a telegram from the mayor of San Francisco, asking for the bat to be raffled off in a war bond drive.

"Hell," Tom said, "give him any ball bat. He won't know the difference." Adds Henrich: "I don't know if he did or not."

So I wrote to Joe, asking what became of the bat. DiMaggio is almost impossible to interview. I tried once at an all star game, patiently waiting while a pretty girl reporter interviewed him in his uniform on the Yankee bench. When I finally approached with an "Excuse me. . . .," Joe shot me a withering look and turned away. Undaunted, I asked Dom to get me an interview. Still no success. So I wrote a letter. "Just one question," I wrote. "What became of the bat you broke the record with?" Weeks went by. At last my own letter and SASE were returned. Printed across the bottom were five words without a signature:

"Gave it to Lou Costello."

And there, with the silence of DiMaggio, and the death of the comedian, the mystery must remain, perhaps forever.

Up in Boston, George Kirksey of the Washington *Daily News* asked Williams if he had any desire to break DiMaggio's record. "I sure have," Ted replied. "I'd like to break every hitting record in the book." He said he'd like to play in Yankee Stadium one year "just to see what I could do there." His favorite homer was the one he walloped off Rigney over the roof in Chicago back in May. "They say the only other two players to hit one over there were Ruth and Gehrig. But now they have to say, 'Only Ruth, Gehrig and Williams.' Yes, sir, that's putting the old Stringbean in some pretty fast company."

Then he sauntered out to take batting practice and pumped six shots into the right-field bleachers amid a group of soldiers. If he did that every day, he would lose almost 1,000 balls a year, at a cost of $1.25 a ball, Kirksey calculated.

In the first game Williams faced lefty Ken Chase, who was only 6–18 that year but was always tough for Ted. ("He was a little wild," smiles Washington first baseman Mickey Vernon, "which helped.") Ted got only one hit against Ken.

In the second game, Williams smacked three hits off Bill Zuber (6–4) and Steve Sundra to move his average up to .405. He also leaped against the scoreboard to catch a fly by Vernon. It was a "fancy catch," Povich wrote in the Washington *Post*. (Povich, who is male, once received a letter asking if his sex was a handicap in doing his job. "No," he replied, "I just try to be one of the boys.")

The Sox swept both games.

Then Williams, along with Foxx, Cronin, Doerr, and Dom DiMaggio, caught the train at Back Bay station for Detroit and the All Star Game.

---

*Tuesday, July 8*
# The All Star Game

◆

*The ball once struck off,*
*Away flies the Boy*
*To the next destin'd Post,*
*And then home with Joy.*

"Base-ball"
Little Pretty Pocket-Book
England, 1744

◆

Of the 128 home runs slugged in over half a century of All Star games through 1990, the one remembered most vividly is still the blast that Ted Williams unloaded to win the 1941 game. A few, but not many, have been hit harder, but none has been hit so dramatically. Half a century has passed, but it's still the homer all others are measured against.

This would be Ted's second classic. He wasn't voted to the team in 1939, in spite of his sensational rookie season. He did get into the 1940 game, got to bat twice, but couldn't get a hit as the National League shut the Americans out 4−0. But this time he had been telling Foxx for weeks that he had a feeling he would bust loose in this one.

As the players left the Book Cadillac hotel on the morning of the game, U.S. troops occupied Iceland to safeguard our ships carrying aid to Britain and Russia. The New York *Times* warned:

## U.S. SAID TO BE HEADING FOR WAR

Briggs (now Tiger) Stadium was festooned with red, white and blue bunting. The skies were bright, though the grass was slippery from a morning shower; there would be four outfield errors that day, one by Ted. A partisan American league crowd of more than 56,000 filled the stands. The game was a benefit for the USO, and khaki uniforms dotted the stands, including two worn by Pvt. Hank Greenberg and Pvt. Hugh Mulcahy. Both sat quietly in the grandstand. Today each would throw out a first ball, but strangely, Dom DiMaggio says, neither one was even introduced to the crowd, not even Detroit's own hero, Greenberg!

Ted brought along a movie camera and trained it on Joe DiMaggio in the batting cage. "Want to study his style," he said. "It might help me." When the National Leaguers took their turn in the cage, he had a rare opportunity to study the sensational Dodger rookie Pete Reiser, plus Johnny Mize, Frank McCormick, Mel Ott, Joe Medwick, and others.

The NL hurler was Whitlow Wyatt, the ex-American Leaguer now 32, who was having the best year of his life (22–10) and leading the Dodgers to the pennant.

With two out in the last of the first, Joe DiMaggio stepped up to bat to an ovation and fouled out to third base. There was one unspoken question hanging in the air: What if he didn't get a hit in the game? Since this was not an official league game, would it break the streak? No one wanted even to mention the subject for fear, perhaps, that it might raise questions about Joe's hitless exhibition against Jimmy Halperin.

With Feller pitching no-hit ball for the American League, the game was 0–0 after three. In the fourth, with "Oom Paul" Derringer, the big Cincinnati right-hander (12–14) pitching and Cecil Travis on second, DiMaggio smashed a 415-foot drive to center, which Reiser galloped back to snare, Travis moving to third. Now it was up to Williams. He whipped a 2–0 pitch on a line to right, where Bob Elliott, normally a third

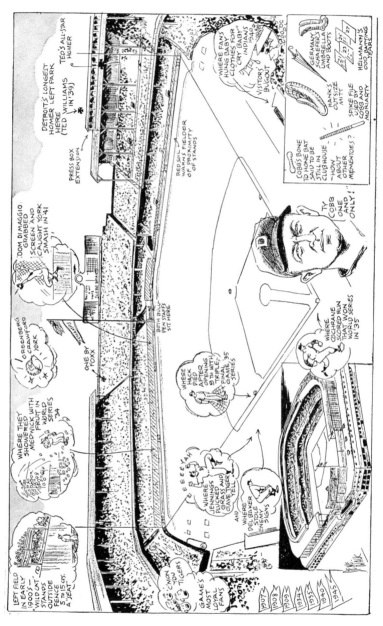

Briggs Stadium (Now Tiger Stadium) *Boston Globe*

baseman, ran in, then reversed himself and ran back, caught his spikes and fell, as the liner whistled over his head for a double to put the AL ahead 1–0.

After four and a half innings, the umpires rotated, and Babe Pinelli, a National Leaguer, strolled in from third to call balls and strikes. (Fifteen years later Pinelli would call Don Larsen's perfect World Series game.). Williams, who studied umpires as closely as pitchers, knew every AL ump's strike zone. But he'd have to feel Pinelli out. Back then NL umpires wore flexible chest protectors under their jackets as they do now, which meant they could crouch over the catcher's shoulder; AL umps wore big, stiff protectors that looked more like swimming-pool floats and forced them to stand erect. As a result, both hitters and pitchers believed, National Leaguers saw—and called—more low strikes than the American Leaguers did.

In the sixth, NL pitcher Bucky Walters hit a line drive down the left-field line and was sacrificed to third. Then Terry Moore hit a long drive to the base of the stands in left. Williams backed against the wall to haul it down and, with seemingly no chance to catch Walters going home, uncorked a tremendous throw that almost nipped Bucky at the plate. The game was now tied.

In the bottom of the sixth, DiMaggio walked, Williams lined out to Reiser, Jeff Heath walked, and Lou Boudreau scored Joe with a single to make it 2–1.

Enos Slaughter opened the seventh with a single to left. Williams bobbled it—"he had to make two or three futile stabs before he came up with it," the *Times* columnist John Kiernan wrote acidly. Then NL shortstop Arky Vaughan, who had hit only four homers in the regular season, drilled one into the upper deck in right to put the Nationals back in front 3–2.

The Cubs' Claude Passeau (14–14) pitched the seventh. He had a natural slider. "Only two or three in the league had a pitch like that then," Passeau said. "They asked how did I throw that ball that just sails and slides? I don't know how I did it; it was just a natural pitch. Ninety percent of my pitches were fastballs that sailed. They'd sail in on left-handed batters. I could get left-handers out where I couldn't get right-handers."

Passeau pitched lefties high and tight, so the ball sailed into the thin part of their bats. Slaughter, Mize, and Ott would put their good bats back in the rack and tell the batboy, "We don't want to break 'em." Passeau called it his "out" pitch: "If it hadn't been for that, I wouldn't be up there."

Bill Dickey, a lefty, hit the slider on a line to third, where Stan Hack leaped and speared it for the best catch of the day. Charlie Keller, another lefty, took a terrific swing at a third strike and missed. Joe Gordon, a righty, also went out.

In the eighth, with Mize on second Vaughan came up again. Williams said he had a hunch that Arky might park one again, and sure enough he did, to make it 5–2, National League.

As the American Leaguers came up in the bottom of the eighth, Yankee coach Art Fletcher trotted to the third base coaching box, and a National League fan yelled something to him. "This game ain't over yet," Fletcher shot back.

The first man up, DiMaggio, still hadn't gotten a hit. Ordinarily, he might have been taken out of the line-up by this stage of the game, but manager Del Baker of Detroit kept him in, presumably to remove any taint from the streak. Baker's faith paid off as Joe hit Passeau for a double.

Since it came against big league opposition, in fact the *best* competition in baseball, it is only fair to count the hit in the streak, which would make the final total 57 in the history books, not 56. Why didn't the myth-makers add the All Star hit? They always made a point of saying that DiMaggio had a second 16-game streak right after the first one, thus giving the feat an extra superman aura. However, adding the All

Star Game would mean applying the same logic to the Norfolk exhibition, and that would knock 11 games off the streak and bring it down to 46, one more than Pete Rose later attained. All in all, the reporters of the day, and the historians ever since, have evidently decided not to raise the embarrassing question.

Anyway, that brought Williams up with a chance to get one run back. Passeau got two strikes on him, then threw a slider low. Pinelli's thumb went up in the air: strike three. Ted muttered that he thought it was a little low—"a National League strike," he would say afterwards. Little brother Dom then came up and singled Joe home to make it 5–3.

Passeau whiffed the mighty Foxx to end the inning. It was a masterful money pitch, and it probably cost him the game. Until then, NL manager Bill McKechnie had been changing pitchers every two innings. He had the great screwball king, Carl Hubbell (6–3 at game time), warmed up to pitch the ninth. Williams had never faced Hubbell before. He would later say he disliked "cutesy" lefties such as Whitey Ford, Warren Spahn, and Bobby Shantz, and Hubbell, with his reverse-breaking scroogie, was in that category. But the strikeout of Foxx impressed catcher Harry Danning. "You go ahead and pitch the ninth," he said. McKechnie agreed.

Still, the Americans were losing by two runs with only three outs left. There seemed little chance that Williams would get to bat again. Yet "I had this funny feeling that I was going to get up there at least one more time and hit one," he said later. "I get hunches that way. I never say anything about 'em, and as sure as I do, they won't come true." He had been right on his hunch about Vaughan's second homer. "Something seemed to tell me he was going to do that. Well, I figured I was going to get up there again."

In the do-or-die ninth, Vaughan, the hero of the game, remained in the dugout, and Eddie Miller, an excellent fielder, went in as defensive insurance at short. When Passeau got right-hander Frankie Hayes on a pop up, many fans began filing out of the exits. Pinch-hitter Ken Keltner, another right-hander, sent a tricky grounder to short, where Miller got a glove on it but couldn't make the throw, and Keltner legged it out for a hit. Now, instead of two outs and the bases empty, the Americans had only one out and a runner on first, with the top of the order coming up.

Joe Gordon, another righty, lined a single, sending Keltner to third, and the fans suddenly stopped and began resuming their seats. Cecil Travis, a lefty, walked to load the bases, and the great DiMaggio advanced to the plate, as the stands grew uproariously noisy.

Williams, meanwhile, knelt in the on-deck circle and began squeezing his bat, a sound that must have unnerved Passeau, who was not used to it, while DiMaggio took his wide-spread stance and waited, impassive. The first pitch was in there and Joe swung. Foul ball. The next one was over too, and DiMag took a hefty cut, missing the ball by a foot. Behind in the count 0–2, Joe couldn't afford to let the third one go by and hit a sharp grounder to Miller, labeled double play all the way. Miller tossed the ball to Billy Herman, a future Hall of Famer, for the second out. A 90-foot throw and the game was over. Herman pivoted—and threw it 12 feet off the bag as big first baseman Frank McCormick made a great stop to keep it from going into the stands. Joe, who had slowed down, now put on speed and crossed first safely, as Keltner scored to make it 5–4.

Some say Travis took Herman out of the play with his slide. Herman denies it. "Travis didn't touch me," he says manfully. "We just didn't complete it, that's all." H. G. Salsinger, veteran writer of the Detroit *News*, said Herman was off-balance and hurried his throw. Billy, a former Cub, was "one of the best second basemen I ever saw," his ex-teammate Passeau says. "He said he just fancy-danned. Like he said, 'I was just shinin'.' "

DiMaggio should have been the fourth out of the inning. Instead, Passeau watched Williams step into the batters' box and pump his bat.

Incidentally, if Herman's throw had gone into the stands, Joe would have been awarded second base, and first base would be open, a sure invitation to a walk. McCormick's great stop, like Passeau's strikeout of Foxx, probably cost the National League the game.

Danning and the infielders hovered solicitously around Passeau. Should McKechnie yank the tiring pitcher and bring in the fresh Hubbell? Or should Passeau walk Williams to load the bases, putting the winning run on second and bringing up Dom DiMaggio (.283 at game time)? The decision was to leave Passeau in and pitch to Ted. Apparently McKechnie didn't know that Williams loved to hit in Detroit. Maybe Passeau thought he could get Ted out again with his slider, as he had the last time. Danning told him to take his time, slapped him on the rump, and trotted back behind the plate.

Williams had been swinging late, he said; he was determined to get out in front this time. "I was nervous," he said, "but I was bearing down a little harder than I ever did in my life."

Passeau's first pitch was low. Ball one. Ted swung at the next one and drilled it foul down the first-base line. Strike one. He said to himself, "Boy, that ball's coming *in* on me. I've got to get just a little quicker." The third pitch was high and inside, probably the slider. Ted took it for ball two. Pinelli called for the ball (did Ted ask him to check it?), inspected it momentarily, and tossed it out.

The next pitch was another slider, the same pitch Williams had struck out on only one inning before (and, Foxx would say, the same one he had struck out on too). But this time it was neither too low nor too high. "The ball got away from me," Passeau would say. "I knew it was going the second I released it. The instant it left my hand, I knew I was a dead duck."

"It was fast and about elbow-high," Ted recalled. "I said to myself, 'This is it.' I shut my eyes and swung. I got under it just a little bit lower than I would have liked. But, Jesus, it kept going."

The ball climbed high into a stiff crosswind as the crowd cheered. When Williams had hit one over the same roof in 1939, he had gotten help from the wind. This time he had to battle it. There was a huge collective gasp as the fans feared the wind would carry it foul. But, Whitman wrote, the wind couldn't stop "this big Bertha." Right-fielder Enos Slaughter turned his back, put his hands on his hips, and craned his head back as the ball whacked the front wall of the press gallery atop the roof, struck some bunting, hung there for a moment, and toppled back onto the field. Another three or four feet and it would have cleared the whole works.

"A towering shot," recalls Sid Hudson. "You knew it was gone as soon as he hit it. He knew it too. He started clapping his hands. Everybody in the park knew it."

Williams watched the ball battle the winds for a few seconds, then shot into the air with a whoop and began galloping and leaping around the bases, not running but frolicking, gamboling, frisking, jumping. As he passed third, Fletcher almost tackled him, then thumped him on the back all the way home. DiMaggio touched home for the winning run, then turned and extended his hand. Merv Shea, first-base coach, hugged Ted. Feller ran out in civvies to embrace him. Cronin jumped in the air, pulled Ted's cap off, mussed his hair, whacked him on the head, and hugged him. "Ted's grin could be seen from the bleachers," wrote Jack Malaney of the Boston *Post*, as Ted hobbled to the dugout with Cronin still pounding him. Half-carrying a dozen players on his back, Williams laughed his way to the runway leading to the clubhouse. A fan

Williams All-Star Home Run *AP Photo*

reached down and snatched his cap. Ted grabbed it back and clapped it on his head and disappeared as straw hats scaled from the stands and littered the field behind him.

In the dressing room, Foxx punched him playfully and nearly broke his chin, Whitman wrote. Jimmie shouted above the din that Ted had been saying for two weeks that he "wants to hit one in that All Star Game." Players pushed each other aside and competed to kiss him, pull his ears, slap his behind, or wrestle him off the stool, while Ted laughed with embarrassed high humor. Baker planted a kiss on his forehead and grinned that he'd "kiss a porcupine" for a hit like that. Even the league president, stuffy Will Harridge, broke down and put one arm around Williams's shoulder for the photographers.

When the panic finally subsided, Whitman wrote, Williams got almost as much kick out of talking about his throw that almost nipped Walters.

Over in the NL dressing room, players were dazed. "He's just inhuman," McKechnie muttered.

Passeau was disconsolate but defiant. More than four decades later he was still defiant. "He didn't hit the ball real well at all," Claude insists. "It was a little short pop fly. If it hadn't been in Detroit, it's only 318 feet. Don't get me wrong, no alibi, but in any other ball park, it would have been a big out."

Williams agrees. "It wasn't all that tremendously hit," he says. "It was high and looked like it was going a mile. Actually, it was a big high fly. In most ball parks it would not have been a home run, even though I hit it way up on the facade."

But surely any fly that high would have been a home run in the Polo Grounds (257 feet at the foul line), League Park (290 feet), Yankee Stadium (296), Ebbets Field (297), Forbes Field (300), Fenway (301), Sportsman's Park (310), Municipal Stadium (320), and Griffith Stadium (326). In fact, the most distant right-field line in the majors was Cincinnati's Crosley Field, and that was only 366 feet away; surely any fly must have carried an additional 50 feet on its descent.

"It's pretty daggone high there," shrugs Slaughter laconically. Enos, who caught the ball when it fell back to the field, quietly pocketed it and took it home to Carolina, where it rested on his mantel piece for over 40 years until Enos entered Cooperstown in 1985. As Slaughter ended his speech, he called Williams to the podium and presented the ball to him.

Even Ted's old enemy, Bill Cunningham, got caught up in the joyful moment. He described the dressing room and the "Slim Slammer" who sat in the middle of all the uproar: "A lanky neck, flashing teeth, blue-gray eyes, in a suntanned face and a tousled mop of brown curly hair." While Ted thanked

After the Game *AP Photo*

everyone in a bashful sort of way, Cunningham recalled "the brutal and cruel cuffing" he had taken from the press in other, less happy times:

"If the kid didn't have something inside him pretty strong—and I'll even say pretty fine—he could easily have quit under the lashing he took." Like Jack Sharkey, the former heavyweight champ, Ted had a tough exterior. "Now we see what he's really like inside. Anyone can do it the easy way. It takes a real champion to ride out on top when they make it real tough. What Williams built, he built without much help."

Even Dave Egan mellowed. DiMaggio had hit in his 49th straight game, the Colonel wrote, but he was overshadowed by Williams. Formerly a subject for a child psychologist's study, Egan wrote, Teddy had been transformed into "a sunny, pleasant boy . . . who had captured the imagination of a continent . . . He came out of the shadows and stepped up on his own spotlighted pedestal, and looked DiMaggio in the eye, and claimed for himself the title of 'the greatest hitter in baseball.' "

### POP-OFF MAKES GOOD

headlined one Detroit paper.

### FIREMAN COMES THROUGH

said another.

New York's Dan Parker headlined his column in the *Daily Mirror*:

### TED WILLIAMS STILL
### TOPS OUR DIMADGE

And the Boston *Herald* proclaimed:

### TED THE KING
### SUCCESSOR TO
### RUTH'S ROBES

Williams was one of the last to leave the dressing room to avoid the armies of autograph seekers. After peeking out of the players' gate, he decided to duck out a rear door. While he was waiting for a cab, a driver pulled up, offered him a lift, and, not recognizing his passenger, told him all about the dramatic end of the game. Ted listened appreciatively. At the Book-Cadillac hotel, another crowd was lying in wait, so Williams asked the Samaritan to drive around to the back door. "Why?" the puzzled driver asked.

"I'm Ted Williams," he said. "I have a dinner date tonight. If I try to get through that crowd, I'll miss my date."

"Ted Williams!" the guy exclaimed. "Geez!"

Later, in his room that evening, Ted yanked off his shoes and stretched his feet as reporter Gerry Moore knocked.

"Come on in, the door's open," Ted called, and as Moore entered, he saw Ted writing to his mother. Williams showed Moore a letter from her ending with "Loads of love to the most wonderful son in the world.

"PS. I'm glad you are getting along so well with the sports writers."

---

### *Friday,*
### *July 11*

---◆---

Williams stayed in Detroit to resume his pursuit of .400 against the Tigers.

Thursday's game was rained out, but Ted went to the park to take batting practice anyway. He smashed several pitches into the bleachers, then signed autographs and posed for pictures with about a hundred kids, "with whom," wrote Moore, "he is undoubtedly king."

*Newsweek* finally recognized Williams as coming out of DiMaggio's shadow. Its straight-forward page-long review of Ted's controversial career was headlined:

### Ted Williams of Red Sox Cools His Hot Temper but His Angry Bat Hits a New High in Tantrums

On Friday Grove went for #300 against Buck Newsom, who slammed the door on him. Buck shut the Sox out 2–0 and shut Ted out 0-for-4. In the fourth Williams flied to far center, which is 440 feet in Detroit. But otherwise Newsom "toyed" with him. Ted took a called third strike and twice bit on slow pitches, grounding to second each time. His average shrank to an even .400.

DiMaggio kept his streak going with a home run, his 20th, to lead the league.

---

### *Saturday, July 12*

---◆---

The Detroit pitchers wouldn't give Williams anything good to hit. He walked his first two times up. The second time catcher Birdie Tebbetts called for a pitch-out and snapped a throw to first. Ted hurried back safely but twisted his ankle, the same one he had broken in March. Trainer Win Green ran out to look at it, and Ted resumed play, although with a definite limp.

He walked a third time in the fifth, to the boos of the crowd—the first time Salsinger could remember a Detroit crowd booing a Detroit pitcher for walking a man. In his next at bat, Williams finally got a pitch to hit but popped it up to Rudy York at first, falling to .397, and Cronin took him out of the game. Although Green worked on the foot in the training room, there was no report on how bad it was or how long Ted might be out.

Had the *Newsweek* story jinxed him?

---

### *Sunday,*
### *July 13*

---◆---

Williams was out of the line-up for the double-header in Cleveland. He watched from the press box, as the Sox lost both games.

In Chicago DiMaggio ran his streak to 53 games. In his first at bat, he bounced another grounder to Appling, who mishandled it again. Unlike New York, the Comiskey Park announcer quickly informed the fans of the ruling: an error. Joe then slammed three solid hits.

Every radio station was now blaring the new Les Brown song:
"Joe, Joe, DiMaggio—
We want you on ouuur side."

---

### *Monday,*
### *July 14*

---◆---

Ted had the foot X-rayed, and was relieved to learn that there was no sign of a break, just the same chip on his ankle. But he sat out the game again.

That night DiMaggio faced Rigney again, the same man who had almost stopped him back in game #30 on the ball that Appling fumbled.

In the first inning Joe hit a broken-bat pop to second, and Bill Knickerbocker dropped it for an error. (If the game had been played in New York, what would Daniel have scored it?)

DiMag walked on the 3–2 in the fourth.

In the sixth the count was 2–0 when Rigney came in with an inside pitch, and Joe swung with all his might. He topped the ball, just getting a piece of it, and dribbled a slow roller halfway to third base, where the ball died. (It rolled a total of 20 feet, the New York *Daily News* reported.) Third baseman Bob Kennedy, playing deep of course, raced in, but didn't even bother to throw; Joe was already on first "long enough to have taken a bath," Daniel wrote. There was nothing to do but give Joe a hit. It was the worst hit of the 86 he had made so far in the streak, Daniel added.

Ed Burns of the Chicago *Tribune* sneered at it as "a miserable little scratch single."

In his last at bat, DiMaggio sent a long fly to left-center, which Mike Kreevich caught at the wall. So Joe's streak reached 54, though Rigney, who won the game 7–1, went to his grave convinced he had stopped him not once, but twice that summer.

---

**Wednesday,
July 16**

---

◆

---

Ted took batting practice Tuesday and was available to pinch-hit but was not called on as the Sox finally won. His mere presence on the bench gives the team a lift, Moore wrote.

And "the fans are yelling for him to get back into action. When they learn he won't be in the regular line-up, they stay away in appalling numbers."

On Wednesday Boston was tied 0–0 against Chicago in the eighth with a man on third when Cronin nodded to Williams to grab a bat. Ted limped off the bench to applause. With the wind blowing straight into his face, he lashed a long drive to center to score the run, and the Red Sox went on to win 2–1. His blow may have won the game, but it was just an out in the box score, and his average fell two more points, to .395.

DiMaggio meanwhile walloped two hits in Cleveland on Tuesday and three more on Wednesday to run his string to 56.

---

*Thursday,*
*July 17*

---◆---

Williams rode the bench again.

DiMaggio and Gomez left their hotel for the big Cleveland Municipal Stadium and a sell-out night game. The story is that they rode a cab, and the cabbie told them he thought Joe was going to get shut out. Joe said Lefty got mad, and they got out and walked the rest of the way. (Lefty's version is that it was a shoeshine boy, not a cabbie.)

Was Joe nervous? "I don't know about him," Gomez said, "but I threw up my breakfast." Joe was so cool, Lefty said, you could hang him in a coat closet and he'd get a good night's sleep.

Cleveland's Municipal Stadium *National Baseball Library*

More than 67,000 people were there, the biggest crowd in the majors in two years. At an average ticket price of a dollar apiece, Joe alone probably earned the two teams almost $70,000, or almost double his salary of $35,000.

The story of how Joe's streak was ended by pitchers Al Smith and Jim Bagby and third baseman Ken Keltner is well known. DiMaggio walked once against Smith, and Keltner made two great backhand stops to rob him of hits down the third-base line. (Joe suspected the base path had been watered down to slow up any balls.) But there were actually four other key players who stopped him, and one of them is a mystery man.

In the eighth, his last at bat, Joe faced Bagby. Jim, who died in 1988, wasn't able to talk after 1982, when a malignant larynx was removed. He wished he had made a tape recording to answer all the questions he has gotten since, but his wife, who lip reads, relayed his answers to my questions. He threw "just fastballs," Bagby said. "Joe hit one hard, but he just hit it at somebody."

The ball sped straight to shortstop Lou Boudreau, then at the last second it took a sharp bounce over Lou's shoulder, but quick as a cat Boudreau snatched it off his ear with his bare hand and flipped to second to start a double play. Historians like to tell about Keltner's two plays, but they seldom mention the Boudreau catch.

The streak was over.

But wait. The Yankees, leading 4–1, put five men up to bat in the ninth. If the Indians could tie the game, Joe would be the fourth man scheduled to bat in the tenth.

The Yankee starter, Gomez, hadn't lost since May 12 and had held Cleveland to four hits. But when he gave up two singles to start the ninth, manager Joe McCarthy waved in "Grandma Johnny" Murphy from the bullpen. The right-handed Murphy, who later served as general manager of the Mets, was the game's top reliever, the Dennis Eckersley of his day. He made a career out of mopping up for Gomez, and saved a league-leading 15 games in all, with a 1.98 ERA. It was his job to shut the door on the Indians, and if he did, he would be shutting it on DiMaggio as well.

"Does the name Larry Rosenthal mean anything to you?" Tommy Henrich asks. It means virtually nothing to even the most rabid trivia expert. But Larry Rosenthal, a .209 hitter that season, almost saved DiMaggio's streak. He came up to pinch-hit and smacked Murphy's first pitch deep to right-center between Henrich and DiMag. Before either one could flag it down, both runners scored to make it 4–3, and Rosenthal ended up on third with a triple, the only one he hit between 1940 and 1945. Cleveland's Gee Walker had smashed an inside-the-park homer to the same spot earlier in the game. If Rosenthal had been faster, he might have scored, tying the game and giving DiMag a chance to bat again.

Instead, Rosenthal was on third with nobody out.

Hal Trosky (.294), a left-handed hitter with fair power, was sent in to pinch-hit. Any kind of ball over or through the infield would score Rosenthal. Instead, Hal hit a bouncer to first base, where Johnny Sturm fielded it without taking his foot off the bag. One out.

Next lefty Clarence (Soup) Campbell (.250) pinch-hit for Bagby. He rapped a hard grounder back to Murphy, who knocked it down, juggled it, then caught Rosenthal off the bag. Larry scooted back and forth, prolonging the rundown so Campbell could take second. But Soup seemed paralyzed. He watched the play with rapt attention, firmly glued to the right-field foul line. Rosenthal was finally tagged out. Two outs.

The lead-off man, lefty Roy Weatherly (.289) was Cleveland's—and DiMaggio's—last hope. If Campbell had taken second, Sturm could have played off the bag. But now he was holding Campbell close. Weatherly pulled a hot grounder down the line right at Sturm, a ball that might have skipped all the way to the right-field corner for a double if Johnny had been playing off the bag. Instead, Johnny gloved it, stepped on first, and the game—and streak—were over.

The Yanks trooped into the clubhouse as if they had lost the game instead of opening a seven-game lead. "Well, that's over," Joe said, breaking the tension, and suddenly everyone started talking and towels began flying around the room. Will anyone ever break the mark? DiMaggio was asked.

"You have to have plenty of luck," he said. "I had lots of it." (However, in later years he would insist that "there wasn't a cheap hit" in the streak. "I earned every one.")

The streak has now entered American mythology so irrevocably that it can never be dislodged. Joe indeed did have a hot two months, hitting .412 since the streak began. But an unsentimental reading of the news accounts reveals that the streak was riddled with as many holes as an archery target. Jimmy Halperin stopped him after 11 games. Mickey Harris shut him down after #15, except for the easy fly that Pete Fox lost. Johnny Rigney apparently ended it after #29 and Thornton Lee after #30 but for two highly questionable calls by Dan Daniel. Auker seemed to have stopped Joe after #37. Finally Rigney almost got him again after #53 except for a squib roller on a topped ball. So Joe really had six streaks of 11, four, 13, six, 15, and three games.

Over a season or a career, good and bad luck theoretically cancel each other out. But in a streak, all luck must be good; none can be bad. That's what happened to DiMaggio in 1941.

In 1914, reports Larry Amman, the Cobb authority, there were no instance of lucky breaks, for Ty. In 1945 Tommy Holmes had only one lucky break, when a ball struck a tarpaulin in the outfield and eluded the fielder. Pete Rose and Paul Molitor in their streaks had the help of no such fortunate breaks. The media attention was so intense that no gift calls would have been tolerated and would have been immediately exposed by TV's instant replays.

If Joe got some good breaks in 1941, he carried one monumental bad break throughout his career—Yankee Stadium. Statistician Pete Palmer has compiled Joe's record both at home and on the road. Here are some of his conclusions:

|        | Home  |     | Road  |     | Total |     |
|--------|-------|-----|-------|-----|-------|-----|
|        | BA    | HR  | BA    | HR  | BA    | HR  |
| 1937   | .343  | 19  | .349  | 27  | .346  | 46  |
| 1939   | .350  | 12  | .413  | 18  | .381  | 30  |
| 1941   | .346  | 16  | .369  | 14  | .357  | 30  |
| Lifetime | .315 | 148 | .333  | 213 | .325  | 361 |

Assuming that the seven road parks represent a league "average" park,* then the vast distances in Yankee Stadium's left field cost Joe a shot at 60 homers in 1937, and at hitting .400 in 1939. DiMaggio later estimated that "I would have hit 76 home runs if I'd played in a normal park. (Announcer) Mel Allen counted all the balls I hit to the warning track. I'd hit the ball 430 feet, and the guy wouldn't even have to make a sensational catch." That total sounds inflated, but the Stadium might have taken about 130 home runs away from Joe lifetime. And, of course, if he had played in a *very* friendly park, such as Fenway or Briggs or Shibe, he would have done even better.

DiMaggio was a wonderful ballplayer, even without the streak. He hit .325 lifetime with 361 homers, which might have been 450 without a war. He doesn't need a phony streak to make him a genuine immortal.

Hank Greenberg, who is almost Joe's twin statistically (.313, 331 homers), was a right-handed native New Yorker who could not make the Yankees because another New York native, Lou Gehrig (a lefty with a short porch in right field), could not be pushed off first base. So Hank, luckily, wound up in Detroit. In 1938 Greenberg hit 58 home runs—39 at home and only 19 on the road. I once asked his biographer, Ira

---

*They don't. For one thing, the home team always bats in the ninth inning on the road, but not always at home. For another, road stats for Joe do not include Yankee Stadium, which pulls the average down a bit for right-handed hitters on other clubs.

Berkow, what Hank would have done if he had played with the Yankees. Berkow relayed the posthumous answer: "I'd have learned to hit left-handed."

Playing for the Yankees can be both a blessing and a curse. While the Stadium hurt Joe, the powerful New York press put his name on page one all over the country. Greenberg escaped the Stadium, but his 58 homers in Detroit were virtually ignored by the media across the country.

So, although DiMaggio's streak may be tainted, fate had already stolen genuine fame from him in denying him possible shots at 60 homers and a rare .400 season. Joe never complained about the bad fortune the baseball fates dealt him. Perhaps we should not complain when life finally gave him a few breaks to even the balance sheet.

The streak has brought Joe undying fame. But it didn't bring him fortune. In an outburst of generosity, the Yankees offered Joe a bonus of $3,000 —this to a man who had probably brought in at least twenty times that much in extra ticket sales in one game alone. Next spring, wrote a wide-eyed columnist Bob Considine, the bidding might start as high as $60,000! Instead, writes Dom DiMaggio, in 1942 the Yankees asked Joe to take a $5,000 cut!

In 1941 Gary Cooper made $600,000 for playing a baseball player, Gehrig, on the screen; that's almost 20 times as much as DiMaggio made for being a ballplayer in real life. But, then, more people saw Gary than saw Joe. What would a player make today for hitting in 56 straight games or bat .400? Pitcher Bob Muncrief laughed when I asked him: "He'd walk up to the owner and say, 'Hi ya, pardner.'"

Meanwhile, after everyone had left the clubhouse, DiMaggio motioned to Phil Rizzuto to stick around, and they walked silently together up the hill to the hotel. When they passed a bar, Joe said something, and Phil, misunderstanding, started in with him. "But he didn't want me, he wanted some money. He'd forgotten his in the little safes they provided us." Phil dug into his pocket and handed Joe all the cash he had, $18, and Joe walked into the bar alone.

Thirty years later, DiMaggio said, he ran into the cab driver, who apologized abjectly. "He was very serious. Well, my God, I felt awful. I mean, he might have been spending his life thinking he had jinxed me. But I told him he hadn't. My number was up, that was all."

Almost half a century later, I was still intrigued by one overlooked question: Who had made the throw that held Rosenthal on third, Henrich or DiMaggio? The newspaper accounts didn't report it. Henrich couldn't remember. Neither could Sturm nor Dickey. Murphy, Joe Gordon, who would have taken the relay, and Red Rolfe at third base are all deceased.

DiMaggio himself has been uncommunicative, but I made one last appeal with another letter: "Do you remember whether you or Henrich made the throw?"

Again I had to wait weeks for a reply. Again my own letter and self-addressed stamped envelope came back. Across the top was one word printed and underlined:

"No."

So there were many men who stopped DiMaggio's streak: Smith and Bagby, Keltner and Boudreau, Murphy and Campbell, and the mystery outfielder, either Henrich or Jolting Joe himself.

Henrich summed it up best. "It would have been very easy for us to have maneuvered the ball and let them score, and nobody would have suspected. When you write about the integrity of baseball, write about that game.*

---

*Sunday,*
*July 20*

---◆---

Ted's ankle still hurt "if I stop suddenly," and the Red Sox played a night game in Chicago Friday without him. To save money, the White Sox didn't turn the lights on until just before game time, and the teams refused to take batting practice without them. Grove was going for #300 again, against Rigney, and lost in the tenth 4–3.

In St. Louis on Saturday Williams pinch-hit in each game of a double-header; he flied out and got one walk and dropped two more points on his average to .393. The Sox lost both games.

DiMaggio was hitting .375. With the pressure of his hitting streak over, he said his next goal was to overtake Williams for the batting crown. It would be Joe's third straight if he could do it.

On Sunday Boston was losing 6–0 against Niggeling when Ted was called in to pinch-hit in the ninth with two on. "I don't remember Williams hitting the knuckler," catcher Rick Ferrell says. "Niggeling's fastball was pretty straight,

*In 1987 Milwaukee's Paul Molitor saw his streak end at 39 in a similar way, in the tenth inning against the same Cleveland Indians at Milwaukee. With the winning run on base, Molitor, due to hit next, knelt in the on-deck circle as pinch-hitter Rick Manning (.228) singled the run home to end the game.

but if he got behind, he had to come in with it." Niggeling's first pitch almost hit Williams' injured ankle. Ted hit the next one far over the pavilion roof just inside the foul pole for three runs, the only runs scored by Boston in both games that day.

Since Williams' injury, he had come to bat four times and batted in four runs. But as the Red Sox boarded their Pullman for the long trip to Boston, Cronin and the writers were pessimistic. The team had won only three and lost nine and had fallen from 7 ½ games behind to 13 ½. In six of their losses, one hit would have turned the tide. The whole team had gone into a batting slump with only 35 runs in 12 games, and four of those had been driven in by Williams. "There's no question that the early return of All Star hero Ted is the tonic most needed by the Cronin crew," Moore wrote.

But the return would come too late. The four straight defeats to lowly St. Louis virtually ended all dreams of a Boston pennant.

Cronin held out no hope for Ted's early return. "He still can't shift that ankle in the outfield," Joe said. "I don't see how I can risk aggravating it further by having the Kid play regularly just yet."

As usual Ted himself was impatient to get into the game. "I really didn't have to limp as much as I did while trotting out that home run yesterday," he apologized.

Incidentally, although DiMaggio wasn't there, Yankee Stadium hosted another immortal that Sunday, when Satchel Paige pitched for the Kansas City Monarchs against the New York Cubans. It was a silent rebuke to the white leagues.

In 1941 Paige was 7−1 with the Kansas City Monarchs (black teams played only about 50 league games a year). His teammate, Hilton Smith, was 10−0, and many black hitters considered Smith even harder to hit than Paige. "My god," whistles Roy Campanella, "you couldn't tell the difference!"

And the previous year Ray Brown of the Homestead Grays had outdone them both with a Negro league record 24 wins and only four losses.

One wonders: If Paige, Smith, and Brown had played in the American league in 1941, replacing Babich, Hadley, and Arnold Anderson, or Niggeling and Rigney, for instance, could DiMaggio have hit in 56 straight games or could Williams have batted .400? No man has hit .400 since integration. "I'd have knocked a few points off those big batting averages," Satch once said.

Williams had seen Paige pitch back when Ted was a kid in San Diego. He recalls that Satchel had legs so skinny the elastics on his pantlegs hung loose. But he "had a nice, easy windup, he made everything look easy."

Ted would face Satch in 1948, when Paige finally joined the American League at the age of 42. While Ted was admiring Satch's loose and languid style, he suddenly realized, he had gone to bat six times with only one hit.

In their next face-off, Williams remembered, Paige went into his stretch and turned his wrist. "Jesus," Ted figured, "curve ball." Instead, a fastball whooshed into the catcher's mitt for strike three. Next day Paige ambled over to the Red Sox dugout. "Where's Ted? Where's Ted?" he demanded.

"Right here, Satch," Williams replied.

"You ought to know better than to guess with Ol' Sachel," Paige grinned.

## Tuesday,
## July 22

◆

### WILLIAMS EAGER TO GO

the *Herald* headlined as the Sox' train pulled into Boston.

Without waiting for the doctor's permission, Ted went to left field against his favorite cousin, Rigney. He received a tremendous ovation when he came up the first time and hit the third pitch for "a magnificent shot against the right-field bleacher front over the bull pen," the *Herald* reported. It was his only hit in two at bats before Cronin yanked him from the line-up, and the Red Sox snapped out of their slump with a 6–2 victory. Ted was back to .397 now.

In the field, he backed up Dom on Knickerbocker's double and threw Knick out at third on a relay.

Williams kept hitting, with 2-for-5 against Thornton Lee on Wednesday and another 2-for-5 against Dietrich on Thursday. One of his hits came on a hit-and-run when he punched the ball through Appling's deserted shortstop position into left field, as the fans laughed in appreciation of the strategy. Boston split the two games.

## Friday,
## July 25

♦

Old Man Mose would try for #300 again, this time against the Indians. In the fifth, Grove was down by two runs when Williams came up against Harder with one man on and slammed "a high, windswept belt" into the right-field stands to tie the game.

In the eighth he came up again with the score tied and fouled out to third. But Foxx followed with a wallop against the door in center field. Eleven-year-old Bob Ruggiero, who was there, said the ball hit about ten feet high and bounced back right past the transfixed outfielder for an easy triple. Half a century later Ruggiero remembered the Foxx belt but not Williams'. Appropriately, Jimmie's sock won the game for his old buddy, Grove. The two had played together for 15 years on the A's and Red Sox.

Grove was only the 12th man, and the second left-hander, to win 300 games. He'd have won a lot more if he hadn't spent three extra years in the minors back before the major league draft prevented that sort of thing.

Washington scout Joe Cambria was at the game and confided that he had found a great prospect, Early Winn (sic), who also would go on to win 300 games.

Grove posed with Cy Young (511 wins) and Walter Johnson (416)—but not with Ted, who was still pouting over his foul-out in the eighth. Today Williams feels badly about it. "Wouldn't I love to have a picture of Lefty and me," he says.

But Ted did get two hits in three at bats to hike his average back to an even .400.

---

### Saturday,
### July 26

———————◆———————

The great Feller, already 19–6, was pitching, hoping to be the first man in this century to win 20 before August 1.

Bob held a low number in the army draft and said he was not going to ask for a 60-day deferment to finish the season. "I want to serve, because I think every young fellow should," he said. (Bob was such a clean-cut Iowa all-American boy he wouldn't even endorse cigarettes. His reason was "very novel," said Bob Considine: He didn't smoke.) Bob would enlist in the navy right after Pearl Harbor and serve three and a half years, part of it in combat shooting down kamikaze planes in the Pacific.

Who was tougher for him, Williams or DiMaggio? Considine asked.

"Williams," Feller answered. Joe is tough, all right, "but honestly, I just can't get that guy (Williams) out. I can't throw my fastball past him, and I haven't got enough curve to fool him. I'm not kidding when I say I feel pretty lucky when he hits a single off my curve ball. If I give him my fast one, he triples."

In the game Williams blasted three "ripping singles" and scored one run to beat Rapid Robert 4–3 and raise his batting average to .405.

———————◆———————

Joe Heving (5–2) brought his slow side-arm curves to Fenway following Feller's blazing fastballs and shut the Red Sox out.

Indians manager Roger Peckinpaugh pulled a surprise that no one ever remembered seeing before. He called it his "Trosky defense." He moved third baseman Keltner over to the shortstop position, moved shortstop Boudreau to the other side of second base, the normal second base position, put second baseman Ray Mack on the outfield grass in short right field, and had first baseman Hal Trosky hug the first base line.

A's shortstop Al Brancato says Connie Mack experimented with a similar alignment that season. "The third baseman was two feet from second," Phil Marchildon agrees. "Williams still hit it through the shift."

And St. Louis third baseman Clift insists that the Browns also pulled the shift on Ted, although not as extreme as the Cleveland one. "I was almost over at shortstop, shortstop was behind the bag, second baseman over in the hole, and the first baseman on the grass. And he still hit some line shots through there."

Catcher Rick Ferrell agreed. "It's not how you pitch to him," Rick said, "but how you play him. We'd swing around."

All Williams says is, "There's no doubt about it, they were playing me tighter all the time."

Five years later, after Boudreau became manager of the Indians, he pulled the same shift against Ted and made it famous as the "Boudreau Shift." Actually, Lou lifted the idea from his old manager in 1941, and the maneuver should properly be called the Peckinpaugh Shift.

How did the shift succeed? Williams walked, lined out, singled, and doubled to raise his average to .408. Still the shift may have had its effect. Ted's only out, a line drive to Mack, would have been a hit in a normal defensive pattern.

The Indians just held their heads in dismay. They agreed that Williams would hit .500 in League Park, Yankee Stadium, or Sportsmen's Park, all with invitingly short right-field targets.

Again Williams turned in a good play in the field, leaping against the scoreboard to rob Gee Walker of an extra-base hit. The year before, Ted had been "nonchalant" in the outfield, said the *Herald*. "This year he's hustling his head off." He is enjoying "tremendous new popularity and plays the outfield as if he enjoys it." He can be another Babe Ruth with the fans. "Ted has the color, which Joe DiMaggio somehow or other lacks."

Since his return to the regular line-up, Williams had hit .525 (12-for-22), and the Red Sox had won four out of six games.

After the game Williams hopped a plane to New York to pose for high-speed color pictures for *Life* magazine.

The Browns arrived on Tuesday, when Williams clipped Niggeling for another homer, #20, a two-run shot that curved around the foul pole just barely fair. But Johnny shut him down the rest of the game and beat the Red Sox 3–2.

After a rain-out Wednesday, Williams ran into an old problem he still couldn't solve—bases on balls. Four Brownie hurlers walked him four times. They only pitched to him twice, including once with the bases loaded, only the second time all year Williams had come up with three men on base; the only other time, Lyons had walked him in Chicago.

This time Williams hit "a terrific sock" on a 3–2 pitch from Bill Trotter (4–2) across a stiff northeast wind and into the bullpen for a grand slam. It was home run #21 and gave the Sox an 11–7 lead, which they blew 14–11.

And Ted made another of his now famous catches, racing to get a drive, juggling it, and finally bare-handing it for the out. In game two Williams hit a double in three trips against Bob Muncrief to end the day with 3-for-6 and .409 for the year.

In game two Williams hit a double in three trips against Bob Muncrief to end the day with 3-for-6 and .409 for the year.

## Friday,
## August 1

---

After an off-day Thursday, Williams thrilled 1700 GIs in the crowd, including Hugh Mulcahy, by drilling two hits in three at bats against Dizzy Trout of the Tigers. He doubled to the flagpole his first time up, then singled and walked and trotted off the field hitting .414. The Tigers won the game, however, 6–5, as Grove failed to win #301.

## Sunday,
## August 3

---

A curfew on gasoline sales apparently had no effect in saving fuel, as New England highways reported their greatest weekend traffic jams in years. Meanwhile, Britain's Royal Air Force took the war to the Germans, raining fire bombs on Berlin, and President Roosevelt, with his little Scottie, Falla, left New London, Connecticut on an Atlantic cruise, course unknown.

In Fenway Park, after an off-day Saturday, the Tiger rookie, Newhouser, beat the Sox, though he gave up 11 hits. Only one of them was by Williams however. But twice Ted reached over, inches from the leftfield stands which hug the foul line to pluck foul flies. Wrote the *Herald*: "The customers love that outfield hustle by the Kid."

## Monday,
## August 4

Ted got no hits, as Lum Harris (4–4 for the last-place A's) walked him three times. In two official at bats Williams lined out "boisterously" to deep center, and, with the bases loaded, swung on an inviting 2–0 pitch and popped it up. Foxx returned to the line-up with a home run however, as the Sox won 7–6.

## Tuesday,
## August 5

Williams smacked two hits against Jack Knott, the A's biggest winner that year at 13–11. Ted singled, and with two on banged a "ferocious" double to the right-field corner, then scored on Foxx' single, as roommate Charlie Wagner won in relief.

Nazi tanks battled the Soviets in Smolensk and Kiev, and knifed closer to Leningrad. In Washington, with defense costs escalating, the House voted "the greatest tax bill ever imposed by a civilization upon its people." Under the bill, a family making $5,000 a year would have to pay $308 in income taxes.

## Wednesday,
## August 6

Fenway Park was sold out for a midweek double-header against the Yankees. The Sox rapped Chandler and Breuer for 15 hits, but Williams got only one of them in six tries, and that one was "a mild handle safety," according to Dick McGann of the New York *Daily News*. (Whitman of the Boston *Herald* called it "a looping single to center.") Perhaps Ted was trying too hard, wrote Whitman, as he went after a couple of bad pitches.

The teams split the games. Joe DiMaggio went 2-for-7, including a 450-foot homer in the first game and a hard-hit double to win the second. Joe was leading the league in RBI, 97, and was one behind Keller in homers with 26. Williams, who trailed them both with 21 homers, saw his average shrink to .405.

## Thursday,
## August 7

The Senate voted a 2 ½-year term for draftees and granted them a raise of $10 a month after their first year.

Williams had a field day against his favorite patsy, Lefty Gomez, who hadn't lost a game in almost three months. Ted led off the second by pulling a wicked line drive 15 rows up into the Fenway stands—his 22nd homer—reached on an error, and rifled two singles to right. All in all, he scored three runs and knocked in two in a 9–5 victory.

DiMaggio was hitless and uncorked a high throw to the plate letting one run in.

Again Williams turned in the catch of the day, a one-handed snatch of a sinking liner by Joe Gordon inches from the ground. "The Kid has strong hands which close on that ball as a bear trap grabs its victim," Whitman wrote.

But John Drebinger of the *Times* said Ted's baserunning cost the Sox a run. Williams was "the perfect image of Babe Herman" (who once doubled into a double play), when Doerr's line-drive out caught Ted on third base "with his mouth open. . . . By the time Ted got his mouth shut and his long legs in motion," it was too late to score.

### *Saturday, August 9*

Ted went 2-for-6 in two games on Friday and Saturday against the Senators. The Sox split the games.

On Saturday Grove took a 6–4 lead into the seventh, when he loaded the bases. With George Case, the fastest man in the majors (33 steals), on third, Cecil Travis (.359, two points ahead of DiMaggio), flied to short left, and Ted whipped the ball home to double Case. The Senators, however, won in the ninth as Lefty was frustrated once more.

In Europe, Nazi bombers pounded Moscow, setting the Kremlin ablaze. The House voted to extend the draft by a single vote 203–202. And a *Newsweek* headline proclaimed:

**WOMEN DEMAND GREATER ROLE
IN NATIONAL DEFENSE PROGRAM**

---

## *Sunday, August 10*

---

Ted lashed four hits in a double-header against the Senators, as the teams split the two games. He was now hitting .412.

Little Hugh Duffy, a 5'6" mite and the all-time record-holder with .440 in 1894 (it was originally published as .438), opined that Williams might be the man to break his record. The Red Sox' batting coach emeritus, Duffy had been born in Rhode Island 74 years earlier, the year after the Civil War ended. He and his outfield sidekick, Tommy McCarthy, were the Boston Red Stockings' "heavenly twins," leading the team to pennants in 1892 and '93. They're both in the Hall of Fame. Duffy told Washington *Post* sports editor Shirley Povich:

"The funny thing about it is, I never did put much store by that .438 average until Rogers Hornsby threatened to better it in 1924. For more than 30 years I virtually forgot about it. Folks weren't so excited about batting averages in those days. They didn't make so much fuss over 'em. Then when Hornsby came along and hit .424, they started checking up on the old records, and there mine was.

**Ted and Duffy** *Saturday Evening Post*

"Then I began to take some pride in my .438 and was kind of glad Hornsby didn't outdo it. I thought it was safe for all time, because Hornsby was just about the greatest of the modern-day hitters. I didn't think anybody would come close, but now this Williams comes along, and I don't think it's out of his reach.

"I've never seen a better hitter. He's got everything to hit with. A great bead on the ball, the courage to wait up there, and the best arms and wrists I ever did see. The amazing thing is he's mostly a pull hitter. He gets a lot of home runs [Duffy also led the league in homers in 1894, with 14], but the high-average hitters are usually the fellows who hit straight-away, where there's more room for hits. That's where I made most of my hits, toward center field."

Duffy and Williams posed for a picture together sitting on the Red Sox bench, the wizened but wise old master and the young and attentive disciple, as Duffy pointed to .438 painted on the wall between them. I asked Williams if Duffy had given him any tips on hitting. In reply, Ted wrinkled his nose, gave a little shake of his head, and smiled.

---

### *Monday,*
### *August 11*

---◆---

The Sox arrived in New York to challenge the Yanks, who had opened up a 13 ½-game lead over Cleveland (15 ½ over the third-place Red Sox). Boston shut the Bombers out 8–0, as Ted drove in the first, and deciding, run with a single through the left side of the infield, then was walked four times, to lusty boos.

Joe DiMaggio went 0-for-3.

Little Dom outshone his big brother with a great running catch, two singles, and a home run. In the ninth, pitcher Charlie Stanceu hit him in the head and dropped him unconscious to the ground. Joe came running in from center field in alarm, while Dom slowly came to, regained his feet, and tottered to first base. But he complained of a pain in his neck and left the game. Afterwards Joe drove him to the hospital for X-rays. Dom was back in action the next day.

Only one player wore a batting helmet then, Red Sox utility man Skeeter Newsome, who had been skulled twice. (Negro leaguer Willie Wells claimed he invented them when he knocked the jets off a coal miner's hard hat.) A year earlier when Brooklyn's Joe Medwick had been almost killed by a pitch in a game against arch-rival St. Louis, Dodger owner

Larry MacPhail promptly ordered a box of helmets for his team, though it would be another 15 years before they were widely used. Strangely, Williams was one of the last to convert.

Owners then didn't think to protect their players' safety—or their own investments. The Dodgers' rookie Pete Reiser burned up the National League in 1941 with a .343 average, but his meteoric career was ended a few years later when he crashed into one too many outfield fences. No one had yet thought of padding the fences or putting warning tracks in front of them.

Tuesday New York's Spud Chandler shut the Red Sox out and held Williams to one hit, a single that struck the first base bag. Ted also whiffed two times. But Joe Trimble of the *Daily News* wrote: "A great throw by Ted Williams—who isn't supposed to be able to do anything but hit—retired Keller at the plate."

---

### *Thursday,*
### *August 14*

---

In three games in Philadelphia, Williams managed only one hit in each game.

Wednesday night he batted in the first run in a 4–0 win with a fierce drive off the rightfield wall off Marchildon, then walked the next four times, giving him 91 walks for the year.

In Friday's double-header, Williams got only 1-for-5 in the first game, but it was a "titanic" three-run homer off Tom Ferrick (8–10) that tied the game 8–8. Foxx' homer then won it in the 11th.

Ted went 1-for-4 in the second game loss. The Sox loaded the bases in the sixth with none out and Pete Fox, Cronin, and Williams coming up, but right-hander Les McCrabb (9–13) retired them all without a run and won the game 10–8. It dropped Ted's average to .408.

Meanwhile, the world finally learned where FDR had gone during his Atlantic cruise. A five-column photo on the front pages revealed the President with Prime Minister Churchill on a warship in the North Atlantic, where they had proclaimed the "Four Freedoms" and the Atlantic Charter, a blueprint of goals in the war against Hitler.

---

### *Saturday, August 16*

---

◆

---

In Washington on Friday Carresquel (6–2) shut Williams out in two at bats. Ted was now batting .405.

Against Dutch Leonard on Saturday, Williams grounded out weakly in his first two at bats, making six straight at bats without a hit, then smacked three hits to zoom up to .410. The Red Sox rallied to win in the eighth for Dobson, who had relieved Grove August 20; poor Lefty was still looking for #301.

## Sunday,
## August 17

Smiling Sid Hudson (13–14) walked Ted in the first. In the fourth Williams lined a hard foul against the fence before going out. In the fifth he slammed the ball 440 feet, where Doc Cramer caught it at the bleacher wall. And in the eighth Ted blasted another one 430 feet, but Cramer hauled it in too with a leaping catch against the same wall. All that muscle power merely produced three loud outs and a batting average of .404.

## Tuesday,
## August 19

After another long cross-country train trip to St. Louis, the Sox played a double-header before 1,100 fans, which was low, even for the Brownies.

In game one, right-hander Denny Galehouse (9–10) held Ted to one hit, a solo home run, #24, as the Red Sox lost 3–2.

In game two Williams faced Muncrief, who had "held" him to 4-for-12 so far, and smashed two singles and two more "lordly" homers over the pavilion roof. The second homer tied the game in the eighth, and the Sox won it in the ninth 10–7.

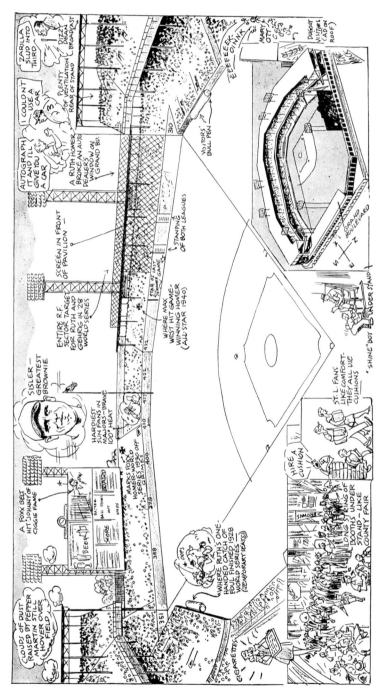

Sportsman's Park, St. Louis  *Boston Globe*

## Wednesday,
## August 20

———————◆———————

The next day the weary teams played two more games, and Williams blasted two more homers, one off Auker in the first and the other off Niggeling in the second.

However, once more Grove was shelled out of the box in the first game, which the Browns won 11−9.

With 8-for-14 in St. Louis, Ted had built his average back up to .411. His five home runs gave him 28 for the year to move him ahead of DiMaggio into second place, though Keller still led the league with 30. But Williams trailed far behind the two Yankees in RBI; he had 93 to Keller's 107 and DiMaggio's 117.

Meanwhile, Kodak came out with the first color slides. The nation reportedly had only a ten-day supply of gasoline left, and some states announced they would begin instituting "gasless Sundays." FDR warned that the war against Hitler might last until 1943. But he also announced that draftees over 28 would be released. Would the 30-year-old Greenberg get his $40,000 job back with the Tigers? (No. Hank was no sooner mustered out than Japan bombed Pearl Harbor, and he turned right around and re-enlisted.)

---

*Thursday,*
*August 21*

---

◆

---

The Red Sox arrived in Chicago to find that Rigney had pitched out of turn the day before, perhaps to avoid facing Williams, who had already rocked him for five monster blasts. Johnny had pitched a shutout, making nine straight victories and 32 straight scoreless innings for Chicago hurlers.

With Ed Smith on the mound, Williams broke the scoreless string when he singled to open the second and scored on Foxx's single and a wild pitch. Ted singled again in the third before walking the last two times up. His average had grown to .414.

---

*Saturday,*
*August 23*

---

◆

---

In the next two games in the Windy City, Buck Ross and Johnny Humphries (4–2) held Williams to 1-for-6.

On Friday Ted's long fly drove in a run in a 2–1 victory, but it looked like just a big out in the box score.

Saturday Humphries (4–2, 1.84 ERA) gave him only one single to shut Boston out 3–0. In the third, Ted popped up with two men on. In the fifth he whipped a long drive to right, which everyone thought was gone, but the wind held it up for another long out.

---

### *Sunday,*
### *August 24*

◆

"Stop Williams, and you stop a good part of the Sox' slugging," Frank Gibbons of the Cleveland *Free Press* wrote as the Red Sox arrived for a double-header against the second-place Indians. And that's what Al Milnar did. Ted struck out once, smacked into a double play, and grounded out before finally getting a single in the ninth, as Milnar shut them out for eight more innings and won the first game 4–3.

Al Smith, the conqueror of DiMaggio, shut Williams out in three tries in game two, which Cleveland also won.

---

### *Monday,*
### *August 25*

◆

The punchless Sox now faced perhaps the best pitcher in baseball and perhaps fastest of all time—Bob Feller—under the lights, which were then still somewhat less bright than they are today. (DiMaggio's streak had ended under these same Cleveland lights). Charlie Wagner was the sacrificial lamb sent out to oppose Rapid Robert.

In the first Williams fouled a fast ball onto the stadium roof, a rare feat in that huge park, then took a called third strike. After a walk and an out, Ted came up in the seventh with the score still 0–0. Feller walked him again and Frankie Pytlak doubled to win the game 1–0. Once again Williams had provided the winning run, but he was 0-for-2 in the box score. He had now gotten two hits in his last 15 at bats, and his average had shrunk to .402.

The next day Jim Bagby walked Ted four times, but he finally got a hit his fifth time, as the Sox won and took over third place.

---

### Wednesday, August 27

◆

Williams arrived in Detroit with a .404 average, down seven points in his last five games. The Tigers' broadcaster, Harry Heilmann, who had reached .401 back in 1923 and had just missed it three other times, huddled with Ted. Forget about home runs, Heilmann urged; just go for singles.

The pep talk may have helped. Williams popped two singles in four tries against Newhouser and Gorsica, raising his average to .404.

## Wednesday, August 27

♦

Ignoring Heilmann's advice, Ted blasted a home run, #29, against Al Benton to almost the same spot he had reached in the All Star game. Then he tripled to left-center and scored on Foxx's fly. Ted left town with 4-for-7 in the series and a .407 average.

"Williams is the best player I've ever seen," Tiger catcher Birdie Tebbetts whistled—he could break Babe Ruth's record in Detroit, New York, or St. Louis. After the war Tebbetts would join the Red Sox as Williams' teammate and would call him an outstanding team player, as well as a great clutch-hitter. Ted was popular with his teammates, "minded his own business," and didn't ask for special favors. "He can run and throw with speed and accuracy and is the best left fielder in the game," Birdie said.

Meanwhile, the government declared that 17.9 cents a gallon would be a "fair price" for gas to prevent profiteering, although many gas stations defied the guidelines. And in the Middle East British paratroopers jumped into Iran, seizing vital oil centers there.

## Friday,
## August 30

———————◆———————

Back home in Fenway, Williams continued his hitting tear against Philadelphia with two hits in three trips, including home run #30 into the bullpen against Bump Hadley (5–6). A's outfielder Sam Chapman leaned over the railing and got a glove on it but couldn't hold it. Ted also slashed a single through first base and drew two intentional walks. One, with two on and two out, backfired when Foxx followed with a double to clear the bases.

"Somewhere on the eastern front," Hitler and Il *Duce* Mussolini ended five days of talks and hinted at a long war ahead. At home Charles A. Lindbergh warned that attacking Germany would be the best way for the United States to lose the war. The 1942 cars were unveiled: Willys came out with a "car for the people" that got 35 miles to the gallon, and Hudson boasted a "Drive Master" with no clutch.

## Sunday,
## August 31

———————◆———————

Williams walloped homer #31 with two men on against Jack Knott to stay one behind Keller and help the Red Sox win the first game 5–3. It also boosted Ted over the 100-mark in RBI.

In game two Williams came to bat three times with men on base, and each time Marchildon issued him an intentional walk. In his only chance to swing at a ball, Ted fouled out. In the seventh Marchildon was leading 3–2 with a man on first and Williams up as the A's stalled, hoping darkness would force the umpires to call the game. The umps wouldn't budge, however, and suddenly manager Connie Mack, who must have been daydreaming, took a look at home plate and leaped to his feet.

Four decades later the memory still makes Williams chuckle. "Funniest thing ever happened to me in the big leagues was the expression Connie Mack got on his face when there were men on base and I'm at the plate. His neck stretched up"—here Ted imitates a pop-eyed giraffe—"and boy, if there was any base open, he'd force them from first to second or second to third to get me the hell of there. He started waving that scorecard. Yeah, he'd force the winning run into position so's not to pitch to me. I had Mack shook. He did some things that were altogether against the percentages of baseball. Got away with it for a while."

The Boston crowd booed, but Connie's strategy worked as Foxx grounded out to end the threat.

Williams was now hitting .407. But he was batting almost 1.000 in the popularity league. Even Bill Cunningham was mellowing:

"The problem child has undoubtedly grown into strapping manhood this summer. He doesn't snarl and snap and slash back the way he did, largely because the various and sundry don't needle him the way they did. He's a personality now, a person of stature." Cunningham saw the terrible temper flare at one writer, but happily a teammate pulled Ted into a corner until he cooled off. "His former tormentors tread with awe. And left alone, he does nicely in the personality league. . . . Let's hope he stays up there."

In the torrid National League race, the Cardinals' Lon Warneke pitched a no-hitter, lifting St. Louis into first place ahead of Brooklyn, as the Dodgers lost to the Giants of New York.

---

### *Monday, September 1*

———◆———

Labor Day. Japan threatened to go to war to break the allies' economic encirclement. FDR replied in a fireside chat that the United States was ready to fight if necessary.

Boston sweltered in 92-degree heat. The beaches were thronged. At Narragansett race track, 200 persons literally toppled over in their chairs and were carried out on stretchers; one died of a heart attack.

At Fenway Park, Williams socked three more homers—#32, 33, and 34—against the Senators to move ahead of Keller, who had 33.

The first one against Carresquel on a 2–0 count had a little help from the wind and tied the game 5–5. It "floated into the stands," wrote Webb of the *Globe*, though the wind almost blew it foul; it was fair by inches.

The second, off Bill Zuber, was a "tremendous drive" 420 feet, over the bullpen and into the bleachers, "one of the most savage of Ted's Boston career," Whitman whistled. Webb called it Ted's longest homer in Boston, "so high the ball almost went out of sight." It drove in the go-ahead run, as the Red Sox went on to win. "The din was terrific," the *Post* reported.

In game two Ted drove a high fly to deep right, "a sure home run anywhere else," Whitman noted. Between innings Ted told the boy in the scoreboard, "I think I've got another one coming. Watch me next time up."

In the sixth, against Arnold Anderson, Williams unleashed his longest drive of all, clear over the right-field roof—foul. It was the first ball ever hit out of Fenway Park to right field, a shot that carried at least 400 feet to the roof, which is 60 feet high, according to SABRs ballpark expert, Bob Bluthardt. Only one man, Carl Yastrzemski, has reached that spot in the half century since then.

Williams followed with another long shot far over the bullpen into the stands. The roar of the crowd could be heard a mile away.

He also walked four times (all "semi-intentional"), and got on base eight times (including an error on his long fly), as the Red Sox swept both games. In all, Williams knocked in five runs and scored five.

His homers gave him 17 for the year in Fenway, breaking his previous high of 14 in 1939 and almost double his total of nine in 1940.

Williams still trailed Keller and DiMaggio in RBI, 106 to 112 for Joe and 119 for Charlie. But the walks gave Ted 123 for the year, way ahead of anyone else. And he raised his average to .410, 50 points ahead of his closest pursuer, Cecil Travis of Washington, and 54 ahead of DiMaggio.

The next day he chided the *Herald* for missing one of his runs: All those walks make it hard to knock in many, "but give me credit for the ones I score after being walked."

"Ted's got to be the whole show with these second-place Red Sox," Whitman exulted in the *Herald*.

The fans were more interested in Ted than in the Sox, Gerry Hern wrote in the *Post*; they blocked the aisles waiting for his last at bat to see if he could hit a fourth homer.

Not even Babe Ruth was a greater attraction, Victor O. Jones wrote in the *Globe*—and Ted is more colorful than DiMaggio.

"What publicity you're getting," one writer told Ted.

"Yeah," he replied. "And what hitting."

---

## Tuesday,
## September 2

---

The Boston press was rushing to clap Ted on the back.

### TED BLOOMS
### INTO MANHOOD

Bill Cunningham admitted.

### Actions, Behavior, Hitting
### Boost Kid to First Place

Even Williams' favorite *bete noir*, "Colonel" Dave Egan, joined the admirers. "The magnificent maypole," he wrote, "is just a thin, nervous, jerky genius who, still in his swaddling clothes, is being compared favorably with the greatest sluggers in the history of baseball." He's already made the fans forget about DiMaggio's streak and almost alone drew some 45,000 customers to Fenway for the series against the woeful Senators. "They pile out of the subways, on the way to the game, talking about Teddy Williams. They pile back into them

again, after the game, still talking about Teddy Williams."
Egan graciously lifted his hat and gave "one loud toot on the
tooter for the Kid who came back."

Ted must have enjoyed his breakfast newspaper before
driving to Cape Cod with his new rifle and pistol to spend the
off-day and await the arrival of the Yankees and a showdown
with Keller.

---

*Wednesday,*
*September 3*

---

Before the Yankee double-header, Williams got a call from
the Boston police. Fourteen-year-old Billy Kane had spent the
night in jail after hitchhiking down from Maine without a
penny to see the Red Sox on Tuesday, only to learn there was
no game. Ted came to headquarters to talk to the boy and
promised him a box-seat ticket to the games that day.

The only contest was between Williams and Keller. New
York was already so far in front—20 ½ games—that they expected to clinch the pennant while in Boston, the earliest
clinching in history.

The Yankee pitchers arrived in town, gushing about
Williams. "He hits them inside, outside, low and high,"
moaned Marius Russo.

"He won't swing at a bad ball," said Johnny Murphy, the
premier reliever. "You don't have much chance to fool him."

Red Ruffing, the ace of the staff (15–6), had pitched against Cobb and Sisler, both good place-hitters and bunters who added points to their averages with those strategies. But Ted didn't do either. "Williams simply overpowers the ball," Ruffing said; "it's a tribute to him that he can hit .400 that way." Ted always could hit Red, and Yankee manager Joe McCarthy refused to let Red pitch against the Red Sox the whole year. If Ruffing had faced Williams the normal five or six times that season, Ted's average might have been several points higher, and Red's won-lost percentage several points lower.

The New York writers were just as awed. Joe King of the *World Telegram* noted that Ted had beaten out only four infield hits all year. He's a shoo-in for .400, King believed: All he needs is one hit a game for the next 19 games.

Charlie Keller wasn't conceding any homers, though. He and Williams had been rivals since they were rookies together in 1939, when Charlie had actually outhit Ted .334 to .327. A picture of "King Kong" with his dark, beetling eyebrows, boning his bat, ran in the *Herald* above the caption: HOPES TO POLISH OFF WILLIAMS.

Prospects for a homer were not good for either man. Williams had hit only one home run off Yankee pitching all year (against Gomez), and Keller, a lefty like Ted, hadn't hit a homer in Fenway yet this season. At home Charlie had a 344-foot power alley to shoot for, compared to 380 feet in Boston. However, Keller didn't pull the ball that much. Many of his drives were to center and left-center, the deepest part of the Stadium, and his speed allowed him to leg out many blows for inside-the-park home runs.

Keller would be facing Charlie Wagner; Ted would go against Tiny Bonham, whose overhand forkball Williams didn't like at all.

Williams and Keller *Bettmann*

Before the game the two matadors posed together, then went out to their *mano a mano* battle. The fans applauded each time Williams stepped up to bat, and held their breath while he dueled the pitcher. Keller also had them hushed, apprehensive of his power.

King Kong opened with a "whistling" 400-foot fly to center, which Dom DiMaggio pulled down.

In Ted's first at bat, with men on second and third, Bonham brazenly pitched to him and got him on a fly to Keller in right.

Thereafter, Wagner gave Keller only one hit, a single. Bonham also held Williams to a single in three at bats. The Yankees won 2−1 in 12 innings and needed just one more victory to clinch the flag.

# Thursday,
## September 4

♦

German armies smashed their way to the outskirts of Leningrad. The U.S. Navy had a close brush with a Nazi sub in the Atlantic, when a torpedo luckily went wide.

### NAVY TO SHOOT
### SUBS ON SIGHT

the Boston *Post* cried.

Williams would be facing Yankee right-hander Atley Donald (9–5), while Keller would face the knuckle-balling Newsome.

In his first at bat, Keller blasted a drive to the bleacher wall in deep right-center. Pete Fox slipped on the soft dirt or he might have caught it, and the ball bounced off the wall for a double to drive in Charlie's 120th run.

Donald, meanwhile, was not taking any chances with Williams. Three times he walked Ted, all on 3–2 counts, twice as the lead-off man in the inning, once with two men on and the Yankees winning 4–0. Once Foxx hit into a double play behind Ted's walk; Jimmie had lost a few steps in the past year, making the strategy of walking Ted that much more valid. Finally, in his last at bat, Ted singled, to boost his average to .411.

Keller got no more hits, but the Yanks won the game 6–3, clinching the flag earlier than any team in history before or since. There was almost no celebration in the clubhouse later. (Remember, Harold Kaese sniffed in the *Post*, the Yanks piled up their big lead while Williams had been out of action after the All Star game.)

Joe Trimble of the New York *Daily News* said Boston owner Tom Yawkey should change the team's name to the Ted Sox. "Williams fans, and they are legion and loud, will also claim another title for their Ted this year: 'Best Drawing Card in Baseball.' Ted, they claim, deserves this more than DiMaggio, hitting streak and all, and Bobby Feller, fireball and all." The Sox seem sure to set a new Boston attendance record of over 800,000, "mainly because of young Williams."

---

## Saturday, September 6

◆

After an off-day the two teams squared off again, this time in Yankee Stadium. This is the game I saw, when Williams went 1-for-4 against Marvin Breuer (9–7): walk, ground out, pop out, fly out—almost a home run—and finally a single.

Keller went hitless with two foul outs and two ground outs against Dobson, who won the game 8–1.

# Sunday,
# September 7

◆

Bobby Riggs beat Frank Kovacs for the U.S. Open tennis title.

Williams, who hadn't hit a homer in New York all year, promised to hit one against his favorite "cousin," Gomez. Instead, he missed two by inches, even fractions of inches.

In the first he smashed one down the right-field line. It hit the foul pole, a one-in-a-million shot, and glanced off into the stands foul. If it had bounced the other way, into fair territory, it would have been a homer. But under Yankee Stadium's crazy ground rules, it was judged a double, though as Jack Malaney of the Boston *Post* pointed out, the foul pole is in fair territory. Williams himself had forgotten all about it until I mentioned it to him, when he quickly agreed with Malaney. So technically, Williams had 38 home runs that year, not 37, and 522 for his career, not 521.

In the third, big Ted singled to right.

In the fifth, he drove one of Gomez' pitches high off the distant center-field wall just inches below the top for a double and scored on Foxx's single.

One inning later Ted came up with the bases loaded, and Gomez, apparently deciding that one run was better than four, walked him on four pitches. It was "almost" intentional, wrote Malaney. Even the New York fans booed.

That was all for Lefty, as reliever Johnny Murphy made his familiar walk in from the bullpen. Murphy finally stopped

Williams in the ninth on a drive that went "a mile into center," where Henrich pulled it down.

Gomez-Murphy had been a formidable pitcher for the Yankees for years. Gomez once cracked that he had won 21 games in 1937 but only 18 in '38, because "Murphy was tired that year." The other secret of Lefty's success was DiMaggio. Gomez said he saw more of Joe's back chasing long flies than he saw of his front. Actually, of course, El Goofy was a good pitcher. He won that afternoon 8−5 and ended the year with a 15−5 record.

Keller had singled home two runs in the first, then hurt his leg sliding home. He hobbled off the field, probably out for the rest of the season. It practically assured Ted of the home run and batting crowns and left him trailing Charlie in RBIs 108 to 122, with a fair shot at overtaking him and Joe (118), who was also out temporarily with injuries.

The game incidentally drew 22,000, putting the Yankees over one million for the year, an excellent total for the Depression. Most of the fans were there that day to see Williams, observed Joe King of the *World-Telegram*. Even the Yankees were pulling for him. "Everybody is saying, 'That's my boy'. . . . As Joe Gordon says, it's a case of one fellow going for something heroic, and that gives everyone a rooting interest." Gordon added that Ted never hits the ball right at someone. "However you look at him, he's a marvel."

## Tuesday,
## September 9

◆

The Tigers came to Fenway, and Ted just missed two more homers off another cousin, Johnny Gorsica (9–11). After a walk and a single, Williams whipped a hard fly that would have gone into the right-field stands if the wind hadn't held it up. He also lashed a foul deep into the stands before grounding out.

In the field, he showed his hustle when he caught Barney McCoskey's foul at the edge of the field boxes in left.

The dean of American sports writers, Grantland Rice, compared Ted to Shoeless Joe Jackson—both were tall, loose, and lean. "When the season opened, the three individual headliners looked to be Bob Feller, Joe DiMaggio, and Ted Williams. But of the three, Williams remains as the individual star for 1941."

The game belonged to Dom DiMaggio however. The donnish little outfielder doubled, tripled, and slugged a grand-slam home run. He tried to bunt for a single to complete the cycle but was thrown out. The Sox won for Newsome 6–0.

Williams left the field hitting .412. On this date two years earlier, Joe DiMaggio had gotten three hits to raise his average to .406. But Joe was already sniffling from a cold, which he may have caught from Ruffing, and beginning the next day went into his fatal 0-for-13 slump, to end his dream of .400. The memory of Joe's dive must have been fresh in Ted's memory. Could he avoid a similar fate?

Williams didn't seem worried. He told *The Sporting News* that he was not going for home runs this year. He wants to hit .400 "like Cobb and Hornsby," then go for Gehrig's RBI mark, and Ruth's 60 homers. "I'm the boy to do it," he beamed.*

---

### *Wednesday, September 10*

---

◆

---

Against Detroit's Buck Newsom, Williams got his customary first-inning walk, then singled to right, as the Sox knocked Bobo off the mound.

Facing reliever Dizzy Trout, Ted doubled off the left-field wall, the second time he'd hit the Monster that year, scoring Cronin for Ted's 111th RBI, one behind DiMaggio. Then he cracked another long drive into the stands, but it curved foul by inches. He finally flied out and grounded out.

The Tigers signed an outfield prospect, Dick Wakefield, to an unheard of bonus contract of $45,000. And in Chicago quarterback Sid Luckman led the Chicago Bears to a 23–6 win over the College All Stars and UCLA's Jackie Robinson.

---

*There are some—Bob Feller is among them—who believe that, but for World War II, Williams might have made good on his boast. He was 23 when he left for the war with 127 homers, more than any man his age except Mel Ott, who had 153. Others: Mickey Mantle 121, Jimmie Foxx 116, Hank Aaron 110, Willie Mays 65, and Babe Ruth 20. Then at age 24 Foxx suddenly smashed 58, Mantle 52, Mays 51, and Ruth broke the old record three years in a row with totals of 29, 54, and 59. Finally, at age 26, Ted's last year in the service, Roger Maris came from nowhere to hit 61. As Joe Cronin said, "If anyone's going to do it, those are the years to do it."

## Friday,
## September 12

Williams faced the Browns' Niggeling, whom he had already slugged for four homers so far this year—but John had also beaten the Red Sox three straight anyway. This time Nig gave Ted another first-inning walk, then got him on two soft flies and a slow roller to first. In the eighth, Niggeling was winning again 5–0 with Lou Finney on third and Williams up. Johnny calmly ignored the hoots of the fans and issued an intentional walk to preserve his shutout. Ted's average was .407.

The next day, against Eldon Auker, Ted got only one pitch to swing at. Breaking his later rule, he swung at the first pitch he saw and popped the ball high to second base. Thereafter, Auker gave him three bases on balls, two intentional and the third "practically intentional." Ted's average dropped to .404.

Foxx slugged a grand slam, giving him 100 RBIs for the 13th year in a row and tying him with Lou Gehrig for that record. The Sox won 7–2.

## Sunday,
## September 14

The third-place White Sox, three games behind Boston, arrived for a double-header, making their last bid to overtake the Red Sox for second place. They would throw two of the toughest pitchers for Williams—Lyons and Lee—and over 36,000 Bostonians, the largest crowd of the year, came out to watch the battle. At an average of a dollar a head, the Red Sox took in on that day alone almost twice Ted's salary for the year. A player's union seemed long overdue, although an effective union was still 25 years in the future.

In game one, Ted, as usual, walked his first time up to load the bases and set the table for Foxx's second grand slam in as many days. Williams walked again his second time up to the disgust of the fans. Then he finally cracked a double and single, driving in run #112, as the Red Sox won 9–2.

In the second game, Lee handcuffed Williams with a strikeout and two infield outs. Then in the eighth, with a man on, Ted slashed Lee's first pitch off the center field wall for a triple, just missing home run territory again. He now had 113 RBIs, and Boston had a 5–1 victory and a virtual lock on second place.

---

*Monday,*
*September 15*

◆

On the screen Abbott and Costello had movie-goers laughing at *Hold That Ghost,* and skating star Sonja Heine starred in *Sun Valley Serenade*, with Glenn Miller's orchestra. On stage, Richard Wright's *Native Son* opened in Boston. The *Herald* called it "a drama of violent rebellion of a Negro against his fate in a white man's world. It's powerful stuff from beginning to end and unpleasant stuff to boot."

Heavyweight champ Joe Louis got his draft call. And, thousands of miles away, unknown to anyone in America, the Japanese navy was conducting battle practice for Pearl Harbor.

Johnny Rigney, also facing a military call-up, would take the mound against the Red Sox. Rig had already given up five home runs to Ted this year, but promised Williams before the game that he would pitch to him. He was true to his word and got Ted the first two times up. Williams did draw a walk in the sixth, #144 of the year; it loaded the bases, and Foxx singled two men in.

In the seventh Ted came up with two men on and Boston leading 3–0. He took a called strike, then unloaded a blast into the bleachers several rows above the bullpen and variously estimated at 420 to 450 feet. It was his 35th homer of the year.

The three RBI's gave Boston a sweep of the series and gave Williams 116 for the year, keeping him even with DiMaggio and six behind the idle Keller. He was also hitting .409.

(Poor Rigney spent the next four years in the service, waiting for revenge. In 1946 he finally got his chance. In their first face-off back from the war, Williams walloped another homer off him.)

---

## *Wednesday, September 17*

◆

Tuesday was an off-day. On Monday night an apprehensive Cronin had watched his star board a plane with pretty

Doris Soule, his fiancee, to fly to New York for the radio show,
"We the People."

On Wednesday Jim Bagby with the now fourth-place Indians decided to give Williams soft stuff and made him ground
out and pop up before Ted got his almost daily walk. In the
eighth Williams drove a 420-foot double to the center-field
corner.

In St. Louis the Associated Press reported that the Cardinals' newest rookie, outfielder Steve Musial (sic), played his
first game and collected two hits.

### SCIENCE UPHOLDS CURVE

the Boston *Post* informed its readers above a report that an
MIT physics professor had confirmed what Williams already
knew, that a curve ball really does curve.

The *Herald* had some other information to impart:

### JANE WYMAN OFFERS
### HAPPY MARRIAGE RECIPE

A two-column picture of the movie star with her baby daughter
and husband, Ronald Reagan, bore the caption: "The couple are
described as among Hollywood's most happily married."

---

*Thursday,*
*September 18*

---

Bobby Feller took the mound, looking twice as fast after
Bagby's slow stuff. Feller was leading both majors in wins

with 23. So far the two great gladiators, Feller and Williams, had faced each other five times, and Williams had gone 8-for-17 — seven singles and one double.

The Indians scored four quick runs in the first inning, so Bobby felt he had a chance to experiment. "Ted's hit everything I threw all year," he said, "so I tried every kind of pitch I knew out there, fast and slow."

In the first he tried a fast ball and Williams slapped it for a long fly to right; it should have been a home run in any other American League park, the Cleveland *Plain-Dealer* wrote. Then Williams grounded to second and walked on a 3−2 curve that was too low. Finally Bobby whiffed him on three pitches.

"It's about time I started to get a little even with Ted," Bob said. "But he's still the best hitter I've ever seen." Bob won the game 6−1 for victory #24. He would finish at 25−13.

The strikeout was one of only 27 that year by Ted, one of a handful of hitters to have more homers than whiffs in a season. Joe DiMaggio was the best of all time in that respect, averaging one strikeout for every home run. In 1941 he had 30 homers and only 13 whiffs; that's one strikeout every 41 at bats.

Compare that to Reggie Jackson, who fanned five times for every home run and once every four at bats. Statistician Pete Palmer says five strikeouts cost a team as much as it gains from one home run, which means that Jackson's strikeouts just about canceled out all his homers. (We all remember Reggie's three World Series homers in one blow-out game in 1977, but we forget his dramatic strikeout by young Bob Welch with the winning run on third a year later.)

*Time* magazine reported that the craters on the moon are from volcanoes, not meteors, since the moon's atmosphere would burn up meteors before they could hit the surface. Today, after men have walked on the moon to check personally, we know that most of the craters are indeed from meteor impacts and that the moon has almost no atmosphere. How much of what we now report as scientific fact will appear to be quaint but inaccurate guesswork to our grandchildren in the year 2041?

---

### *Saturday, September 20*

---◆---

The Nazi armies entered Kiev. At 135 pounds, Sugar Ray Robinson KO'd Maxie Shapiro for his 24th victory in a row since turning pro.

The Yankees came back to Boston, and this time the duel would be between Williams and DiMaggio to see which, if either, could overtake Keller for the RBI crown. DiMaggio would face Charlie Wagner (12–8). Williams would be up against Brooklyn-born Marius Russo (14–10). In later years Ted would call Russo one of the toughest pitchers he faced, but in 1941, the lefty was a pushover. In fact, both Russo and his fellow Yankee left-hander, Gomez, put Williams over .400. The rest of the league held him to .398.

"A round of applause greets (Williams') every appearance," wrote Louis Effrat in the *Times.* "When he connects the ovation is tremendous."

The Boston *Post* kept a detailed account of every pitch to Ted:

First inning: ball inside, called strike, ball low, called strike, foul back, single.

Third inning: outside, called strike, single.

Fifth inning: low outside, called strike, high outside, foul, foul, strikeout.

Eighth inning: low, outside, swing and a miss, foul, inside, high fly to short center. (Shortstop Phil Rizzuto back-pedaled to catch it, "and somehow or other wasn't driven into the sod by what you might call a falling star," Whitman of the *Herald* noted.)

With 2-for-4, Ted was hitting .405, five points higher than Bill Terry on that date in 1930.

But DiMaggio got the better of the RBI duel, as Russo limited the Sox to one run. Joe knocked in two for the Yankees, to go two ahead of Ted, 118 to 116.

That night was one of the most unforgettable of my childhood, the night the East Coast from Maine to Virginia was treated to a magnificent spectacle of northern lights. As the news rushed from house to house, all the neighbors ran into the streets in pajamas, bathrobes, and hair curlers, craning our heads upward, pointing, and oohing and ahing as some giant invisible artist hurled a canvas of colors—reds, blues, yellows—dancing all over the sky.

While an aesthetic sensation, the display had its negative practical aspects, destroying radio communications among ships at sea. Intimate phone conversations were broadcast nationwide over network radio. Frantic Brooklyn fans feverishly but futily twisted their dials to get Red Barber's report of the Dodgers' game. But they had to wait until morning to read that the Cards had won, cutting the Bums' lead to a game and a half.

# 8

## *The Autumn of '41*

## Sunday,
## September 21

◆

The aurora borealis also lit the battlefield in far-away Leningrad. Reports called it the most wonderful display in years. Attacking Nazi bombers crisscrossed the shifting colored lights like balls of fire moving across the heavens amid the rumble of the guns and thudding of the bombs.

Farther south

### KIEV ABANDONED, REDS ADMIT

and

### EX-SHAH CEDES SON PROPERTY, FLEES FOR SOUTH AMERICA

Footballs were starting to replace baseballs on the playgrounds and in the Sunday morning sports pages. College football was the big rage—Tommy Harmon of Michigan was the number-one star. The pro's were less famous—the two best known were Slingin' Sammy Baugh of the Redskins and Don Hutson, the pass-catching end for Green Bay. Another star was running back Byron "Whizzer" White, the future Supreme Court Justice. Players played both offense and defense; and some players, such as the famous 1940 Iowa Ironmen played all 60 minutes. We used the old drop kick as much as the present-day place kick; the kicker dropped the ball and kicked it just as it hit the ground. If the sport insisted on drop kicks today, it would return the suspense to the point after touchdown and the field goal.

In Boston 28,070 fans turned out to see the Red Sox and Yankees in the final game of the year in Boston. Since there was no pennant race, one assumes they were there to see

Williams and DiMaggio wage their duel for RBI king. DiMag went into the game two ahead of Ted and four behind Keller, who was still on the bench. Tiny Bonham was out to stop Ted; lefty Mickey Harris would try to hold Joe. Again the *Post* gave readers a blow-by-blow of Williams' day:

In the first, he took two called strikes but had the discipline to let two low balls (dipping forkballs?) go by. But Bonham finally got him on a pop up to short.

In the fourth the big pitcher threw a called strike past Williams, then Ted lashed a fierce, "treacherous," sinking line drive which DiMaggio caught without moving.

In the sixth, with Cronin on third, Tiny defiantly decided to pitch to Ted. The first pitch was outside. The next one flew off the bat on a high arc toward the New York bullpen, dropping into the stands behind it for home run #36 and two RBIs to draw even with DiMaggio.

In the eighth, with the Sox leading 4−1, Johnny Murphy (8−3, 1.98) put Williams in a hole with two quick strikes. Again Ted worked the count even, taking one pitch low and inside and another high and outside. He fouled one to the roof, then took another low inside ball, and finally walked on another low pitch.

DiMaggio did not have a good day after cracking his arm trying for a catch against the wall.

The Sox won the game 4−1, clinching second place.

Ted trotted off the field with a batting average of .4055. His homer was only his second against Yankee pitching that year. Both came in Boston, and for the first time in three seasons he failed to hit at least one in every park— Washington also still eluded him. But he had fattened his average off New York pitching that year, swatting .470 against them. And that was without his favorite Yankee pitcher, Ruffing. Red, a future Hall of Famer, sat resolutely on the bench whenever the Yanks met the Sox. He had a 15–6 record for the year, making it doubly strange that manager Joe McCarthy would hold him out of all games against the Yankees' closest rival.

That evening Ted and the Red Sox filed out of the Fenway Park dressing room for the last time and boarded Pullmans at Back Bay for the long ride to Washington. Ted had six games left, all on the road, three in Washington and three in Philadelphia. Although the Senators and A's were the weakest teams in the league, the games would not be as easy as they looked. In his eight previous games in Washington, Ted had hit only .319; in Philadelphia, .316.

The team debarked at Washington's Union Station on a hot, 90-degree day and hailed cabs to the Mayflower Hotel past news boys hawking the *Post*:

### GERMANS DRIVEN BACK
### 25 MILES ON MOSCOW
### FRONT, RUSSIANS CLAIM

A U.S. freighter was sunk off Iceland with 34 on board. The Duke and Duchess of Windsor were in town, asking support for Britain's war effort. Errol Flynn and Fred MacMurray were starring in *Dive Bomber*, Dottie Lamour was playing *Aloma of the South Seas* in a sarong, although Ted probably headed for *Texas* with Glenn Ford and William Holden.

◆

Williams would face Sid Hudson. In their only face-off thus far this year, Ted had managed no hits off him in three tries. Sid, who later became pitching coach under Ted when Williams managed the Senators, said he used to bear down extra hard against Williams and DiMaggio. "I met Ted going out the clubhouse before the game," he recalled. "They used to dress in the clubhouse next to ours, and he came out of his and we walked up the stairs to the field together."

"You're pitching today?" Ted asked.

"I sure am," Hudson replied. "And I'm gonna get you today. You're hitting .400 now. Are you going to stay there?"

"Against you, I am," Ted bantered.

Sid smiled. "I'll just throw you a lot of fastballs until I get in trouble. Then you might see something else."

"I don't know if he believed me," Hudson would say later, "but I just fed him mostly fastballs all day."

"I hit the ball," Williams insists. "But, damn it all, that Washington park was kind of big."

In his first at bat Ted grounded out.

Then he sent a deep smash to center field. "A low outside pitch," Ted recalls. "I hit it 420 feet to left-center. Doc Cramer [Washington center fielder] was out deep. He could make plays out deep." Cramer gave it a long chase, got a glove on it, then dropped it.

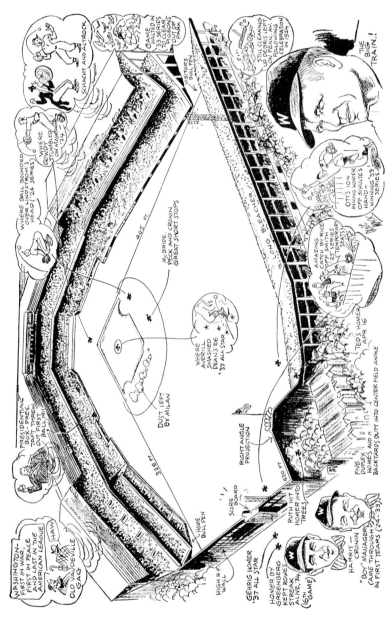

Griffith Stadium, Washington *Boston Globe*

The official scorer gave Ted a double, though there were some eyebrows raised on the call. "Stricter scoring might have deprived Williams of a hit," Frank "Buck" O'Neill of the *Times-Herald* wrote. "Truth to tell, Cramer should have caught Teddy the Kid's wallop, which was just a fly ball, and Cramer made contact ten feet from the fence." What O'Neill didn't add was that in almost any other park in the country, no one could have caught the ball.

In today's modern "toilet bowl" stadia, with outfield fences standardized at about 405 feet to centerfield, Cramer would have watched the ball sail over the low fences. In fact, ten times that season the deeper and more irregular old-fashioned parks had cost Williams ten home runs, compared to the smaller parks of today. Five times he had lost potential homers in Boston, twice in Yankee Stadium, and once each in Detroit, Comiskey Park, and Washington. With a little luck, Williams might have hit 47 homers instead of 37. And he lost not only ten homers, but ten hits as well. Ten extra hits would have boosted his final batting average to .428. Other sluggers—Ruth, DiMaggio, Greenberg, Mantle—had also lost homers to unfriendly fences. But Roger Maris for one missed no homers when he hit 61 in 1961. In fact, I saw one of them drop into the new center field bullpen in Washington 408 feet away, a drive that would have been an out in 1927 or 1941.

Finally Ted hit one to deep right, which Buddy Lewis "took off the wall," as Hudson recalls. That gave Ted 1-for-3 for the day.

Oddly, the Washington papers didn't think Williams' pursuit of .400 was news. The game involved a seventh-place club against a second-place team 20 games out of first. Yet Merrill Whittlesy of the *Post* almost didn't mention Ted at all. Not until his final paragraph did he write, literally as an afterthought, that Williams had dropped one percentage point to .405.

---

## *Wednesday,*
## *September 24*

◆

General Douglas MacArthur, American commander in Manila, called up the Philippine reserves. Colonel Charles de Gaulle formed a French government-in-exile in London. President Roosevelt called for the arming of U.S. merchant ships.

Williams faced two puzzling pitchers who hoped to de-rail his bid.

The first was Dutch Leonard. The wily knuckle-baller was gunning for his 19th win. Leonard was "a hittable guy," Williams says—"except when he threw his knuckle ball." Ted admits that he never could hit a knuckler. "But I think I hit a couple balls good that day. I hit one in left-center."

Dutch liked Ted. "You ask any ballplayer or clubhouse man, and they'll tell you Williams was one of the great ones," Leonard told me. "If he got two or three hits off you, he'd hit you on the shoulder and say, 'I was lucky as hell.' I'd say, 'Get out of here, you long drink of water.'"

But Ted wasn't lucky that first game. The Red Sox got nine hits, unfortunately none of them by Ted. He walked twice, fouled out, grounded out, and flied out. His average shrank three more points, to .402.

The second game would pose a challenge of a different sort. Ted would face an unknown quantity, a left-handed knuckle-baller just up from Washington's Class-B Trenton farm team, a kid named Dick Mulligan. Mulligan was hungry. Now a sales manager for a Houston import company, he recalls the day he was signed by a big-league scout. "I nearly knocked him down to take the pen out of his hand," he laughs. "I didn't say, 'How much?' I said, 'Give me a chance!' "

Today Ted can't remember Dick at all. But Mulligan remembers him. "My God," the youngster whistled to himself as he walked to the mound. "I've got my chance now." It was his first big-league game. He would have come up earlier, but Trenton got into the league playoffs; the series went seven games, while Dick, who had already been picked in the army draft, fretted that his big chance was slipping away.

"Here I am," Mulligan thought, as he stepped onto the mound and exhaled. "I'm going to give it my best, see what I can do. You either do or you don't. Of course you're a little nervous—butterflies. But then they give you the sign for a fastball, and you rare back and throw it."

What was the book on Mulligan? Williams wondered. Was he wild? A "head-hunter"?

"I had a funny philosophy pitching to left-handers," Mulligan says. "I felt it was my job to get them out. If I can't get the left-hander out, I'm really in trouble. Since Williams is on top of the plate, you crowd him with the ball. If he pulls it, he pulls it foul. You don't let him look at anything too many times. I threw him anything and everything from all directions. Never showed him the same pitch twice: three-quarters, side-arm, overhand, cross-fire, knuckle ball—the whole schmeer."

The kid got two strikes on the big slugger. "Until then I hadn't thrown him an overhand curve. I threw one right at his shoulder. He dipped back with his shoulder, and the ball busted right over the plate. He walked away and smiled all the time as if to say, "Yep, it was over.' Didn't even wait for the umpire to say strike." (Dick "fooled Ted completely," O'Neill nodded in the press box.)

Next time up Ted drilled a grounder to second baseman Jimmy Bloodworth. The play at first was close. Umpire Bill Grieve started to raise his thumb, then quickly changed his mind and spread his palms instead, signifying safe, though most fans hooted at the call. The hit was "a gift of the umpire," O'Neill typed.

On his last at bat, Williams hit a smash to first, where rookie Mickey Vernon made a fine pickup for the out. Ted, who had started the day hitting .405, left with sagging shoulders and an average of .40009. The Sox made 20 hits, only one of them by Ted. If it hadn't been for Grieve's "gift hit," the Boston *Post* admitted, he'd be hitting .399.

The Sox won both games, but O'Neill commented that "one tiny light flickered through the pall. . . . That was the pitching of Mulligan, a spindle-shanked left-hander" from Trenton. His nine strong innings against the murderous Red Sox right-handers promised great things for next year.

Burt Hawkins of the Washington *Star* also remarked on Mulligan's "mighty curve and considerable poise."

It was the last big league game the kid pitched for almost five years. The war would rob him of the best years of his baseball life. In '46 he won three and lost two for the Phillies and dropped out of the majors.

Meanwhile, the *Star* didn't mention Williams at all!

◆

## WILLIAMS' BACK TO WALL
## IN BID FOR .400 AVERAGE

the *Globe* told its readers as Williams arrived in Philadelphia for the last three games of the year. The mathematics of the problem were formidable. Ted would have to hit almost .500 in order to finish over .400. Assuming 12 at bats in the three games, he would need five hits. Four hits would bring him down to .399. Was the pressure getting to him?

"It seemed like under pressure Ted got tougher," Doerr says. But Bob admits that Ted was "a little over-anxious" and swung at some bad pitches. As George Brett would say when he faced the same challenge in 1980, "You get just a shade over-anxious and start going outside the strike zone."

Charlie Wagner agrees. "They say you can hit that ball low and outside, but you can't. They pitched around Ted. I don't think anybody ever threw him a fastball down the middle. Low outside, inside slider, change-up—he never got a pitch to his liking unless the guy made a mistake." Williams was like the fastest gun in the West—every young buck was gunning to shoot him down. "When every pitcher is pitching his best at you every minute in every game, that shows how great you are," Wagner says. But pressure never bothered him. "Whatever pressure there was, Ted generated on himself."

"I was feeling a little pressure," Williams admits. He had been tight in Washington, had taken too many good pitches. "But I was hitting the ball at somebody. I was going 1-for-4.

When you're up there over .400, Jesus, does it come down fast!"

Cronin was feeling the pressure too. If Ted hit well in the first two games in Philly, should Joe bench him for the final one? "I might yank him," Cronin was quoted as saying, "even if he doesn't like it."

Williams was stubborn on that point, however. He was gambling with his pay check—if he could hit .400, he could expect to double his salary to $35,000 for 1942. Nevertheless, he would not hit .400 sitting on the bench. The autumn shadows at Shibe would be a "headache," but "I'm not alibiing. I want to hit .400, but I'm going to play in all three games, even if I don't get a ball out of the infield."

To make matters worse, the weather had turned cold. "I've always been a warm weather guy," he says. "The hotter, the better. Jesus Christ, I could hit when it was hot. The cold weather, I never could hit well. And at the end of the year, God, the winds are not prevailing, and lights get low, the shadows come sooner, and, oh Jesus, it's cold. You can't get going." Williams blames today's long schedule, from early April to late October in the case of the World Series, for the demise of the .400 hitter.

---

### Friday, September 26

---

The Sox had two days off before facing the A's on Saturday. So Ted collected Shellenback and catcher Frankie Pytlak and hailed a taxi to the park. He experimented with a new stance, moving his front foot around in the box, wrote Whitman. Usually Ted pointed his toe toward short when he strode; now he was pointing more toward third. Ted doesn't remember that, although "anytime I would get into a rut, I would try to close up my stance a little bit (that is, turn his back more toward the pitcher) and think of hitting through the middle more. I might have been doing that. I was trying not to pull the ball. In other words, I wanted to hit the ball at right angles to the direction of the pitch rather than having the bat at 45 degrees, where the hitting surface would be down near my hand." Also, by hitting the ball when it was over the plate instead of in front of it, he could wait an extra split-second before swinging. For two straight days Ted took swings, slamming ball after ball against the fence from the batting cage 50 feet behind the plate. Some of the shots cleared the fence.

Up in New York the Yankees and Senators opened a meaningless series with only one thing at stake, the batting race between DiMaggio and Washington's Cecil Travis for second place behind Williams. Joe entered the final four games with the edge, .359 to Cecil's .357.

In the Friday double-header, the Yankee starters, Chandler and Russo, were tough, each hurling three-hitters. Travis went 2-for-7 to drop a point to .3567. DiMaggio got one hit in five tries, an RBI-double against Ken Chase in the first game. That broke Joe's tie with the idle Charley Keller and put him ahead in the RBI race to stay.

Rookie Early Wynn, with a 3–0 record in his first year in the majors, held DiMaggio hitless in game two (though Early lost the game 1–0, the first defeat in his big league career).

## Saturday,
## September 27

$\blacklozenge$

In New York DiMaggio managed only one hit, a "lusty" double against Walt Masterson good for two more RBI's for a season's final total of 125. Meanwhile, Travis was having a splendid day against Gomez, Bonham, and Murphy. He swatted three hits in four at bats to move ahead of his Yankee rival, .359 to .3575.

Down in Philly Connie Mack had cooked up three surprises for Williams. Connie, then 73, had started playing in 1886, had managed the A's since 1901, and had been trying to get Ted out since 1939. He named three rookies to start the weekend games—three youngsters Williams had never seen before. As Wagner said, Ted much preferred to face someone he knew. To make the challenge tougher, Shibe was the worst park to hit in late in the year. The high grandstand cast shadows that would leave the hitter in the shade, blinking at the pitcher in the sun. And Sunday would be the first day of standard time, when clocks are set back one hour. For Sunday's second game, as Yogi Berra would say, it would get late even earlier.

The first mystery Ted would have to solve was Roger Wolff. "He had the best knuckle ball I ever saw," says A's pitcher Phil Marchildon. And Roger himself proudly recalls that Ted would later call him the toughest pitcher in the league. Once, when the two teams were traveling on the same train, Ted stopped in the dining car and sat down beside Wolff. "My God," he said, "I just can't hit you. I can hit Leonard, I can hit Niggeling, but I can't hit you." Wolff replied modestly that Dom DiMaggio had just hit one off his knuckler, and Dom, at the next table, nodded that it was true. "Well," said Ted, "the son of a bitch didn't break then."

**274**

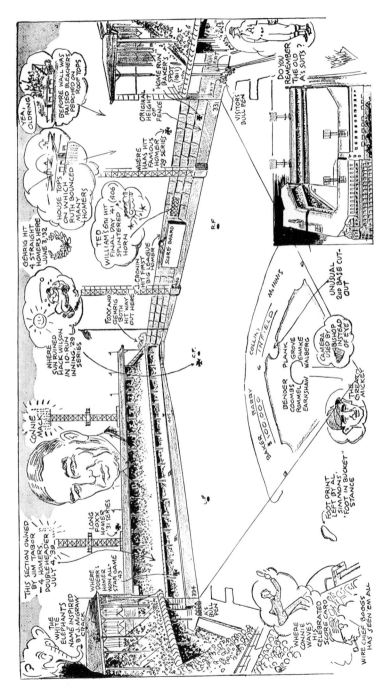

Philadelphia Shibe (later Connie Mack Stadium) *Boston*
*Globe*

"I respected the guy very much," says Wolff, "but I felt I could get him out any time. He had to hit my best pitch. I felt like I wanted to make a good showing against him. I wanted him to hit .400 — but not against me."

A's shortstop Al Brancato recalls the game vividly. "Mr. Mack wanted everyone to go all out and not let up," he says. "He told our pitchers, 'You're not to give him anything to hit. He's out there to hit the ball. You're out there to win the game.'"

A's coach Al Simmons, who had hit .390 in 1931, sneered that Williams could never have hit .400 back in that year. He sidled up to Ted and bet that he wouldn't do it this time either.

"Hell, I'm not going to bet on that," Ted replied. "I might not hit .400." As confident as he seemed to be, he now admits, "I knew that was a hell of a mark. If I hit it, a lot of little things had to happen." Was Al trying to psych him out? "He wasn't well liked," Ted says. "I admired him more than he knew, still, he was a fellow that was a little crude in some of the things he said."

The world news was crowding sports off the front page. The Nazis reached Leningrad and opened a siege that would last 900 days. Another U.S. ship was sunk off Iceland.

## U S ON THRESHOLD
## OF WAR, KNOX SAYS

the Philadelphia *Inquirer* headline blared.

The gas crunch on the East Coast sent prices to 17 cents a gallon, and a 40 mph speed limit was imposed to save fuel. Philadelphians were closing their summer homes on the Jersey shore. Those who stayed in town could take in a movie — Bette Davis in *Little Foxes* — or curl up with a bestseller — *My Friend Flicka*, A.J. Cronin's *The Keys of the Kingdom*, *Claudia*, *Mildred Pierce*, or *The G-String Murders* by ecdysiast

Gypsy Rose Lee, all of which would become movies. On the radio Vaughan Monroe was crooning "Sam, You Made the Pants Too Long," band-leader Freddy Martin had transformed Tchaikovsky's piano concerto into the danceable "Full Moon and Empty Arms." There were also clarinetists Artie Shaw and Woody Herman and his Herd, or the syrupy Guy Lombardo.

Pro football was still a minor sport. After the baseball game that afternoon, the Brooklyn Dodgers would play the Philadelphia Eagles under the lights. Ticket prices ranged from $1.25 to $2.25.

Only 1,000 baseball fans turned out that afternoon to see if history would be made. Imagine that happening today!

Brancato recalls that as Williams stepped up to bat, the infielders shifted, like a backfield in T-formation, over toward the first-base side.

And Wolff had his knuckler dancing around the corners of the plate. On the 2−2 count to Williams, he uncorked another butterfly. "I never threw a better knuckler in my life," he says. "The ball just exploded into the middle of the plate." He was sure it was strike three. The umpire, however, called it a ball, and Ted got one more swing. The next pitch missed the corner, and Williams walked, having been spared a precious out.

On his next trip, Ted looked at another ball and then a knuckler that dipped into the strike zone. He "walloped it with his customary vigor and ferocity deep to right-center," Whitman reported. A clean two-base hit, and the meager crowd applauded. He was now hitting .402.

But on his next two at bats, Williams flied to right and fouled to first. His average dropped to .4004.

That should have been all. But in the ninth, with two out, DiMaggio and Finney both hit, bringing Williams up for one more time. He took a called strike, slashed a savage foul just inches outside the first-base line, then swung at a low knuckler and missed for strike three.

He was now hitting .3995535 with one more day to go. Ironically, the rest of the Red Sox collected 11 hits that day. Every man would gladly have given his to Ted if he could have.

Rounded off, Williams was batting exactly .400. But was it a real .400? The skies were cloudy as the players left the park. What if it rained tomorrow? Would it go into the books with an asterisk? Would the fans consider him a bona fide .400 hitter? Most important, would he himself?

Williams' challenge was formidable. Assuming eight at bats in the double-header, he would have to hit at least .500 in order to finish over .400. Three-for-eight would bring him down to .399.

"Of course he's worried," Burt Whitman wrote. "But you can't get him to admit it." The rest of the players were worried too. "They consider him a favorite younger brother. They have a strong affection for him. He's certainly grown up from the problem child he was a year ago."

The others avoided talking to him. Cronin had warned them not to give him advice. It would only upset him, knock his timing off, and besides, Joe reasoned accurately, no one else was as qualified to diagnose his swing as Ted was himself.

Cronin offered to take him out on Sunday.

Many another hitter has chosen to win his title, or hit .400, sitting on the bench. In 1990 George Brett and Rickey Henderson, fighting for the American League batting championship, took turns ducking games against pitchers they couldn't hit. Brett had done the same thing in 1980 to protect his .390 average.

In 1921 Rogers Hornsby was hitting .398 on the morning of September 30, when St. Louis fans gave him a "day" with two diamond rings and $2,000 worth of Liberty Bonds with which to buy a home. He responded with three hits—a home run and two doubles—against three Pittsburgh pitchers to raise his average to .402 with three more games left.

The next day Rajah went 0-for-4 against Earl Hamilton (13–14 with the second-place Pirates) to fall to .39966.

A double-header was scheduled for Sunday, which dawned to a steady rain. Fans brought umbrellas to the bleachers, and the players sloshed through mud as Pittsburgh's lefty Wilbur Cooper, the league's biggest winner that year with 22–14, warmed up. Since the Pirates were fighting for second-place money, Cooper would be bearing down.

Should Hornsby play or not? Hitting .400 was not that newsworthy in 1921—the eastern papers didn't even mention his average. At any rate, Rogers quietly decided to play.

Cooper gave up 11 hits with the wet ball, but none of them to Hornsby, who popped up in the fifth with the bases loaded to drop to .397. When the umpires called the second game off, Rog lost all chance of .400, a fact that his home-town *Globe-Democrat* noted briefly in paragraph ten of its story.

The next year Hornsby made another assault on .400, a challenge made doubly difficult since all 24 of his final games would be on the road, ending in Chicago against the fifth-place Cubs with two games on Saturday and the final contest on Sunday.

On Friday Hornsby went 0-for-4 to cut his average to .398. But he swatted four Cubs' pitchers for three hits in the opener Saturday to pull to .40065.

In game two against left-hander Percy Jones (8–9) Rog got one hit in two at bats, while again dark rain clouds covered the field. Neither team could see the ball, the *Globe-Democrat* reported. In the fifth, against right-hander Virgil Cheeves (12-11) Hornsby lifted a fly to right field, and the umpires called the game, as Rogers sprinted through the puddles, carrying a .3997 batting average with him. The *Globe-Democrat* reporter didn't even mention it.

The weather on Sunday was not reported, implying that the sun may have come out over Wrigley Field. Right-hander Tony Kaufman (7–13) was warming up for the Cubs. Should Rogers play or not? Hornsby was a gambling man, and the fact that the Cards had a shot at some third-place money if they won may have influenced him to take the field and bet everything on one cut of the cards.

He singled in the first to climb safely over .400, singled again in the third to solidify his hold, and collected a third single on a bunt to end the day with 3-for-5 and a .401 average. The *Post-Dispatch* gave the feat a two-column story on page two of the sports section.

That same afternoon over in the American League, 35-year-old Ty Cobb was bidding for his third .400 season. A day earlier he had slapped two hits in four at bats against left-hander Sherry Smith (5–8 with Brooklyn and Cleveland), which left Ty batting exactly .400.

In those days the official figures would not be published until November or December. The unofficial average given in the newspapers was .397 (209/526), instead of the actual .400 (210/525). Whether Cobb knew the correct figure is not clear, but Ty was an astute student who took advantage of every angle he could, and so he may have known what the public did not, that he was right on the verge of a .400 season.

His opponent for Sunday's finale would be George Uhle (22-16). Cobb, who was also manager, had reportedly said that if he had .400 safely in hand, he'd bench himself. In the first inning he singled to make his average .401, and a few minutes later scored, sliding home ahead of the throw, then limped to the bench, where he watched the rest of the game, claiming he had aggravated a charley horse. Comments Cobb scholar Larry Amman: "The whole business sounds very questionable."

In 1925 Hornsby once more found himself facing the dilemma: to play or not to play? This time ending the season on a long home stand, he climbed steadily until he had lifted his average to .403 with two games left to play against the last-place Cubs in St. Louis. Right-hander Sheriff Blake (10−18) would hurl the Saturday game, and left-hander Percy Jones (6−6) the Sunday contest.

By now Hornsby had been promoted to manager, and one of his final managerial decisions of the season was to bench second baseman Hornsby for the rest of the year, the third .400 season of his career safely engraved in the record books.

In 1941, 23-year-old Ted Williams faced the same question that these other, older gladiators had wrestled with: Should he play it safe, or gamble everything on one roll of the dice? (Philadelphia's Wally Moses elected to sit out the final double-header to preserve a .301 average.)

"A batting title is no good unless you play every game of the season," Ted told Joe Cronin. He was going to play.

On Saturday night Ted called his buddy, Johnny Orlando, the clubhouse attendant, and, he says, they must have walked ten miles through the streets, walking and talking Ted's nerves away. Johnny wasn't much of a walker, however, Ted writes, so he ducked into a couple of bars to keep his strength up. "The way he tells it, he made two stops for Scotch, and I made two stops for ice cream." They got back to the hotel at 10:30. Cronin and the coaches were sitting in the lobby talking. They chinned a while, then Ted turned in.

Wagner was already in bed. Williams didn't say anything, Charlie says; he seemed relaxed, not nervous, even confident.

But Ted *was* nervous, he later admitted. "I went to bed early, but I just couldn't sleep. I tossed and turned and finally went to sleep, still thinking about that .400 average."

---

### *Sunday, September 28*

---◆---

Up in New York, DiMaggio and Travis were in the final day of their duel. Travis went 1-for-4, a fifth-inning double into right-center, to end the day at .358553.

DiMaggio had clipped a single in three trips against Sid Hudson, who was shutting the Yankees out with a change-up and "a crackling curve that broke around the batters' knees." Joe was hitting .357 when he stepped in to bat with two out in the ninth. One more hit would let him slip in just ahead of Travis with a final figure of .358595. Instead, on a two-strike count, Joe swung and missed to end the year at .3567, good for third place.

Rounded off, that was .357 for DiMaggio, .359 for Travis, the runner-up to Ted. As Cecil would shrug half a century later from his Georgia farm, "second place don't mean anything anyway." Yet Travis' .359 has been surpassed by only ten hitters in the 50 years since then. Joe's .357 has never been topped by a right-handed batter, although Roberto Clemente tied it in 1967. Amazingly, Travis received exactly three votes for MVP in 1941. Like Hester Prynne's scarlet letter, the white "W" on Cecil's cap branded him as an outcast among the great players of baseball.

Travis ended the year with a lifetime average of .324 after nine years in the major leagues. Only one shortstop in history had ever hit higher, Honus Wagner with .327.

Cecil, 28 years old, spent the next three and a half years in the army, suffering frost-bitten toes in the Battle of the Bulge. When he came back after the war, he played another two and a half years but hit only .245. It brought his final, lifetime average down to .314, still good enough for third place among shortstops behind Wagner and Arky Vaughan (.318). Some stories say Travis had some toes amputated in Europe, accounting for his poor performance. Travis denies it. He didn't lose any toes, he insists; he "just couldn't get going" again after the long lay-off.

While New York shortstops Pee Wee Reese (.269) and Phil Rizzuto (.273) push him out of line for the Hall of Fame, Cecil just says, "It doesn't worry me." Today hardly anyone knows that he beat Joe DiMaggio out in batting the year Joe hit in 56 straight games.

Meanwhile, 100 miles away in Philadelphia, Sunday dawned "cold and miserable," Williams writes. However, SABR's Harrison (Kit) Crissey contradicts Ted. According to the Philadelphia papers, the weather was actually mild and sunny.

For many it was a good morning to stay in bed with the Sunday funnies—the Gumps, Jiggs and Maggie, Smokey Stover, Henry, Tillie the Toiler, the Katzenjammer Kids, Barney Google, Joe Palooka, Smilin' Jack, and Skippy.

In the afternoon other Philadelphians had tickets for the Philadelphia Orchestra under Eugene Ormandy to hear Jascha Heifitz play Brahms' violin-cello concerto.

Williams and Doerr got to the park five hours before game time and shot the breeze with the boys at the concession stands, says one of the kids, Eddie "Dutch" Doyle. Then it was time to suit up for batting practice.

Philadelphia *Bulletin* writer Frank Yeutter spied Ted biting his fingernails on the bench. "His mammoth hands were trembling," Yeutter wrote. Was he nervous? I asked.

"Maybe I was, I don't remember," Williams says. "I don't remember anything before the game."

Imagine the crowd today if Kirby Puckett or Don Mattingly were going into the final game with a .3995 average! But only 10,000 showed up in Shibe Park in that pre-media-hype era. They let out a roar, however, as Ted advanced to the plate to lead off the second inning. "I was shaking like a leaf," he admitted after the game.

Umpire Bill McGowan stopped the game to brush off home plate. "They always have their ass toward the pitcher," Ted recalls. Without looking up, McGowan said, "In order to hit .400, you gotta be loose. You gotta be loose." Then he went back behind the plate.

A's catcher Frankie Hayes squatted down behind Ted. "Mr. Mack told us today we're gonna pitch to ya," he said. "We're not gonna give ya anything, but he told us to pitch to ya. He told us if we let up on you, he'll run us out of baseball.

I wish you all the luck in the world, but we're not giving ya a damn thing."

Dick Fowler, a tall Canadian left-hander just up from Philadelphia's Toronto farm, was waiting on the mound. He had pitched twice already in the majors, splitting the two decisions, but Ted had never seen him before. The first pitch was low outside, the next inside.

Ted was ready to jump on the 2−0 pitch if it was in there. It was, and he cracked a "fierce low grounder" to the right of first baseman Indian Bob Johnson. Whitman called it "a sizzling single."

"When I got that first hit, I was all set," Williams said later. "I felt good."

"He was loose as a goose," nods A's shortstop Al Brancato.

Back on the bench, Ted's adrenaline was still pumping; he was yelling and screaming at every pitch, Doerr says. And each time he came to bat, the crowd yelled too, especially the fans in left field. And Ted gave them plenty to shout about.

In the fourth he took a ball high and outside, then slammed a 1−0 pitch over the high right-field wall, at least 440 feet, Whitman estimated. It was his 37th homer of the year, tops in both leagues.

In the sixth another lefty, Porter Vaughan, was in the box. In his second year with the A's, mostly in relief, he had a 2−11 record. Vaughan was "a real cute little left-hander," Williams says (though Vaughan was only two inches shorter than Ted himself). The lefty threw two curves, one high, the other inside. Then, with Ted ahead again 2−0 in the count, Vaughan crossed up the book and threw a third straight curve, this one over the plate. "I looked for a curve ball, and here it was," says Ted. "I hit a bullet right through the middle—base hit."

Williams now had three of the four hits he needed. One more would put him over .400 no matter what he did for the rest of the afternoon.

In the seventh, with a man on first, Mack waved Johnson away from the bag and onto the edge of the outfield grass—the A's would rather stop Williams than hold the runner close. "They wanted him to earn it," Cronin said. Johnson, a right-handed outfielder, was playing in place of the regular first baseman, left-handed Dick Siebert, one of the best fielders in the game. This might have been a break for Ted.

Vaughan poured a called strike over the plate, but then he threw three straight pitches below Ted's knees. Williams now had the count 3–1 in his favor, but he wasted the chance when Porter courageously threw the next one over the plate and Williams looked at it for strike two. Vaughan then threw what McGowan would call "as beautiful a curve ball as I've seen."

Ted smashed it down the first base line to Johnson's left, or glove side. If Indian Bob had been holding the runner close, it would have been right to him. And if Siebert had been playing first, he would have had to reach across his body for the bullet, and it is doubtful if he could have caught it. "The ball was hit sharply, and Johnson was way back," Brancato said. "He got a glove on it. It bounded off his glove and went into right field. I don't know if the glove went off Johnson's hand or not. I think that was the one that put Ted over."

On the bench Cronin almost cried with relief. "I never came closer to bawling right out loud on a baseball diamond than when Ted got that hit," he said. "I really filled right up. I was so happy that the Kid had done the trick without asking or getting any favors."

In the ninth rookie right-hander Newman Shirley (0–1) got a called strike on Ted, then finally got him on a ground ball to second, which was ruled an error. The Associated Press wrote that "a very ponderous" scoring decision "robbed" Ted of his fifth straight hit, although no other reporter objected to the ruling.

After wolfing a sandwich between games, Williams ran back onto the field for game two to face right-hander Fred Caligiuri (1–2 so far this year). Ted took two low balls, then jumped on the 2–0 for a single on the ground between first and second. In the fourth he slammed another 2–0 pitch into the loudspeaker atop the wall for a double, punching a hole clear through the horn. Mack had to get it fixed that winter, he chuckles. Finally, with the shadows growing "dim, even murky," he flied to right on the 1–1 pitch. His final average for the history books: .406.

The fans burst over the railings and tried to mob him, and Ted fought his way through them while the Sox tried to form a human bodyguard around him. In the dressing room, they mobbed him playfully. Cronin rumpled his hair. Coach Moe Berg dropped a spiked shoe on his foot. It was so crowded, Dom DiMaggio said, he had to walk sidewise. Frankie Pytlak squirted ice water on his chest. Jim Tabor smacked him so hard he almost dislocated a rib.

All the while Ted "laughed like a kid," Yeutter reported. To Jimmie Foxx he yelled, "Just think—hitting .400. What do you think of that, Slug? Just a kid like me hitting that high?"

"Do you think you'll win the MVP?" someone shouted across the room.

"Do you think there's a chance?" he asked.

The answer was no; the writers chose DiMaggio in the closest voting till then in the history of the contest. But Dave "The Colonel" Egan surprised Ted and even himself by voting for the Kid:

"Certainly DiMaggio sparked the Yankees to the pennant, but he was sparking a smart and nimble and intelligent and ambitious team. It did not require very much to set them off. . . .

"On the other hand, Master Williams was carrying, on his slim, young shoulders, a lot of tired veterans and pleasant yes-men and family retainers. The Red Sox are not a baseball team. They are a country club . . . .

"I hereby cast one unanimous vote for Master Teddy Williams."

After listening to Williams recall the details of the year, I was still dissatisfied. "But why did *you* do it," I kept asking, "when everyone since you has failed?"

"I've got a picture of Gene Tunney upstairs in my room," Williams shrugged. "I'm convinced after talking to Tunney one day, all day long, that, everything being equal, he'd beat you. The proof of it is, he got beat pretty badly by Harry Greb, a super fighter, one of the greatest. But the second fight Tunney beat him awful bad. And the third time he damn near killed him. That's the feeling I got after talking to him. You knew he had to be the fiercest competitor the game ever had. He had a super, super body—strong and fast and daring and gritty, and he went all-out every second. That was the margin.

"With Ty Cobb I had the same feeling. Everything being equal, he'd beat you, he'd take advantage. And the next one to them, I believe, is Mr. Rose."

Williams mentioned a golfer who had been quoted as saying it didn't matter whether he won or lost. A guy like that, Ted said, "just doesn't have it as far as I'm concerned."

Meanwhile, as darkness descended over Philadelphia, sports editors around the country began making up their pages for the morning editions. The Boston *Globe* and *Herald* both ran the story of Ted's .406 on page one just under the banner news from the war front. Both gave it two columns, including a picture of Ted kissing his bat.

The rest of the nation yawned. One can imagine the headlines if DiMaggio rather than Williams had hit .400, or if Wade Boggs or Tony Gwynn were to do it today. But in 1941 the *Times* buried the story beneath a single column on the sports page, under the news that the Dodgers had won their 100th game. No picture, no quotes, no sidebar.

On the front page, the *Times* editors were dummying in their lead story.

## NAZIS CLAIM 665,000 CAPTIVES WITH END OF KIEV BATTLE; STUKAS* BOMB SERB TOWN

♦

### Roosevelt Insists Seas Be Kept Open

Meanwhile the players finished dressing, gathered their bags, shook hands one last time, and drifted out into the night. Ted, as usual the last to leave, walked into a mob of 2,000 fans who had kept vigil, waiting for him. They soon pinned him against a wall, demanding autographs, until a couple of cops rescued him. "But he enjoyed the ordeal," Yeutter wrote, "and left only when he was shoved into a taxicab."

Ted said later he didn't remember celebrating that night. "But I probably went out and had a chocolate milk shake."

The summer of '41 was over. The long winter had begun.

*Nazi dive bombers

*"Forgotten they that
cast the curses,
"Remembered only
those they cursed."*

—Ukrainian poet
Yevgeni Yevtushenko

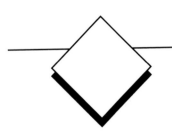

# *Appendix*
# *The Math of the*
# *.400 Hitter*

# Williams' 1941 Breakdown

## by Team and City

Williams was not a .400 hitter on the road; he hit only .380 away from home, but .426 at Fenway Park. For one thing, he said that he probably got better pitchers to hit at home where the distant fences gave pitchers more confidence.

However, he hit better in Yankee Stadium than anywhere else, with a .485 average there. In fact, the Yankees put him over .400; the rest of the league held him to a .394 mark.

Washington was the worst city for him—he hit only .281 in that spacious field, though he hit Washington pitchers freely when they came to Boston—.484. Cleveland was the worst city for him; luckily he played only seven games there.

Williams hit .415 for all games outside of Washington and .411 for all games outside of Cleveland. He hit .394 against all clubs except New York, .394 against all clubs but Philadelphia, and .419 against all clubs except Detroit.

Detroit was supposed to be his favorite park, but he hit only .342 there. Why didn't Ted hit better in Detroit? A clue was furnished by *The Sporting News,* which reported that a measurement of all the pitching mounds in the league revealed that Detroit's was twice as high as any other.

| Team | At Boston | | | Away | | | Total | | |
|---|---|---|---|---|---|---|---|---|---|
| | G | BA | HR | G | BA | HR | G | BA | HR |
| New York | 11 | .457 | 2 | 11 | .485 | 0 | 22 | .470 | 2 |
| Philadelphia | 10 | .469 | 4 | 9 | .407 | 4 | 19 | .431 | 8 |
| Washington | 11 | .484 | 3 | 11 | .281 | 0 | 22 | .381 | 3 |
| Detroit | 11 | .333 | 2 | 10 | .342 | 3 | 21 | .338 | 5 |
| Cleveland | 11 | .474 | 2 | 7 | .300 | 1 | 18 | .414 | 3 |
| St. Louis | 11 | .394 | 2 | 10 | .464 | 7 | 21 | .426 | 9 |
| Chicago | 11 | .405 | 4 | 9 | .333 | 3 | 20 | .377 | 7 |
| Totals | 76 | .426 | 19 | 67 | .380 | 18 | 143 | .406 | 37 |

John Tattersall, the nation's foremost home run authority, reported that playing in Fenway cost Williams perhaps 25 home runs throughout his career. He hit 248 at home but 273 on the road.

# Against Lefties and Righties

One supposed advantage of being a left-handed hitter in Boston was that most clubs refused to pitch lefties against the Red Sox' right-handed power there. However, this may actually have hurt Ted. Williams loved lefties, feasting on them for a .429 average. He once said he learned to hit them at Minneapolis, where opposing clubs *did* like to pitch left-handers to try to offset the short right-field wall.

However, he had not been successful against them in his first two years in the American league. He also says that against lefties, he shortened up on the bat and tried to hit up the middle—only one of his 37 homers came against a southpaw. One wonders: If he had tried to do the same thing against right-handers, he might have ended up as the last of the .500 hitters!

|           | AB  | H   | BA   | HR |
|-----------|-----|-----|------|----|
| Lefties   | 84  | 36  | .429 | 1  |
| Righties  | 372 | 149 | .401 | 36 |

Against selected lefties, Williams hit as follows:

|          | AB | H  | BA   | HR |
|----------|----|----|------|----|
| Gomez    | 12 | 10 | .833 | 1  |
| Russo    | 8  | 5  | .625 | 0  |
| E Smith  | 11 | 6  | .545 | 0  |
| Milnar   | 15 | 4  | .267 | 0  |
| T Lee    | 12 | 3  | .250 | 0  |

# Day Versus Night

Williams said lights didn't bother him after three years playing at night in the minor leagues. However, he hit only .333 at night in 1941. Luckily, he played only two games after dark. Within a decade most games would be at night. No man, including Williams, has ever reached .400 since the era of unlimited night baseball began.

|       | AB  | H   | BA   | HR |
|-------|-----|-----|------|----|
| Night | 6   | 2   | .333 | 0  |
| Day   | 450 | 183 | .407 | 37 |

# Sacrifice Flies and .400

Williams is the only .400 hitter who did not have the sacrifice fly rule working for him. The rule deducts a time at bat for a fly ball that scores a man from third. In 1930 it deducted a time at bat for advancing a man from second to third as well.

In 1941 Ted hit six long flies that drove a runner in from third. That's relatively low for his era, statician Pete Palmer says; perhaps that's because pitchers seldom pitched to him with a man on third. If he had played in almost any other year this century, he would have had six less at bats, which would have raised his average six points to .412 —thus removing all the drama from that final double header.

Of 12 .400 seasons, six would have been under .400 without the rule.

Palmer says the average player 1908–1925 collected about seven SFs a year. The average for 1926–1930 was about 12. If we add these numbers to the at bats of all other .400 hitters (except Lajoie, for whom we have no estimates), Cobb, Heilemann, and Terry would have lost .400 seasons, and Hornsby would have lost two.

| Year | Hitter | AB | H | BA | w/o SF |
|------|--------|-----|-----|------|--------|
| 1911 | Cobb | 591 | 248 | .420 | .413 |
| 1911 | Jackson | 571 | 233 | .408 | .403 |
| 1912 | Cobb | 553 | 227 | .410 | .405 |
| 1920 | Sisler | 631 | 257 | .407 | .403 |
| 1922 | Hornsby | 592 | 235 | .401 | .392 |
| 1922 | Sisler | 586 | 246 | .420 | .411 |
| 1922 | Cobb | 526 | 211 | .401 | .396 |
| 1923 | Heilmann | 524 | 211 | .403 | .397 |
| 1924 | Hornsby | 536 | 227 | .424 | .414 |
| 1925 | Hornsby | 504 | 203 | .403 | .397 |
| 1930 | Terry | 633 | 254 | .401 | .394 |

Note that if all had played under the same rule, only three men in this century (not counting Lajoie) would have had a higher batting average than Ted: Cobb, Sisler, and Hornsby.

## At Bats and .400

Today's 162-game schedule is an important factor working against our seeing another .400 hitter.

As Williams points out, the season starts earlier in April and lasts until later in October, which generally means chilly weather and longer shadows.

Then there is the fatigue factor. Today's players play six games more than their fathers or grandfathers did.

But even more important is the fact that hitting .400 is defying the law of averages. No matter how good one is—even for Ty Cobb with a lifetime .367 —to hit .400 is far outside the law of averages, and as every gambler knows, sooner or later the law of averages will straighten itself out. You may pitch nine heads out of ten, but it is infinitely harder to do it again— 18 out of 20. The longer you go on pitching pennies, the closer your total average will return toward normal.

Williams came to bat officially less than any other .400 hitter ever, a factor that worked in his favor. He swung at only 456 balls that year. By contrast, Terry had 633 at bats in 1930, the highest total for any .400 hitter in this century, or 177 more at bats than Ted.

It is interesting to note that George Brett, who in 1980 came closer than anyone since Williams to reaching .400, came to bat only 449 times.

The 20th century .400 hitters ranked in order of times at bat are:

| | | | |
|------|----------|-----|------|
| 1930 | Terry    | 633 | .401 |
| 1920 | Sisler   | 631 | .407 |
| 1922 | Hornsby  | 592 | .401 |
| 1911 | Cobb     | 591 | .420 |
| 1922 | Sisler   | 586 | .420 |
| 1911 | Jackson  | 571 | .408 |
| 1901 | Lajoie   | 544 | .426 |
| 1924 | Hornsby  | 536 | .424 |
| 1922 | Cobb     | 526 | .401 |
| 1923 | Heilmann | 524 | .403 |
| 1925 | Hornsby  | 504 | .403 |
| 1941 | Williams | 456 | .406 |

Other near misses were:

| 1977 | Carew | 616 | .388 |
| 1980 | Brett | 449 | .390 |
| 1957 | Williams | 420 | .388 |

---

# Walks and .400

One of the raps against Williams has always been that he took too many walks, that he sacrificed his team rather than swing at a pitch an inch outside the strike zone. Yet the new science of SABRmetrics proves that Williams and his mentor Hornsby were right to take the sure walk instead of gambling on the possible hit or home run. The base on balls is actually the most under-rated offensive play in baseball—and the intentional walk the most over-rated defensive play. Here's why:

On the simplest level, the game of baseball is about outs. The defense wants to get 27 of them as fast as possible; the offense wants to give up as few as possible—if everyone walked, the first game ever played would still be going on. John Thorn and Pete Palmer, who studied every at bat ever recorded in the major leagues since 1900, concluded in their seminal book, *The Hidden Game of Baseball*, that every out costs the offensive team, on average, one-third of a run. They also concluded that various offensive plays have the following run-producing values*:

*Includes runs scored, RBI, runners advanced who later scored, and runs that scored after two outs because the player had kept the inning alive.

| | |
|---|---|
| home run | 1.4 runs |
| triple | 1.0 |
| double | 0.8 |
| single | 0.5 |
| walk | 0.3 |

Let's take Williams' lifetime stats and see what this means.

Ted walked 2,019 times, second only to Babe Ruth—and the Babe came to the plate almost 700 times more than Ted did:

| | Williams | Ruth |
|---|---|---|
| At bats | 7706 | 8399 |
| Walks | 2019 | 2056 |
| Total | 9725 | 10,455 |

In other words, Williams was the most feared batter in baseball history. His Pitcher Fear Factor (walks/total plate appearances) was .208; Ruth's was .197.

Williams' lifetime batting average was .344. Assuming that, instead of walking those 2,019 times, he got hits 34.4% of them, he would have gotten 695 more hits, including an additional 137 home runs. (To simplify the calculations, I'm going to assume that all his other hits were singles). Then what do we have?

$$2,019 \text{ walks} \times .3 = 606 \text{ runs}$$

compared to

$$137 \text{ additional homers} \times 1.4 = 192 \text{ runs}$$
$$558 \text{ additional singles} \times .5 = 279 \text{ runs}$$
$$\text{total} \qquad\qquad\qquad\quad 479$$

That means if Williams had never taken a walk and had put the ball in play (or struck out) in every time at bat, he would probably have produced an extra 479 runs for his team. But by taking the walks, he produced an extra 606 runs, or a profit of 127 runs for the Red Sox.

With the fence-busters Ted had batting behind him in Boston, his walks probably produced even more than 606 runs. And, as he would be quick to point out, those 2,019 walks were on bad pitches, when his batting average would have been considerably less than .344.

As he also points out, with him on first base the next man—Foxx, York, Dropo, Doerr, Stephens—got better pitches to hit.

Joe DiMaggio walked half as much as Williams. He must have been either swinging at too many bad pitches, or the hurlers didn't fear him as much as they did Ted and gave him more strikes to hit. If Joe had walked more, he would have helped his team score more runs, especially with Gehrig, Keller, Berra etc coming up behind him. Joe would also have raised his own batting average several points. (But he would have come to bat considerably less often, and thus would probably not have been able to put together a 56-game hitting streak.)

When Williams walked, the writers wrote that he was hurting his team. Now, he points out, they complement a hitter who is "selective" or "patient at the plate."

The moral to the story is: Yes, Tom Lasorda was right to pitch to Jack Clark in the final game of the 1985 play-off. Clark upset the law of averages by hitting a homer and winning the pennant, but over the long run Lasorda made the right call. Hornsby knew it, and Williams knew it, even if most of the writers and opposing managers haven't figured it out yet.

Perhaps other .400 hitters didn't know it either. Only Hornsby came close to grasping the truth that his most famous disciple, Williams, put into practice. Following are this century's .400 hitters, with their bases on balls:

| Year | Player | AB | BB | BA |
|------|--------|-----|------|------|
| 1901 | Lajoie | 544 | 24 | .426 |
| 1912 | Cobb | 553 | 43 | .410 |
| 1911 | Cobb | 591 | 44 | .420 |
| 1920 | Sisler | 631 | 46 | .407 |
| 1922 | Sisler | 586 | 49 | .420 |
| 1922 | Cobb | 526 | 55 | .401 |
| 1912 | Jackson | 571 | 56 | .408 |
| 1930 | Terry | 633 | 57 | .401 |
| 1922 | Hornsby | 623 | 65 | .401 |
| 1923 | Heilmann | 524 | 74 | .403 |
| 1925 | Hornsby | 504 | 83 | .403 |
| 1924 | Hornsby | 536 | 89* | .424 |
| 1941 | Williams | 456 | 145* | .406 |

*Led league*

Cobb was among Williams' most vocal critics for taking so many pitches. One can only assume that the hurlers were trying not to give Ty anything good to hit and that therefore he must have been swinging most of the time at pitches on the corners. One wonders how well Cobb might have done if he had waited, as Williams did, until he had the pitcher in a hole and the hurler had to come in with a good ball to hit.

# Einstein's Theory
## of Baseball
## Relativity

Why don't we see .400 hitters again? Until 1941 fans yawned at .400 hitters. In the 1890s there were no less than ten of them—four in one year, 1894, and three of those on one team, Philadelphia! (One wonders what their park was like.) In the 11 years, 1920–30, baseball saw eight more. In 1922 there were three in the same year. Altogether, in baseball's first 55 years, there were no less than 26 men who reached the magic mark. In the last 60 years there has been only one, Ted Williams.

Williams says today's players don't hit .400 because they're not dedicated enough, but I have to disagree. There are only two ways to raise batting averages, both of them largely out of the control of the players themselves.

Everything is relative, and if Einstein were alive today, and a Red Sox fan, he would dash to the blackboard and scribble the E-mc2 of baseball relativity:

$$LBA \times RBA = BA,$$

which means league batting average times relative batting average equals (individual) batting average.

For baseball's 12 .400-hitters since 1901, the numbers look like this:

|      |                 | LBA    |   | RBA  |     | BA     |
|------|-----------------|--------|---|------|-----|--------|
| 1901 | Larry Lajoie    | .277   | × | 1.54 | =   | .426   |
| 1911 | Ty Cobb         | .273   | × | 1.54 | =   | .420   |
| 1941 | Ted Williams    | .266   | × | 1.53 | =   | .406   |
| 1924 | Rogers Hornsby  | .283   | × | 1.50 | =   | .424   |
| 1911 | Joe Jackson     | .273   | × | 1.49 | =   | .408   |
| 1922 | George Sisler   | .285   | × | 1.47 | =   | .420   |
| 1920 | George Sisler   | .283   | × | 1.44 | =   | .407   |
| 1923 | Harry Heilmann  | .282   | × | 1.43 | =   | .403   |
| 1922 | Ty Cobb         | .285   | × | 1.41 | =   | .401   |
| 1925 | Rogers Hornsby  | .292   | × | 1.38 | =   | .403   |
| 1922 | Rogers Hornsby  | .292   | × | 1.37 | =   | .401   |
| 1930 | Bill Terry      | .303   | × | 1.32 | =   | .401   |

Williams had to overcome the lowest league batting average of any .400-hitter in this century. To do it, he had to excel 53% above average, and only two .400 hitters in that period have ever done that—Lajoie in 1901 and Cobb in 1911—and they did it when the competitive level was much lower than in 1941.

Sixteen years later, in 1957, Ted was again 53% better than the average batter in his league, but the league average had fallen 11 points to .255, and the best Ted could do was .388:

$$.255 \times 1.53 = .388$$

To change the individual's batting average, then, one must change either the league average or the relative average, or both.

What is the league average? Nothing more than the point at which the league defense exactly equals the league offense. It's a function of the rules and equipment of the game—the size of the gloves, the size of the strike zone, the height of the mound, the brightness of the lights, the distance to the fences etc etc.

Thus, to change the league average requires manipulating the rules and equipment to favor either offense or defense. When Bill Terry hit .401 in 1930, the National league *average* was .303; it has been steadily falling ever since, until today it's about .250. That would require a relative average of 1.60 in order to hit .400, a feat no man has ever achieved in 115 years of trying.

If a player comes to bat 500 times a season, each hit is worth two points on his batting average. Only one extra hit a week will raise a .250 hitter to a .300 hitter, and a .350 hitter to a .400 hitter. How many hits do today's batters lose to bigger gloves alone?

Suppose—just suppose—that Wlliams had been 53% better than average under the same conditions as 1930, when the league average was .303. He would have hit .464:

$$.303 \times 1.53 = .464$$

But, just as it is harder and harder to hit for a high absolute average, so is it now relatively hard to hit for a high *relative* average. That's because the population noose grows tighter with every new baby born. In great-great grandfather's day, around 1901, every major leaguer represented the best of about 76,000 white North American males. Today, with the population exploding even faster than the big leagues can expand, the average player stands atop a pyramid of about 300,000 western hemisphere males—white, black, and brown—from the Arctic circle to the equator. No one has hit .400 since integration, which is not coincidental.

Old-timers like to scoff at the "dilution" of today's expanded game. Actually, the game was diluted in their day, not in this.

Today the pool has grown so great that only the cream of the cream is chosen. Where Cobb had faced a Walter Johnson or an Ed Walsh about once every series, today's hitters must face a man of that calibre once a game, maybe twice, since relief pitchers are now as good as, or better than, the starters.

To raise the individual's relative average, one must manipulate the competition, i.e., expand the number of teams. When Larry Lajoie hit .426 in 1901, he did it in an expansion year, the first season of 16 teams, replacing the old 12-team National league of the 1890s. It would take at least three times the number of major league teams today to return the player-population ratio to where it had been in Lajoie's or Cobb's day.

In addition, we know there is a third factor not in Einstein's formula for baseball relativity.

Quite apart from the numbers of athletes and the changing rules, we know that athletes today are better than in their father's day. The dizzying succession of new Olympic records tells us that. And they're bigger. In 1927 the Yankees' starting foursome averaged 180 pounds. Today the littlest man on the staff is bigger than that. And the extra power of today's pitchers is not off-set by greater power of the hitters. Because extra size does not mean extra quickness, and pitched balls get to home plate several feet sooner than they used to.

As Mike Schmidt said, "You can't hit 60 homers today. The pitchers won't let you."

But that all could change. And when it comes, it will not be accomplished by the players in their uniforms down on the field but by the governors of the game in their business suits high above Park Avenue.

There are two things commissioner Fay Vincent could do to bring back the .400 hitter (or 60-homer man etc):

1. approve a major expansion of teams, returning baseball to the player:population ratio of 60–70 years ago; it would take about triple the present big league teams to do that.

2. reverse the trend toward stronger defense and return to league averages of .280-.300, where they were in the 1920s and '30s, then the .400 hitter will return as well. This could be done with new rules (a longer pitching distance) or new equipment (aluminum bats).

Warning: There is a price to pay, however. As expansion will cut down competition among individuals, allowing the best to rise 50% or more above the crowd again, so will it cut down on the competition among teams. In the "good old days" of Cobb and Ruth, pennant play-offs were unheard of, and seven-game World Series were rarities. Now teams fight to the last day of the season, or beyond, once or twice a decade, and most Series are in doubt right down to the last inning. Eighty years ago the last-place team might stagger home 50 games behind the champ. That's unthinkable today. And today's tendency to crown a new champ every year will be replaced with the dynasties of old, where the same team stays on top year after year.

# Ty Cobb's .420 in 1911

In 1911, 30 years before Williams' feat, Ty Cobb combined a high relative average, 54%, with a high league average, .273 to attain a personal average of .420. Larry Amman offers some interesting data on Cobb's season:

"Batting averages and scoring were up all over the majors. Writers used the term "lively ball" to describe the new cork-centered baseball. Ty was having trouble bunting, because the ball was hard to deaden. . . .

"On the seventh of May Cobb opened a series in the new Comiskey Park and went 4-for-5 against the veteran southpaw, Doc White. It had taken Cobb several years in the league to hit White's drop ball at all. . . . For several years White made Ty look foolish. This year Cobb was 9-for-18 against him. Sportswriters noted that teams saved their left-handers to use against the Tigers to try to neutralize left-handed swingers Cobb and Sam Crawford (.378). Two southpaws especially tough on Cobb this season were Earl Hamilton and Vean Gregg. It is significant that both men were rookies; Ty never hit a pitcher well until he had seen him a few times.

For the year, Ty hit .405 against left-handers and .426 against righties.

"On June 3 Cobb had a three-hit day against Walter Johnson and a perfect day on the eighth against Eddie Plank, the league's best southpaw. . . .

"He led the league in every defensive category except home runs, where he finished one behind Home Run Baker. His totals for runs, hits, and stolen bases set American league records, as did his 40-game hitting streak. . . .

Amman reports that Cobb hit .418 at home, .421 away. His record against selected pitchers:

|  | R–L | W–L | BA |
|---|---|---|---|
| Joe Wood | R | 23–17 | .555 |
| Jack Coombs | R | 28–12 | .529 |
| Walter Johnson | R | 25–13 | .500 |
| Doc White | L | 10–14 | .500 |
| Russ Ford | R | 22–11 | .428 |
| Eddie Plank | L | 23– 8 | .388 |
| Ed Walsh | R | 27–18 | .291 |
| Vean Gregg | L | 23– 7 | .285 |
| Earl Hamilton | L | 5–12 | .260 |
| Ray Collins | L | 11–12 | .250 |

# Climbing the Hill

Hitting .400 is like running a marathon. Stamina and pacing are both important. Some hitters have built up huge leads early and barely held on at the finish line. Others have started slowly and crossed the finish with a powerful closing kick. Here's how their races look when charted graphically:

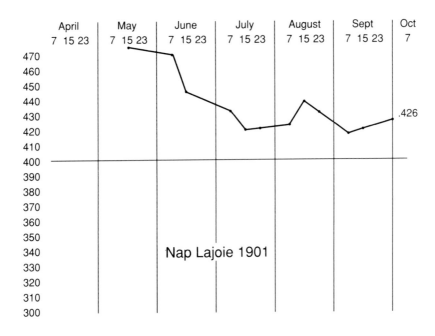

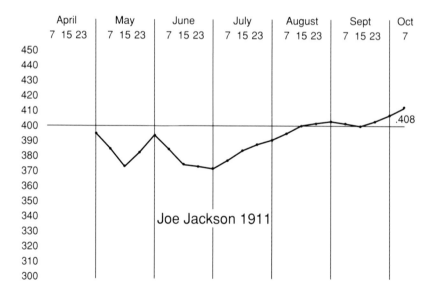

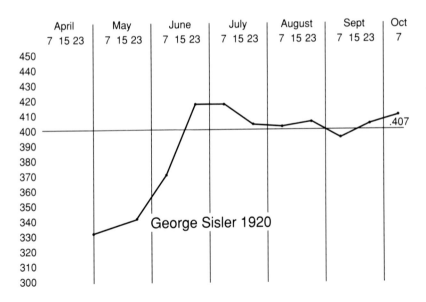

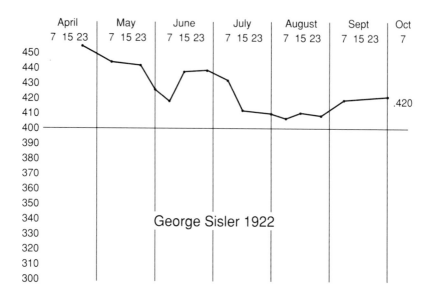

George Sisler 1922

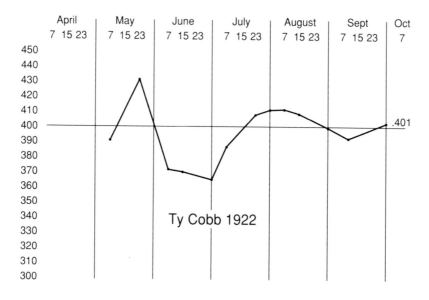

Ty Cobb 1922

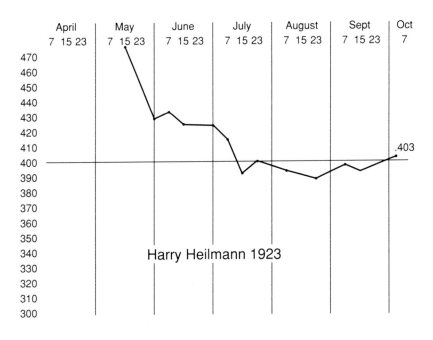

Rogers Hornsby 1922

Harry Heilmann 1923

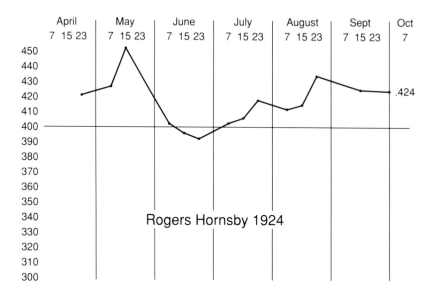

Rogers Hornsby 1924

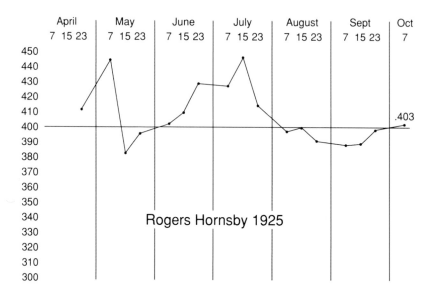

Rogers Hornsby 1925

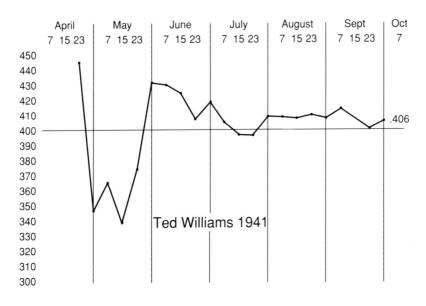

# Those Who Came Close

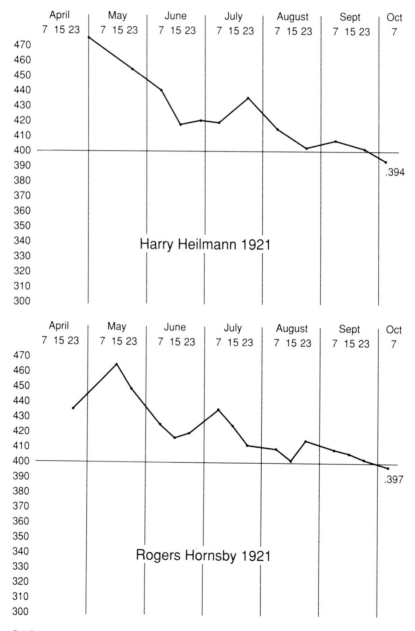

|  | April | May | June | July | August | Sept | Oct |
|---|---|---|---|---|---|---|---|
|  | 7 15 23 | 7 15 23 | 7 15 23 | 7 15 23 | 7 15 23 | 7 15 23 | 7 |

Harry Heilmann 1921

.394

|  | April | May | June | July | August | Sept | Oct |
|---|---|---|---|---|---|---|---|
|  | 7 15 23 | 7 15 23 | 7 15 23 | 7 15 23 | 7 15 23 | 7 15 23 | 7 |

Rogers Hornsby 1921

.397

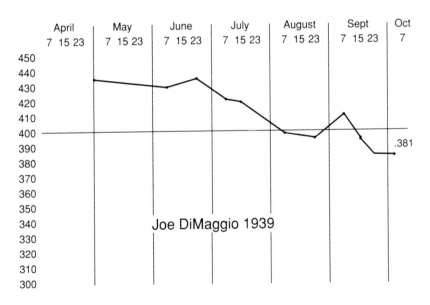

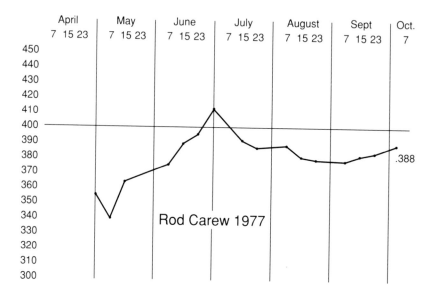

Ted Williams 1957

Rod Carew 1977

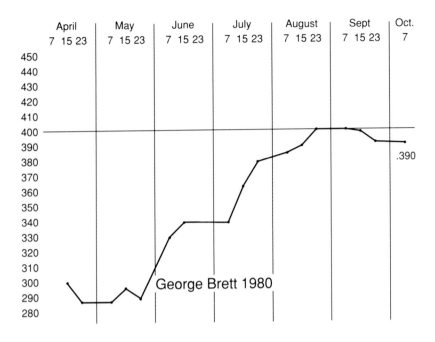

George Brett 1980

.390

# MVP
# Does 56 Beat .406?

Today Williams says magnanimously that DiMaggio deserved the award. "He carried the club with that streak, and they got going. They won the pennant by 17 games. That's an awful big factor when you consider the two." He is bitter about several later votes when the writers ignored him for the honor. But "there's *never* been any question in my mind about that one. Never. Never."

I however think Williams is overly modest.

The MVP vote is a subjective, inexact science at best, a popularity poll at worst. Several scholars have made attempts to put a more objective quantitative value on players' performances.

For one thing, the pitchers voted overwhelmingly for Ted—they gave him twice as many walks as Joe.

For another, Joe hit .412 during his streak, .322 in the other two-thirds of the season; Ted hit .406 for the whole season.

Third, the Yankees had been picked for first or second before the season. They won by 17½ games and clinched the pennant earlier than any team in history, even the Yankee powerhouses of Ruth and Gehrig or the '39 juggernaut. The Red Sox were picked to finish fourth or fifth; they finished second, seven gamed ahead of Chicago. Surely the Yankees would have won the pennant without DiMaggio, although by a smaller margin. The Red Sox could not have finished second without Williams.

# IVP
# Individual Victory
# Percentage

Beginning in 1944 I compiled each player's "Individual Victory Percentage," or how well his team did when he was in the line-up compared to when he was out. The results were published in *Baseball Digest* magazine in November 1959.

In 1939, Williams missed three games, and the Red Sox lost two of the three.

DiMaggio missed 34 games, and the Yankees won 27 of them. The Yanks were considerably better without Joe than with him. Yet he was voted Most Valuable Player, presumably on the basis of his batting title and his reputation.

In 1941, with Williams out of the line-up, or pinch-hitting only, the Sox were a losing team (11–12). On the other hand, the Yankees played almost as well without DiMaggio, .625, as with him, .664. They would have easily won the pennant whether he had been on the team or not.

# Teammates
# Table Setters

Every great hitter needs a lot of help. One unsung source of help is the men in his line-up, both ahead of him and behind him.

In 1941 Williams had about 45 more runners to drive in than DiMaggio had. Dom DiMaggio and Lou Finney, the 1-2 hitters in the Red Sox batting order, got on base 418 times that year. Red Rolfe and Tom Henrich, the two men who hit ahead of DiMaggio, reached base only .373.

But also important is getting on first base, as Bill James has demonstrated that batting averages go up with a man on first; pitchers must pitch more carefully, since there is no open base to invite a walk. Again Ted had a slight advantage. Dom and Lou were on first base with walks or singles 326 times; Red and Tom, 308.

---

### *Power on Deck*

---

◆

---

Of course the other factor in Runs Produced—and in forcing pitchers to put the ball over the plate—is the quality of the man in the on-deck circle:

| Red Sox | HR | RBI | SA* | Yankees | HR | RBI | SA |
|---------|----|-----|-----|---------|----|-----|-----|
| Foxx | 19 | 105 | .505 | Keller | 33 | 122 | .580 |

*Slugging Average*

Both Ted and Joe were fortunate to have formidable men coming up behind them, though the younger Keller was more formidable than the aging Foxx. Advantage DiMag.

# TOTAL RUNS
# PRODUCED

◆

In total runs produced (runs scored and teammates batted in), the two men were just about even: Ted just topped Joe, 218–217. But Ted's runs were more crucial to his team than Joe's were to his.

## GWAB
## Games Won at Bat

This was my own invention back in 1944.

A run or RBI in a losing game is wasted; one might as well have gone hitless. So is a run in a 10–0 blow-out victory. But a run produced in a 10–9 victory is a Game Won At Bat. Without it, the team would have tied and perhaps lost. A total of two runs produced (scored or batted in) in a 10–8 victory is also a GWAB, and so forth.

Williams' hits won more games than DiMaggio's did. Again, the Yankees had a power-packed line-up—plus the best pitching in the league. Yankee hurlers gave up only 631 runs; the Red Sox' staff yielded almost 100 more. The Boston batters were the most efficient in either league, scoring 865 runs; the Yankees were second with 830. In other words, New York outscored their foes by 199 runs; Boston, by 135

The Yankees won more games, giving each player more opportunities to score a GWAB. But they won by lop-sided scores, such as 14−6, 12−1, 9−0 etc. It's almost impossible for one man to supply the margin of victory very often for a team like that. But that's what the "V" in "MVP" means—or should.

GWAB are roughly similar to pitchers' victories—20 is very good, 30 is superior—which permits us to compare hitters and pitchers as MVP candidates.

Unfortunately, after I discovered girls, and went to college, my time grew suddenly short as I stopped pursuing baseball stats and began pursuing beauty and a diploma. But with the help of Paul Doherty and Tim Joyce, I have filled in GWAB for all the top players each season in Williams' career.

I with I could add Assists. This would include:

1. runners moved into scoring position who later score on someone else's RBI
2. runners replaced on the bases through a force out or pinch-runner by a man who later scores
3. runs that score after two outs when a player has prolonged the inning with a hit or walk
4. runs that score in extra innings after a player has helped tie the game through a run, an RBI or an Assist.

Assists would be a particular boon to hitters in the second and third positions in the batting order; they often set the table for the clean-up man who gets the RBI.

I tabulate Assists when I score a game. But they cannotbe derived from present box scores.

Ted's runs or RBIs were the margin of victory in 29 Red Sox wins. Joe supplied the key runs in 22 games. Interestingly, 18 of Joe's 22 came during the streak. He contributed only three before the streak started and only one after it ended.

DiMaggio was not even the unchallenged MVP on the Yankees. Red Ruffing won 15 games on the mound and seven more at bat, either as pinch-hitter or by producing runs that helped his reliever win. Ruffing tied DiMaggio with 22.

Four other Yankees—Rolfe, Gordon, Henrich, and Keller—chippin in with 19 games won each.

But Ted had to carry the Red Sox' offensive burden with little help from the other bats. Foxx supported him with 17 wins; the next highest, Doerr and Lou Finney, contributed only 13 each.

**1939**

| MVP Vote | | Total Runs | | GWAB | | | |
|---|---|---|---|---|---|---|---|
| DiMaggio | 280 | Williams | 245 | **Williams** | 29 | | |
| Foxx | 170 | **Williams** | 206 | C Brown | 29 | (11 + 18)@ | |
| Feller | 155 | Johnson | 205 | Foxx | 28 | | |
| **Williams** | 126 | Rolfe | 204 | Feller | 25 | (24 + 1)@ | |
| Ruffing | 116 | DiMaggio | 200 | Rolfe | 21 | | |
| | | Foxx | | | | Ruffing | 21 |
| | | | | | | Dickey | 18 |
| | | | | · · · | | | |
| | | | | **Williams** | 4 | DiMaggio | 18 |

@ *Wins plus saves*

**1940**

| MVP Vote | | Total Votes | | GWAB | | |
|---|---|---|---|---|---|---|
| Greenberg | 292 | Greenberg | 238 | Feller | 31 | (27 + 4) |
| Feller | 222 | **Williams** | 224 | Greenberg | 29 | |
| DiMaggio | 151 | York | 206 | Gehringer | 27 | |

| | | | | |
|---|---|---|---|---|
| Newsom | 120 | DiMaggio | 195 | Cronin 26 |
| Boudreau | 119 | Cronin | 191 | York 25 |
| | | | | Doerr 25 |
| | | | | Doerr 25 |
| | | | | Benton 23 (6+17) |
| | | | | **Williams** 22 |
| | | | | Foxx 22 |
| | | | | Keller 21 |
| | | | | Milnar 21 (18+3) |
| | | | | Cramer 20 |
| | | | | McCoskey 20 |
| | | | | Trosky 19 |
| | | | | Higgins 19 |
| | | | | DiMaggio 18 |
| | | | | Boudreau 16 |

| **Williams** | 16 | (14th) | Boudreau | 0 | **Williams** | 29 |
|---|---|---|---|---|---|---|

**1941**

| DiMaggio | 291 | **Williams** | 218 | **Williams** | 29 |
|---|---|---|---|---|---|
| **Williams** | 254 | DiMaggio | 217 | Feller | 27 (25+2) |
| Feller | 174 | Travis | 200 | Lee | 23 (22+1) |
| T Lee | 144 | Keller | 191 | DiMaggio | 22 |
| Keller | 126 | Heath | 188 | Ruffing | 22* |

*15 pitching, plus seven at bat.

## 1942

| MVP Vote | | Total Votes | | GWAB | |
|---|---|---|---|---|---|
| Gordon | 270 | Williams | 242 | **Williams** | 36 |
| Williams | 249 | J. DiMaggio | 216 | Hudson | 26 (22 + 4) |
| Pesky | 143 | Keller | 188 | Pesky | 25 |
| Stephens | 140 | Gordon | 173 | Bonham | 21 |
| Bonham | 102 | Spence | 169 | D. DiMaggio | 20 |
| | | | | Doerr | 19 |
| | | | | Finney | 19 |
| | | | | Lupien | 18 |
| | | Stephens | 162 | J. DiMaggio | 17 |
| | | Pesky | 154 | Chandler | 16 |
| | | | | Borowy | 15 |
| | | | | Murphy | 15 (4 + 11) |
| | | | | Henrich | 12 |
| | | | | Keller | 12 |
| | | | | Gordon | 11* |
| | | | | Donald | 11 |

*(tied for #34)

In his first four seasons in the major leagues, Williams never won the nod of the human electors for MVP. But he won the vote of the computer three of the four years.

## Ted Williams Batting Record
## San Diego Padres, 1936

| Date | | Score | Opp. | AB | H | R | RBI | |
|------|------|-------|------|----|----|----|-----|----|
| June | 27 | 7– 6 | Sac | 1 | 0 | 0 | 0 | ph struck out on 3 pitches |
| July | 3 | 9–14 | @LA | 2 | 2 | 2 | 0 | p, lf; 1.1 IP, 2 H, 2 BB, 2 R |
| | 4 | 3– 4 | | 1 | 0 | 0 | 0 | ph |
| | | 3– 4 | | 4 | 1 | 1 | 0 | |
| | 5 | 1– 3 | | 3 | 0 | 0 | 0 | |
| | | 3– 4 | | 3 | 0 | 0 | 0 | |
| | 15 | 1– 2 | Seat | 1 | 0 | 0 | 0 | ph |
| | 17 | 2– 4 | Port | 1 | 0 | 0 | 0 | ph |
| | 22 | 1– 3 | Miss'n | 1 | 0 | 0 | 0 | ph |
| | 24 | 4– 3 | | 0 | 0 | 1 | 0 | pr scored winning run in 10th |
| | 26 | 1– 4 | | 2 | 1 | 0 | 0 | |
| | 30 | 5–10 | LA | 1 | 0 | 0 | 0 | ph |
| Aug | 7 | 2– 3 | @Port | 0 | 0 | 0 | 0 | |
| | | 10– 0 | | 4 | 1 | 1 | 1 | |
| | 8 | 6– 9 | | 3 | 2 | 1 | 0 | |
| | | 1– 8 | | 3 | 0 | 0 | 0 | |
| | 9 | 4– 1 | | 4 | 2 | 0 | 2 | 2B |
| | | 4– 1 | | 3 | 1 | 1 | 0 | 2B |
| | 11 | 2– 0 | @Miss'n | 3 | 0 | 0 | 0 | |
| | 12 | 1– 5 | | 4 | 0 | 0 | 0 | |
| | 16 | 4–15 | | 1 | 1 | 0 | 0 | ph |
| | | 2– 6 | | 1 | 0 | 0 | 0 | |
| | 19 | 8–10 | @Sac | 1 | 0 | 0 | 0 | ph |
| | 23 | 3– 7 | | 1 | 0 | 0 | 0 | ph |
| | 28 | 3– 2 | Oak | 0 | 0 | 0 | 0 | pr |
| Sep | 1 | 14– 3 | Sac | 3 | 2 | 1 | 2 | 2B, 3B |
| | 2 | 11– 1 | | 3 | 0 | 0 | 0 | SH |
| | 3 | 0– 1 | | 3 | 0 | 0 | 0 | |
| | 4 | 13– 1 | | 3 | 2 | 1 | 2 | |
| | 5 | 10– 3 | | 3 | 1 | 0 | 1 | |

| Date | | Score | Opp. | AB | H | R | RBI | |
|---|---|---|---|---|---|---|---|---|
| | 6 | 15–3 | | 4 | 1 | 2 | 1 | three brilliant catches |
| | | 1–0 | | 1 | 1 | 0 | 0 | SB |
| | 7 | 5–1 | | 3 | 1 | 1 | 1 | |
| | | 3–0 | | 3 | 1 | 1 | 0 | SB |
| | 9 | 0–6 | @SF | 3 | 0 | 0 | 0 | |
| | | 2–3 | | 3 | 1 | 1 | 1 | |
| | 10 | 8–2 | | 4 | 1 | 1 | 0 | |
| | 11 | 5–7 | | 5 | 1 | 0 | 0 | |
| | 12 | 3–4 | | 4 | 0 | 0 | 0 | |
| | | 4–1 | | 6 | 3 | 1 | 1 | 3B |
| | 13 | 3–5 | | 4 | 2 | 1 | 0 | |
| | | 4–0 | | 4 | 1 | 1 | 1 | |
| | | 42 | games | 107 | 29 | 18 | 11 | .271 |
| | | | home | 33 | 10 | | | .303 |
| | | | away | 74 | 19 | | | .257 |
| Playoffs | | | | | | | | |
| Sep | 15 | 3–6 | @Oak | 3 | 1 | 1 | 2 | HR vs Willie Ludolph |
| | 16 | 3–4 | | 4 | 0 | 0 | 0 | |
| | 19 | 4–5 | Oak | 3 | 0 | 1 | 0 | |
| | 20 | 7–1 | | 2 | 0 | 1 | 0 | |
| | 21 | 6–7 | | 4 | 2 | 1 | 0 | |
| | | | | 16 | 3 | 4 | 0 | .198 |

## Ted Williams Batting Record
## San Diego Padres, 1937

| Date | | Score | Opp | AB | H | R | RBI | |
|------|---|-------|-----|----|----|----|----|---|
| Apr | 3 | 7– 9 | @LA | 1 | 0 | 0 | 0 | |
| | 4 | 0– 6 | | 1 | 0 | 0 | 0 | |
| | 7 | 4– 3 | Mission | 2 | 0 | 0 | 0 | |
| | 9 | 1–15 | | 1 | 0 | 0 | 0 | |
| | 11 | 3– 2 | | 4 | 1 | 0 | 1 | |
| | | 4– 0 | | 3 | 1 | 1 | 2 | HR vs Bolen |
| | 13 | 5– 4 | @Oakland | 0 | 0 | 0 | 0 | lifted for ph in 12th |
| | 15 | 3– 4 | | 1 | 1 | 0 | 0 | ph |
| | 16 | 2– 7 | | 3 | 0 | 0 | 0 | |
| | 18 | 2– 1 | | 4 | 1 | 0 | 1 | |
| | 23 | 9– 8 | Sac | 5 | 1 | 1 | 1 | |
| | 24 | 10– 4 | | 4 | 1 | 1 | 1 | 2B |
| | 25 | 4– 5 | | 4 | 1 | 0 | 0 | |
| | | 2– 0 | | 3 | 1 | 0 | 1 | |
| | 27 | 18– 3 | Oakland | 4 | 3 | 3 | 5 | HR |
| | 28 | 4– 2 | | 2 | 0 | 0 | 0 | |
| | 29 | 4– 8 | | 4 | 1 | 0 | 1 | 2B |
| | 30 | 3– 4 | | 4 | 1 | 0 | 0 | |
| May | 4 | 3– 4 | @SF | 4 | 1 | 0 | 0 | |
| | 6 | 4– 8 | | 2 | 0 | 0 | 0 | |
| | 7 | 2–10 | | 4 | 1 | 1 | 0 | |
| | 8 | 7– 0 | | 4 | 1 | 0 | 1 | |
| | 9 | 6–12 | | 3 | 0 | 0 | 0 | |
| | | 2– 8 | @SF | 2 | 1 | 0 | 0 | |
| | 13 | 5– 0 | @Sac | 4 | 0 | 0 | 0 | |
| | 14 | 3– 4 | | 3 | 0 | 0 | 0 | |
| | 15 | 6– 3 | | 4 | 1 | 0 | 2 | |
| | 16 | 4– 1 | | 5 | 1 | 0 | 0 | |
| | | 1– 4 | | 3 | 1 | 0 | 0 | 2B |
| | 20 | 0– 5 | Seattle | 1 | 0 | 0 | 0 | ph |
| | | 5– 4 | | 3 | 1 | 1 | 0 | |
| | 28 | 2– 6 | @Seattle | 1 | 0 | 0 | 0 | ph |

**333**

| Date | | Score | Opp | AB | H | R | RBI | |
|------|---|-------|-----|----|---|---|-----|---|
| Jun | 2 | 3– 4 | @Portland | 1 | 1 | 0 | 0 | |
| | 3 | 2– 6 | | 1 | 0 | 0 | 0 | ph |
| | 5 | 7– 8 | | 1 | 1 | 0 | 0 | ph |
| | 6 | 12– 1 | | 5 | 3 | 2 | 3 | |
| | | 8– 5 | | 3 | 2 | 1 | 3 | |
| | 8 | 1– 5 | SF | 4 | 0 | 0 | 0 | |
| | 9 | 4– 6 | | 0 | 0 | 0 | 0 | ph |
| | 15 | 1– 4 | @LA | 1 | 0 | 0 | 0 | ph |
| | 16 | 2–10 | @LA | 2 | 1 | 0 | 0 | |
| | 18 | 8–10 | | 1 | 1 | 1 | 0 | 2B |
| | 19 | 5– 1 | | 4 | 0 | 0 | 0 | |
| | 20 | 1– 4 | | 5 | 1 | 1 | 3 | HR |
| | 22 | 3– 2 | Portland | 3 | 1 | 1 | 2 | HR (great catch) |
| | 23 | 3– 2 | | 3 | 1 | 1 | 0 | 2B |
| | 24 | 13– 7 | | 4 | 2 | 1 | 4 | HR, SB |
| | 25 | 6– 1 | | 4 | 2 | 1 | 1 | HR |
| | 26 | 11– 9 | | 4 | 2 | 2 | 2 | |
| | 27 | 2– 3 | | 4 | 1 | 1 | 1 | HR |
| | | 6– 2 | | 3 | 2 | 1 | 4 | 2B, HR |
| | 29 | 3– 6 | LA | 4 | 0 | 0 | 0 | |
| | 30 | 4– 0 | | 3 | 2 | 1 | 2 | 2B |
| Jul | 1 | 4– 6 | | 3 | 1 | 0 | 0 | |
| | 2 | 11– 2 | | 5 | 4 | 1 | 4 | 2B, HR |
| | 3 | 5– 3 | | 4 | 1 | 1 | 2 | 2B |
| | 4 | 2– 1 | | 3 | 1 | 0 | 1 | 2B |
| | | 12– 1 | | 2 | 0 | 2 | 0 | |
| | 5 | 5– 0 | | 4 | 1 | 0 | 2 | |
| | | 3– 5 | | 3 | 1 | 1 | 1 | |
| | 6 | 4– 5 | @Mission | 3 | 0 | 0 | 0 | |
| | 7 | 5– 1 | | 4 | 2 | 0 | 2 | |
| | 8 | 7– 2 | | 2 | 0 | 1 | 0 | SH |
| | 9 | 7– 2 | | 3 | 1 | 2 | 0 | |
| | 10 | 7– 9 | | 5 | 3 | 2 | 0 | 2B |
| | 11 | 2–10 | | 4 | 2 | 0 | 0 | 2B |

| Date | | Score | Opp | AB | H | R | RBI | |
|------|------|-------|-----|-----|---|---|-----|------|
| | | 5–2 | | 4 | 0 | 0 | 1 | |
| | 13 | 8–3 | Mission | 3 | 2 | 3 | 3 | HR, HR |
| | 14 | 8–6 | | 2 | 2 | 0 | 3 | |
| | 15 | 3–0 | | 2 | 0 | 0 | 0 | |
| | 16 | 8–3 | | 4 | 1 | 0 | 0 | |
| | 17 | 5–4 | | 2 | 1 | 0 | 0 | |
| | 18 | 6–9 | | 4 | 0 | 0 | 0 | |
| | | 1–0 | | 2 | 1 | 0 | 0 | |
| | 20 | 4–0 | Seattle | 4 | 0 | 0 | 0 | |
| | 21 | 5–1 | | 3 | 1 | 1 | 3 | HR |
| | 22 | 2–3 | | 3 | 1 | 0 | 0 | 2B |
| | 23 | 1–5 | @Oakland | 3 | 0 | 0 | 0 | |
| | 24 | 8–6 | | 5 | 2 | 1 | 0 | |
| | 25 | 1–2 | | 3 | 0 | 0 | 0 | |
| | | 1–2 | | 2 | 0 | 0 | 0 | |
| | 27 | 6–5 | @Seattle | 4 | 0 | 0 | 0 | |
| | 28 | 12–2 | | 5 | 2 | 1 | 1 | |
| | 29 | 4–1 | | 3 | 0 | 1 | 0 | |
| | 30 | 1–6 | | 4 | 1 | 0 | 0 | |
| | 31 | 3–7 | | 4 | 0 | 0 | 0 | |
| Aug | 1 | 0–5 | | 4 | 1 | 0 | 0 | |
| | 3 | 11–3 | @Portland | 5 | 2 | 2 | 4 | HR |
| | 4 | 2–3 | | 4 | 0 | 0 | 0 | |
| | 5 | 5–1 | | 4 | 0 | 0 | 0 | |
| | 6 | 4–3 | | 5 | 1 | 1 | 0 | |
| | 6 | 4–3 | | 5 | 1 | 1 | 0 | |
| | 7 | 0–6 | | 4 | 2 | 0 | 0 | 2B |
| | 8 | 6–5 | | 5 | 3 | 0 | 0 | 2B |
| | | 1–4 | | 1 | 1 | 1 | 0 | |
| | 10 | 4–3 | Oakland | 4 | 0 | 0 | 0 | |
| | 11 | 2–4 | | 3 | 0 | 0 | 0 | |
| | 12 | 2–4 | | 4 | 0 | 0 | 0 | |
| | 14 | 9–2 | Sac | 3 | 0 | 1 | 0 | |
| | 15 | 3–2 | | 4 | 0 | 0 | 0 | |

| Date |    | Score | Opp | AB | H | R | RBI | |
|------|----|-------|-----|----|---|---|-----|--|
|      |    | 0– 5  |     | 0  | 0 | 0 | 0   | lifted for a ph |
|      | 17 | 6– 1  | @Sac | 4 | 1 | 0 | 0   | 2B |
|      | 18 | 5– 7  |     | 4  | 2 | 1 | 0   | 2B |
|      | 19 | 8– 0  |     | 1  | 0 | 0 | 0   | |
|      | 20 | 7– 6  |     | 2  | 2 | 1 | 3   | 2B |
|      | 21 | 2– 4  |     | 4  | 3 | 0 | 1   | 2B, HR |
|      | 22 | 5– 7  |     | 4  | 2 | 1 | 0   | |
|      |    | 1– 2  |     | 2  | 2 | 0 | 0   | |
|      | 24 | 1– 2  | Portland | 4 | 1 | 1 | 1 | Hr |
|      | 25 | 1– 3  |     | 3  | 1 | 0 | 0   | |
|      | 26 | 1– 0  |     | 2  | 1 | 0 | 0   | |
|      | 27 | 4– 8  |     | 4  | 1 | 1 | 1   | HR |
|      | 28 | 3– 2  |     | 3  | 2 | 1 | 1   | HR |
|      | 29 | 1– 3  |     | 4  | 0 | 0 | 0   | |
|      |    | 10– 1 |     | 4  | 1 | 1 | 0   | 2B |
|      | 31 | 4– 2  | SF  | 4  | 2 | 2 | 3   | HR |
| Sep  | 1  | 10– 5 |     | 3  | 2 | 3 | 3   | HR, HR |
|      | 2  | 4– 0  |     | 2  | 0 | 1 | 0   | hp |
|      | 3  | 15–16 |     | 6  | 2 | 2 | 3   | |
|      | 4  | 3– 4  | @SF | 5  | 1 | 0 | 1   | |
|      |    | 1– 2  |     | 3  | 0 | 0 | 0   | |
|      | 5  | 4– 6  |     | 5  | 1 | 1 | 0   | 3B |
|      | 6  | 2–11  |     | 4  | 3 | 0 | 2   | 3B |
|      |    | 1– 2  |     | 4  | 2 | 0 | 0   | |
|      | 7  | 2– 7  | @LA | 4  | 1 | 0 | 0   | |
|      | 8  | 2– 1  |     | 4  | 3 | 1 | 2   | HR |
|      | 9  | 7–11  |     | 5  | 3 | 2 | 0   | 2B |
|      | 10 | 4– 3  |     | 5  | 1 | 0 | 1   | |
|      | 11 | 5– 0  |     | 4  | 1 | 0 | 1   | |
|      | 12 | 2– 5  |     | 4  | 1 | 1 | 1   | HR |
|      |    | 8– 3  |     | 3  | 2 | 1 | 2   | 2B |
|      | 14 | 2– 3  | @Mission | 4 | 1 | 0 | 0 | |
|      | 15 | 3– 6  |     | 4  | 0 | 0 | 0   | |

| Date | | Score | Opp | AB | H | R | RBI | |
|------|------|-------|-----|-----|-----|-----|-----|------|
| | 16 | 3–4 | | 3 | 0 | 0 | 0 | lifted for ph |
| | 17 | 4–2 | | 2 | 0 | 0 | 0 | |
| | 18 | 2–1 | | 4 | 0 | 0 | 0 | |
| | 19 | 2–5 | | 4 | 3 | 0 | 1 | 2B |
| | | 4–5 | | 4 | 1 | 1 | 1 | HR |
| | 138 | | games | 454 | 132 | 66 | 98 | .291, 24 2B, 2 3B,23 HR |
| | | | home | 180 | 57 | | | .317, 17 HR |
| | | | away | 274 | 75 | | | .274, 6 HR |
| Play-offs | | | | | | | | |
| Sep | 21 | 6–4 | @Sac | 5 | 4 | 2 | 0 | 2B, 3B |
| | 22 | 4–1 | | 3 | 0 | 1 | 0 | hp |
| | 23 | 6–4 | | 3 | 0 | 0 | 0 | |
| | 25 | 2–1 | Sac | 4 | 2 | 1 | 1 | HR |
| | 28 | 4–3 | Portland | 4 | 0 | 0 | 0 | |
| | 29 | 3–1 | | 4 | 3 | 0 | 0 | |
| | 30 | 5–1 | | 4 | 1 | 0 | 0 | |
| Oct | 3 | 6–4 | @Portland | 4 | 1 | 1 | 0 | 2B |
| | 8 | | games | 35 | 11 | 5 | 2 | .314, 2B, HR |

## Ted Williams Batting Record
## Minneapolis Millers, 1938

| Date | | Opp. | AB | R | H | RBI | Home Run No. |
|------|----|------|----|----|----|----|--------------|
| April | 16 | @ Indianapolis | 5 | 0 | 0 | 0 | |
| | 17 | | 4 | 0 | 0 | 0 | |
| | 18 | | 3 | 0 | 0 | 1 | |
| | 19 | @ Louisville | 1 | 2 | 1 | 1 | |
| | 20 | | 5 | 1 | 2 | 2 | 1 and 2 |
| | 21 | | 4 | 2 | 3 | 2 | 2 inside the park home runs. First one 425 ft. to right– second 500 ft to center. Dimensions of Parkway Field in Louisville: LF-331, CF-512, RF-350 |
| | 22 | @ Columbus | 5 | 1 | 1 | 1 | |
| | 23 | | 6 | 0 | 1 | 0 | |
| | 24 | | 5 | 0 | 2 | 1 | |
| | 25 | @ Toledo | 5 | 1 | 1 | 0 | |
| | 26 | | 5 | 1 | 1 | 1 | 3 |
| | 27 | | 4 | 0 | 2 | 0 | |
| | 29 | Louisville | 4 | 3 | 3 | 4 | 4 Long hr to right; lands on roof of building across Nicollet Avenue |
| | 30 | | 3 | 0 | 1 | 0 | |
| May | 1 | | 6 | 2 | 3 | 6 | 5 and 6 |
| | 3 | Rain | | | | | |
| | 4 | Rain | | | | | |
| | 5 | Rain | | | | | |
| | 6 | Rain | | | | | |
| | 7 | Rain | | | | | |
| | 8 | Rain | | | | | |
| | 8 | Rain | | | | | |

| Date | | Opp. | AB | R | H | RBI | Home Run No. |
|------|----|------|----|----|----|----|----|
| | 9 | Rain | | | | | |
| | 10 | Columbus | 2 | 1 | 0 | 0 | |
| | 11 | | 4 | 1 | 2 | 1 | 7 |
| | 12 | St. Paul | 4 | 2 | 1 | 1 | 8 |
| May | 13 | @ St. Paul | 2 | 2 | 1 | 1 | |
| | 14 | St. Paul | 4 | 2 | 1 | 0 | |
| | 15 | @ St. Paul | 4 | 1 | 1 | 0 | |
| | 17 | Rain | | | | | |
| | 18 | Rain | | | | | |
| | 19 | Rain | | | | | |
| | 20 | Kansas City | 3 | 0 | 1 | 1 | |
| | 21 | | 4 | 1 | 2 | 0 | |
| | 22 | | 4 | 3 | 2 | 3 | 9 |
| | 22 | | 2 | 1 | 1 | 0 | |
| | 23 | @ Milwaukee | 3 | 1 | 1 | 1 | 10 |
| | 24 | | 3 | 0 | 0 | 0 | |
| | 25 | | 2 | 0 | 1 | 2 | |
| | 26 | @ Kansas City | 3 | 1 | 1 | 1 | 11 |
| | 27 | | 4 | 0 | 0 | 0 | |
| | 28 | | Did Not Play | | | | Missed Games |
| | 29 | St. Paul | Did Not Play | | | | Because of Stiff Neck |
| | 30 | St. Paul | Did Not Play | | | | |
| | 30 | @ St. Paul | 3 | 1 | 2 | 1 | 12 HR on top of Coliseum roof in left-center |
| June | 1 | @ Toledo | 5 | 2 | 2 | 1 | 13 |
| | 2 | | 4 | 1 | 1 | 1 | |
| | 3 | @ Columbus | 4 | 0 | 1 | 1 | |
| | 4 | | 3 | 3 | 2 | 4 | 14 and 15 |
| | 5 | @ Louisville | 2 | 1 | 1 | 0 | |
| | 5 | | 4 | 0 | 2 | 2 | |
| | 6 | | 2 | 0 | 1 | 0 | |
| | 7 | @ Indianapolis | 5 | 1 | 2 | 5 | 16 |
| June | 8 | @ Indianapolis | 5 | 1 | 1 | 0 | |

| Date | | Opp. | AB | R | H | RBI | Home Run No. |
|------|---|------|----|----|----|-----|--------------|
| | 9 | | 4 | 1 | 1 | 1 | |
| | 11 | St. Paul | 4 | 1 | 1 | 0 | |
| | 12 | @ St. Paul | 4 | 1 | 2 | 1 | 17 |
| | 13 | Toledo | 3 | 2 | 1 | 0 | |
| | 14 | Columbus | 4 | 0 | 1 | 0 | |
| | 15 | Rain, Wet Grounds | | | | | |
| | 16 | Columbus | 3 | 1 | 3 | 0 | |
| | 17 | Toledo | 3 | 2 | 2 | 2 | |
| | 17 | | 5 | 3 | 3 | 3 | 18 and 19 |
| | 18 | | 4 | 1 | 1 | 3 | 20 |
| | 19 | Indianapolis | 4 | 1 | 1 | 1 | 21 Hitting streak extended to 21 games |
| | 19 | | 2 | 1 | 1 | 0 | |
| | 20 | | 4 | 0 | 0 | 0 | |
| | 20 | | 3 | 1 | 2 | 1 | 22 |
| | 21 | Louisville | 2 | 1 | 1 | 0 | |
| | 22 | | 3 | 1 | 1 | 0 | |
| | 23 | @ Kansas City | 4 | 1 | 2 | 3 | |
| | 24 | | 3 | 2 | 1 | 1 | |
| | 25 | @ Milwaukee | 4 | 0 | 0 | 0 | |
| | 26 | | 4 | 0 | 2 | 0 | |
| | 26 | | 2 | 0 | 0 | 0 | |
| | 27 | Kansas City | 5 | 0 | 1 | 0 | |
| | 28 | | 1 | 1 | 1 | 0 | |
| | 29 | Milwaukee | 5 | 1 | 2 | 3 | |
| | 29 | | 4 | 1 | 1 | 0 | |
| | 30 | | 4 | 1 | 2 | 1 | |
| July | 1 | @ St. Paul | 2 | 1 | 1 | 0 | |
| | 2 | @ St. Paul | 3 | 1 | 1 | 2 | |
| | 3 | St. Paul | 3 | 1 | 0 | 0 | |
| | 4 | @ St. Paul | 4 | 0 | 0 | 0 | |
| | 4 | St. Paul | | Rain | | | |
| | 6 | @ Louisville | 4 | 1 | 1 | 1 | |

| Date | | Opp. | AB | R | H | RBI | Home Run No. |
|---|---|---|---|---|---|---|---|
| | 7 | | 4 | 0 | 1 | 0 | |
| | 8 | @ Indianapolis | 5 | 0 | 1 | 0 | |
| | 9 | | 5 | 0 | 1 | 1 | |
| | 10 | @ Toledo | 3 | 2 | 2 | 3 | 23 |
| | 10 | | 5 | 1 | 0 | 0 | |
| | 11 | | 4 | 1 | 1 | 1 | |
| | 12 | @ Columbus | 4 | 1 | 2 | 2 | |
| | 13 | | 5 | 2 | 3 | 4 | 24, 430-ft Grand Slam |
| | 14 | AA All-Star Game | 4 | 0 | 1 | 0 | |
| | 15 | St. Paul | 3 | 0 | 0 | 2 | |
| | 16 | Louisville | 4 | 0 | 3 | 0 | |
| | 17 | | 4 | 1 | 1 | 1 | 25 |
| | 17 | | 3 | 0 | 1 | 0 | |
| | 18 | Indianapolis | 5 | 2 | 2 | 1 | 26 |
| | 19 | | 4 | 1 | 1 | 1 | 27 |
| | 20 | | 3 | 0 | 0 | 0 | |
| | 20 | | 3 | 1 | 1 | 0 | |
| | 21 | Toledo | 2 | 0 | 1 | 0 | |
| | 22 | | 5 | 1 | 2 | 1 | 28 |
| | 22 | | 3 | 1 | 2 | 0 | |
| | 23 | | 3 | 0 | 2 | 2 | |
| July | 24 | Columbus | 3 | 1 | 1 | 3 | 29 |
| | 24 | | 3 | 1 | 3 | 2 | |
| | 25 | | 4 | 1 | 2 | 1 | |
| | 26 | Milwaukee | 4 | 0 | 2 | 0 | |
| | 27 | | 3 | 1 | 1 | 0 | |
| | 28 | | 4 | 3 | 2 | 2 | 30 |
| | 28 | | 4 | 1 | 1 | 1 | 31 |
| | 29 | Kansas City | 2 | 0 | 1 | 0 | |
| | 30 | Rain | | | | | |
| | 31 | @ St. Paul | 5 | 0 | 1 | 0 | |
| Aug | 1 | St. Paul | 5 | 2 | 2 | 2 | 32 |
| | 2 | @ St. Paul | 4 | 0 | 2 | 0 | |

| Date | | Opp. | AB | R | H | RBI | Home Run No. |
|------|------|------|-----|---|---|-----|--------------|
| | 3 | @ Milwaukee | 2 | 1 | 2 | 4 | Beaned in 5th taken out of game |
| | 4 | | | Did Not Play | | | |
| | 5 | Rain | | | | | |
| | 6 | @ Kansas City | 4 | 1 | 2 | 4 | 33 |
| | 7 | | 4 | 0 | 1 | 0 | |
| | 7 | | 3 | 1 | 2 | 2 | 34 |
| | 8 | | 4 | 1 | 1 | 4 | 35 Grand slam |
| | 9 | St. Paul | 5 | 0 | 1 | 2 | |
| | 10 | @ St. Paul | 3 | 0 | 1 | 0 | |
| | 11 | @ Toledo | 3 | 2 | 1 | 0 | |
| | 12 | | 4 | 0 | 2 | 0 | |
| | 13 | | 5 | 2 | 3 | 0 | |
| | 14 | @ Columbus | 4 | 2 | 3 | 0 | |
| | 14 | | 3 | 0 | 0 | 0 | |
| | 15 | | 3 | 1 | 0 | 0 | |
| | 16 | @ Columbus | 4 | 1 | 2 | 1 | 36 |
| | 17 | Rain | | | | | |
| | 18 | @ Louisville | 4 | 1 | 2 | 1 | 37 |
| | 18 | | 4 | 1 | 1 | 3 | 38 |
| | 19 | | 4 | 0 | 1 | 0 | |
| | 20 | @ Indianapolis | 4 | 1 | 1 | 0 | |
| | 21 | | 3 | 1 | 1 | 1 | |
| | 21 | | 3 | 0 | 1 | 0 | |
| | 22 | Louisville | 3 | 0 | 1 | 2 | |
| | 23 | | 4 | 0 | 1 | 0 | |
| | 24 | | 3 | 1 | 2 | 1 | 39 |
| | 25 | Indianapolis | 3 | 1 | 1 | 0 | |
| | 26 | | 4 | 1 | 2 | 0 | |
| | 26 | | 3 | 2 | 2 | 4 | 40 |
| | 27 | Toledo | 2 | 2 | 2 | 5 | 41 HR cleared bldgs on Nicollet and landed in alley between Nicollet & 1st Ave |

| Date | | Opp. | AB | R | H | RBI | Home Run No. |
|------|------|------|-----|---|---|-----|--------------|
| | 28 | | 1 | 2 | 0 | 0 | |
| | 28 | | 3 | 0 | 1 | 1 | |
| | 29 | Columbus | 2 | 1 | 1 | 0 | |
| | 29 | | 2 | 1 | 0 | 0 | |
| | 30 | | 4 | 2 | 3 | 2 | |
| | 30 | | 1 | 1 | 0 | 0 | |
| | 31 | @ Kansas City | 3 | 1 | 1 | 0 | |
| Sept | 1 | | 3 | 0 | 0 | 0 | |
| | 2 | @ Milwaukee | 4 | 1 | 2 | 0 | |
| | 2 | | 2 | 1 | 1 | 0 | |
| | 3 | | 4 | 0 | 0 | 0 | |
| | 4 | St. Paul | 4 | 1 | 1 | 0 | |
| Sept | 5 | St. Paul | 4 | 0 | 2 | 0 | |
| | 5 | @ St. Paul | 4 | 0 | 1 | 0 | |
| | 6 | Rain | | | | | |
| | 7 | Kansas City | 3 | 1 | 0 | 0 | |
| | 7 | | 4 | 1 | 1 | 0 | |
| | 8 | Rain | | | | | |
| | 8 | Rain | | | | | |
| | 9 | Rain | | | | | |
| | 10 | Milwaukee | 4 | 0 | 1 | 1 | |
| | 10 | | 3 | 2 | 2 | 2 | 42 |
| | 11 | | 4 | 1 | 4 | 4 | 43 |
| | 11 | | 2 | 0 | 1 | 0 | |

148 games

| | |
|------|------|
| 528 | AB |
| 130 | R |
| 193 | H |
| 142 | RBI |
| 30 | 2B |
| 9 | 3B |
| 43 | HR |
| 370 | TB |
| .366 | AVG. |

Won Triple Crown

also lead AA in runs and total bases

*Copyright-Stew Thornley 1981*

## Ted Williams Batting Record
## 1939 Boston Red Sox

| Date | | Score | AB | R | H | 2B | 3B | HR | RBI | Home Run No. | Opp. Pit |
|------|----|-------|----|----|----|----|----|----|-----|------|-----|
| April | 20 | NY 2 Bos 0 | 4 | 0 | 1 | 1 | 0 | 0 | 0 | | |
| | 21 | Bos 9 Phil 2 | 5 | 1 | 1 | 0 | 0 | 0 | 1 | | |
| | 22 | Bos 5 Phil 2 | 4 | 1 | 2 | 1 | 0 | 0 | 1 | | |
| | 23 | Phil 12 Bos 8 | 5 | 2 | 4 | 1 | 0 | 1 | 3 | 1 | Thomas |
| | 24 | Was 10 Bos 9 | 6 | 0 | 1 | 1 | 0 | 0 | 0 | | |
| | 25 | Bos 6 Was 5 | 4 | 1 | 1 | 0 | 0 | 0 | 0 | | |
| | 29 | Bos 3 Phil 2 | 4 | 0 | 1 | 0 | 0 | 0 | 0 | | |
| | 30 | Bos 3 Phil 1 | | | | | | | | Ted out sick | |
| May | 3 | Bos 5 Cle 1 | 4 | 0 | 1 | 0 | 0 | 0 | 1 | | |
| | 4 | Bos 7 Det 6 | 4 | 2 | 2 | 0 | 0 | 2 | 5 | 2 | Lawson |
| | | | | | | | | | | 3 | Harris |
| | 5 | Bos 4 Det 1 | 3 | 0 | 0 | 0 | 0 | 0 | 0 | | |
| | 6 | Bos 5 Det 4 | 3 | 0 | 0 | 0 | 0 | 0 | 0 | | |
| | 7 | StL 6 Bos 3 | 4 | 0 | 1 | 1 | 0 | 0 | 2 | | |
| | 9 | Bos 10 Stl 8 | 6 | 1 | 1 | 0 | 0 | 1 | 3 | 4 | Cole |
| | 11 | Chi 3 Bos 2 | 4 | 0 | 1 | 0 | 0 | 0 | 1 | | |
| | 14 | Bos 5 Was 4 | 5 | 0 | 0 | 0 | 0 | 0 | 0 | | |
| | 15 | Bos 9 Was 2 | 5 | 0 | 0 | 0 | 0 | 0 | 0 | | |
| | 16 | Bos 18 Chi 4 | 4 | 2 | 2 | 1 | 0 | 0 | 1 | | |
| | 17 | Chi 6 Bos 3 | 3 | 0 | 0 | 0 | 0 | 0 | 0 | | |
| | 18 | Bos 5 Chi 3 | 4 | 0 | 0 | 0 | 0 | 0 | 0 | | |
| | 19 | Bos 15 StL 7 | 4 | 1 | 3 | 0 | 0 | 0 | 2 | | |
| | 20 | StL 9 Bos 5 | 4 | 0 | 3 | 1 | 0 | 0 | 1 | | |
| | 21 | Bos 8 Det 3 | 4 | 1 | 2 | 1 | 0 | 0 | 2 | | |
| | 23 | Det 7 Bos 2 | 4 | 0 | 0 | 0 | 0 | 0 | 0 | | |
| | 24 | Cle 6 Bos 2 | 4 | 0 | 0 | 0 | 0 | 0 | 0 | | |
| | 25 | Cle 11 Bos 0 | 4 | 0 | 0 | 0 | 0 | 0 | 0 | | Feller pitched one hit win |
| | 26 | Bos 4 Was 2 | 4 | 1 | 1 | 0 | 0 | 0 | 1 | | |

| Date | | Score | AB | R | H | 2B | 3B | HR | RBI | Home Run No. | Opp. Pit |
|------|---|-------|----|----|----|----|----|----|----|----|------|
| | 27 | *Bos* 11 Was 4 | 5 | 0 | 1 | 0 | 0 | 0 | 2 | | |
| | | *Bos* 7 Was 6 | 4 | 1 | 3 | 1 | 1 | 1 | 4 | 5 | Krakauskas |
| | 28 | *Bos* 12 Was 7 | 4 | 2 | 2 | 0 | 0 | 1 | 2 | 6 | Masterson |
| | 29 | NY 6 *Bos* 1 | 2 | 1 | 1 | 1 | 0 | 0 | 0 | | |
| | 30 | *Bos* 8 NY 4 | 4 | 1 | 1 | 0 | 0 | 1 | 2 | 7 | Ruffing |
| | | NY 17 *Bos* 9 | 5 | 1 | 1 | 0 | 0 | 1 | 2 | 8 | Pearson |
| June | 1 | Bos 14 *Det* 5 | 5 | 2 | 2 | 1 | 0 | 0 | 1 | | |
| | 2 | *Det* 8 Bos 5 | 5 | 1 | 1 | 0 | 0 | 0 | 0 | | |
| | 4 | *Cle* 10 Bos 2 | 2 | 0 | 1 | 0 | 1 | 0 | 0 | | |
| | | Bos 7 *Cle* 1 | 4 | 0 | 2 | 1 | 0 | 0 | 1 | | |
| | 5 | *Cle* 7 Bos 5 | 3 | 1 | 1 | 1 | 0 | 0 | 0 | | |
| | 6 | *Cle* 8 Bos 7 | 1 | 0 | 0 | 0 | 0 | 0 | 0 | | |
| | 8 | Bos 8 *StL* 7 | 5 | 0 | 1 | 0 | 0 | 0 | 0 | | |
| | 9 | Bos 4 *StL* 3 | 3 | 0 | 0 | 0 | 0 | 0 | 0 | | |
| | | Bos 18 *StL* 7 | 5 | 3 | 3 | 2 | 0 | 1 | 6 | 9 | Kimberlin |
| | 11 | *Chi* 7 Bos 5 | 4 | 1 | 1 | 0 | 1 | 0 | 0 | | |
| | | Bos 4 *Chi* 3 | 4 | 1 | 0 | 0 | 0 | 0 | 0 | | |
| | 14 | Det 9 *Bos* 8 | 3 | 0 | 2 | 1 | 0 | 0 | 3 | | |
| | | Det 6 *Bos* 2 | 3 | 1 | 0 | 0 | 0 | 0 | 0 | | |
| | 15 | Det 6 *Bos* 3 | 2 | 0 | 0 | 0 | 0 | 0 | 0 | | |
| | 16 | Det 8 *Bos* 7 | 4 | 0 | 2 | 0 | 0 | 0 | 2 | | |
| | 18 | *Bos* 5 Cle 4 | 4 | 0 | 0 | 0 | 0 | 0 | 0 | | |
| | | *Bos* 5 Cle 3 | 4 | 0 | 1 | 1 | 0 | 0 | 3 | | |
| | 20 | *Bos* 8 StL 1 | 2 | 0 | 0 | 0 | 0 | 0 | 2 | | |
| | 21 | StL 6 *Bos* 3 | 4 | 0 | 0 | 0 | 0 | 0 | 0 | | |
| | 22 | *Bos* 7 StL 3 | 3 | 1 | 2 | 1 | 0 | 0 | 1 | | |
| | 24 | Chi 14 *Bos* 6 | 5 | 0 | 0 | 0 | 0 | 0 | 0 | | |
| | 26 | *Bos* 3 Was 0 | 4 | 0 | 4 | 1 | 1 | 0 | 2 | | |
| | 27 | *Bos* 8 Was 0 | 5 | 2 | 2 | 0 | 0 | 0 | 0 | | |
| | 29 | Phil 8 Bos 6 | 4 | 3 | 3 | 1 | 0 | 1 | 1 | 10 | Potter |
| July | 1 | *Bos* 5 NY 3 | 4 | 2 | 1 | 0 | 1 | 0 | 0 | | |
| | 2 | *Bos* 7 NY 3 | 3 | 2 | 1 | 0 | 0 | 1 | 3 | 11 | Gomez |
| | | NY 9 *Bos* 3 | 2 | 1 | 0 | 0 | 0 | 0 | 0 | | |

| Date | | Score | AB | R | H | 2B | 3B | HR | RBI | Home Run No. | Opp. Pit |
|---|---|---|---|---|---|---|---|---|---|---|---|
| | 4 | Bos 17 *Phil* 4 | 4 | 3 | 2 | 1 | 0 | 1 | 4 | 12 | Pippen |
| | | Bos 18 Phil 12 | 4 | 2 | 1 | 1 | 0 | 0 | 0 | | |
| | 5 | *Bos* 6 Phil 4 | 4 | 0 | 3 | 2 | 0 | 0 | 2 | | |
| | 7 | Bos 4 *NY* 3 | 3 | 1 | 2 | 0 | 0 | 0 | 1 | | |
| | 8 | Bos 3 *NY* 1 | 3 | 0 | 2 | 1 | 0 | 0 | 1 | | |
| | | Bos 3 *NY* 2 | 4 | 0 | 0 | 0 | 0 | 0 | 0 | | |
| | 9 | *Bos* 4 NY 3 | 3 | 1 | 1 | 0 | 0 | 0 | 1 | | |
| | | Bos 5 *NY* 3 | 3 | 1 | 1 | 0 | 0 | 0 | 0 | | |
| | 13 | Bos 6 *Cle* 5 | 3 | 0 | 1 | 1 | 0 | 0 | 1 | | |
| | 15 | Bos 9 *Cle* 5 | 4 | 2 | 1 | 0 | 0 | 1 | 1 | 13 | Broaca |
| | 16 | Bos 9 *Det* 2 | 4 | 1 | 1 | 0 | 0 | 0 | 0 | | |
| | | Bos 3 *Det* 0 | 4 | 0 | 0 | 0 | 0 | 0 | 0 | | |
| | 17 | *Det* 13 Bos 6 | 5 | 2 | 2 | 1 | 0 | 1 | 2 | 14 | Newsom |
| | 18 | Bos 13 *Chi* 10 | 5 | 1 | 3 | 0 | 0 | 1 | 3 | 15 | Brown |
| | | *Chi* 8 Bos 5 | 5 | 1 | 3 | 0 | 0 | 0 | 1 | | |
| | 19 | *Chi* 4 Bos 1 | 4 | 0 | 1 | 0 | 0 | 0 | 0 | | |
| | | *Chi* 8 Bos 0 | 3 | 0 | 0 | 0 | 0 | 0 | 0 | | |
| | 20 | *Chi* 4 Bos 0 | 4 | 0 | 1 | 0 | 0 | 0 | 0 | | |
| | 21 | Bos 6 *StL* 5 | 6 | 0 | 4 | 0 | 0 | 0 | 2 | | |
| | 22 | Bos 6 *StL* 3 | 5 | 1 | 1 | 1 | 0 | 0 | 0 | | |
| | 23 | Bos 13 StL 5 | 5 | 1 | 3 | 2 | 0 | 0 | 3 | | |
| | | Bos 11 StL 3 | 4 | 2 | 1 | 0 | 0 | 1 | 2 | 16 | Kramer |
| | 25 | *Bos* 3 Chi 2 | 4 | 2 | 2 | 0 | 1 | 0 | 0 | | |
| | | *Bos* 6 Chi 5 | 5 | 1 | 2 | 0 | 0 | 0 | 0 | | |
| | 26 | Chi 8 *Bos* 1 | 2 | 0 | 1 | 0 | 0 | 0 | 0 | | |
| | | *Bos* 6 Chi 5 | 4 | 0 | 2 | 0 | 0 | 0 | 0 | | |
| | 27 | Chi 12 *Bos* 7 | 3 | 1 | 2 | 0 | 1 | 0 | 0 | | |
| | 28 | StL 11 *Bos* 6 | 4 | 1 | 1 | 1 | 0 | 0 | 1 | | |
| | 29 | StL 4 *Bos* 3 | 5 | 1 | 2 | 0 | 0 | 0 | 0 | | |
| | 30 | *Bos* 6 StL 4 | 4 | 0 | 0 | 0 | 0 | 0 | 0 | | |
| Aug | 1 | *Bos* 1 Cle 5 | 3 | 1 | 0 | 0 | 0 | 0 | 1 | | |
| | 2 | Cle 8 *Bos* 2 | 4 | 0 | 0 | 0 | 0 | 0 | 0 | | |
| | | *Bos* 5 Cle 4 | 2 | 2 | 0 | 0 | 0 | 0 | 0 | | |

| Date | | Score | AB | R | H | 2B | 3B | HR | RBI | Home Run No. | Opp. Pit |
|------|---|-------|----|---|---|----|----|----|-----|-------------|----------|
| | 3 | *Bos* 17 Cle 6 | 6 | 3 | 1 | 0 | 0 | 0 | 2 | | |
| | 5 | Det 16 *Bos* 4 | 3 | 1 | 1 | 0 | 0 | 0 | 0 | | |
| | 6 | Det 10 Bos 1 | 4 | 0 | 1 | 0 | 0 | 0 | 0 | | |
| | | *Bos* 8 Det 3 | 3 | 2 | 0 | 0 | 0 | 0 | 0 | | |
| | 8 | Bos 4 Phil 2 | 4 | 1 | 2 | 1 | 0 | 0 | 2 | | |
| | 9 | *Bos* 5  Phil 3 | 4 | 0 | 0 | 0 | 0 | 0 | 1 | | |
| | | *Bos* 6 Phil 5 | 5 | 0 | 2 | 0 | 0 | 0 | 3 | | |
| | 10 | *Bos* 7 Phil 5 | 4 | 1 | 1 | 0 | 0 | 0 | 0 | | |
| | 12 | *Bos* 9 Was 5 | 4 | 2 | 2 | 2 | 0 | 0 | 0 | | |
| | 13 | *Bos* 9 Was 1 | 3 | 2 | 3 | 0 | 0 | 0 | 1 | | |
| | | Was 6 *Bos* 3 | 3 | 2 | 3 | 0 | 1 | 1 | 1 | 17 | Carrasquel |
| | 15 | *Phil* 3 Bos 0 | 4 | 0 | 2 | 0 | 0 | 0 | 0 | | Ted singled in first AB for nine straight hits |
| | 17 | Bos 7 *Phil* 1 | 4 | 0 | 2 | 1 | 0 | 0 | 0 | | |
| | 18 | Bos 6 *Was* 2 | 3 | 1 | 0 | 0 | 0 | 0 | 1 | | |
| | 19 | Bos 8 Was 6 | 5 | 1 | 2 | 0 | 0 | 1 | 4 | 18 | Appleton |
| | | *Was* 2 Bos 1 | 4 | 0 | 0 | 0 | 0 | 0 | 0 | | |
| | 20 | *Was* 2 Bos 0 | 4 | 0 | 0 | 0 | 0 | 0 | 0 | | |
| | | Bos 10 *Was* 5 | 4 | 1 | 0 | 0 | 0 | 0 | 0 | | |
| | 22 | Bos 10 *StL* 3 | 3 | 3 | 3 | 0 | 1 | 1 | 4 | 19 | Harris |
| | 23 | Bos 9 *StL* 1 | 4 | 1 | 2 | 0 | 0 | 0 | 1 | | |
| | 24 | *Chi* 3 Bos 1 | 4 | 0 | 0 | 0 | 0 | 0 | 0 | | |
| | 25 | *Chi* 9 Bos 2 | 3 | 0 | 0 | 0 | 0 | 0 | 0 | | |
| | 26 | *Chi* 5 Bos 4 | 4 | 0 | 1 | 0 | 0 | 0 | 2 | | |
| | 27 | *Cle* 1 Bos 0 | 4 | 0 | 0 | 0 | 0 | 0 | 0 | | |
| | | *Cle* 5 Bos 3 | 4 | 0 | 1 | 0 | 0 | 0 | 0 | | |
| | 28 | Bos 6 *Cle* 5 | 4 | 2 | 2 | 0 | 0 | 1 | 3 | 20 | Harder |
| | 29 | Bos 7 *Cle* 4 | 3 | 1 | 1 | 0 | 0 | 1 | 5 | 21 | Eisenstat |
| | 30 | *Det* 7 Bos 6 | 4 | 1 | 1 | 0 | 0 | 1 | 3 | 22 | Hutchinson |

| Date | | Score | AB | R | H | 2B | 3B | HR | RBI | Home Run No. | Opp. Pit |
|------|----|-------|----|----|----|----|----|----|----|----|----|
| | 31 | Det 11 Bos 4 | 4 | 0 | 2 | 1 | 0 | 0 | 2 | | |
| Sept | 1 | *Det* 14 Bos 10 | 3 | 3 | 3 | 1 | 0 | 0 | 1 | | |
| | 2 | *Bos* 12 NY 7 | 5 | 3 | 3 | 1 | 0 | 0 | 1 | | |
| | 3 | *Bos* 12 NY 11 | 2 | 1 | 1 | 1 | 0 | 0 | 0 | | |
| | | NY 5 *Bos* 5 | 3 | 2 | 2 | 0 | 0 | 2 | 4 | 23 | Hadley |
| | | | | | | | | | | 24 | Hadley |
| | 4 | Was 7 *Bos* 6 | 3 | 1 | 2 | 2 | 0 | 0 | 1 | | |
| | | Was 6 *Bos* 4 | 3 | 1 | 0 | 0 | 0 | 0 | 0 | | |
| | 6 | *NY* 2 Bos 1 | 4 | 0 | 1 | 0 | 0 | 0 | 1 | | |
| | 7 | *NY* 5 Bos 2 | | | | | | | | | |
| | 8 | *NY* 4 Bos 1 | | | | | | | | | |
| | 9 | *Phil* 2 Bos 1 | 4 | 1 | 0 | 0 | 0 | 0 | 0 | | |
| | 10 | Bos 10 *Phil* 7 | 4 | 3 | 3 | 0 | 1 | 1 | 2 | 25 | Dean |
| | | Bos 5 *Phil* 1 | 3 | 2 | 2 | 0 | 1 | 1 | 1 | 26 | Nelson |
| | 11 | Bos 11 Phil 9 | 2 | 2 | 0 | 0 | 0 | 0 | 0 | | |
| | 12 | *Bos* 2 Det 1 | 3 | 2 | 2 | 0 | 0 | 0 | 0 | | |
| | 13 | *Bos* 1 Det 0 | 3 | 0 | 0 | 0 | 0 | 0 | 0 | | |
| | 14 | Cle 8 *Bos* 7 | 3 | 1 | 2 | 0 | 0 | 0 | 3 | | |
| | 15 | Cle 7 *Bos* 1 | 3 | 0 | 2 | 1 | 0 | 0 | 1 | | |
| | 16 | Cle 2 *Bos* 1 | 4 | 1 | 1 | 0 | 0 | 1 | 1 | 27 | Harder |
| | 17 | Chi 6 *Bos* 1 | 3 | 1 | 1 | 0 | 0 | 1 | 1 | 28 | Lee |
| | | *Bos* 11 Chi 1 | 3 | 2 | 1 | 0 | 0 | 0 | 0 | | |
| | 19 | *Bos* 6 StL 2 | 4 | 0 | 0 | 0 | 0 | 0 | 0 | | |
| | 20 | StL 11 *Bos* 8 | 3 | 3 | 1 | 0 | 0 | 1 | 2 | 29 | Lawson |
| | 21 | *Bos* 6 StL 2 | 4 | 1 | 0 | 0 | 0 | 0 | 0 | | |
| | 22 | *Bos* 7 Phil 5 | 4 | 0 | 3 | 0 | 0 | 0 | 1 | | |
| | 23 | *Bos* 10 Phil 8 | 3 | 3 | 2 | 0 | 0 | 1 | 2 | 30 | Page |
| | 24 | *Bos* 8 Phil 4 | 4 | 3 | 3 | 1 | 0 | 0 | 0 | | |
| | 28 | Bos 4 *Was* 2 | 4 | 0 | 0 | 0 | 0 | 0 | 0 | | |
| | | *Was* 6 Bos 1 | 4 | 0 | 0 | 0 | 0 | 0 | 0 | | |
| | 30 | *NY* 5 Bos 4 | 4 | 1 | 1 | 1 | 0 | 0 | 0 | | |
| | | Bos 4 *NY* 2 | 2 | 1 | 1 | 0 | 0 | 1 | 1 | 31 | Sundra |

## Ted Williams Batting Record
## 1940 Boston Red Sox

| Date | | Score | AB | R | H | 2B | 3B | HR | RBI | Home Run No. | Opp. Pitcher |
|------|----|------------|----|---|---|----|----|----|-----|------|---------|
| April | 16 | Bos 1 *Was* 0 | 4 | 0 | 2 | 1 | 0 | 0 | 0 | | |
| | 18 | Bos 7 *Was* 0 | 2 | 2 | 1 | 0 | 0 | 0 | 0 | | |
| | 19 | *Bos* 7 Phil 6 | 3 | 0 | 0 | 0 | 0 | 0 | 0 | | |
| | | Phil 3 *Bos* 1 | 4 | 0 | 0 | 0 | 0 | 0 | 0 | | |
| | 23 | *Bos* 7 Was 2 | 3 | 1 | 2 | 0 | 0 | 1 | 1 | 32 | Leonard |
| | 24 | Was 9 *Bos* 6 | 4 | 0 | 0 | 0 | 0 | 0 | 0 | | |
| | 26 | *Bos* 8 NY 1 | 4 | 1 | 0 | 0 | 0 | 0 | 0 | | |
| | 27 | *Phil* 8 Bos 3 | 4 | 0 | 0 | 0 | 0 | 0 | 1 | | |
| | 28 | Bos 5 *Phil* 4 | 6 | 1 | 2 | 1 | 0 | 0 | 0 | | |
| | 29 | Bos 11 *Phil* 3 | 5 | 2 | 4 | 0 | 2 | 0 | 3 | | |
| | 30 | Chi 9 *Bos* 4 | 4 | 2 | 2 | 1 | 0 | 0 | 0 | | |
| May | 1 | *Bos* 12 Chi 4 | 4 | 3 | 2 | 0 | 0 | 0 | 1 | | |
| | 3 | *Bos* 9 StL 8 | 4 | 3 | 2 | 1 | 0 | 1 | 3 | 33 | Kramer |
| | 4 | *Bos* 4 StL 1 | 3 | 1 | 2 | 0 | 0 | 0 | 1 | | |
| | 5 | Clev 6 *Bos* 1 | 4 | 0 | 2 | 0 | 0 | 0 | 1 | | |
| | 6 | *Bos* 8 Clev 5 | 4 | 0 | 2 | 2 | 0 | 0 | 2 | | |
| | 7 | *Bos* 6 Clev 4 | 4 | 1 | 1 | 1 | 0 | 0 | 0 | | |
| | 8 | *Bos* 5 Det 4 | 4 | 0 | 1 | 0 | 0 | 0 | 0 | | |
| | 9 | *Bos* 6 Det 5 | 4 | 1 | 2 | 0 | 0 | 0 | 0 | | |
| | 10 | Bos 3 *NY* 2 | 2 | 0 | 0 | 0 | 0 | 0 | 0 | | |
| | 11 | Bos 9 *NY* 8 | 5 | 1 | 2 | 0 | 0 | 0 | 0 | | |
| | 12 | *NY* 4 Bos 0 | 3 | 0 | 1 | 0 | 0 | 0 | 0 | | |
| | 14 | Bos 7 *Chi* 6 | 5 | 0 | 1 | 1 | 0 | 0 | 1 | | |
| | 16 | Bos 7 *StL* 5 | 4 | 1 | 1 | 0 | 0 | 0 | 1 | | |
| | 20 | *Det* 10 Bos 7 | 5 | 1 | 2 | 0 | 0 | 0 | 1 | | |
| | 21 | Bos 11 *Det* 8 | 2 | 3 | 2 | 0 | 0 | 1 | 1 | | |
| | 22 | *Clev* 9 Bos 6 | 4 | 1 | 2 | 0 | 0 | 0 | 1 | | |
| | 26 | NY 7 *Bos* 2 | 4 | 1 | 1 | 0 | 0 | 1 | 1 | 35 | Murphy |
| | 28 | Bos 4 *Phil* 1 | 4 | 2 | 3 | 0 | 0 | 0 | 1 | | |
| | 29 | Bos 8 *Phil* 3 | 3 | 2 | 1 | 0 | 0 | 0 | 0 | | |

| Date | | Score | AB | R | H | 2B | 3B | HR | RBI | Home Run No. | Opp. Pitcher |
|------|----|-------|----|---|---|----|----|----|-----|------|---------|
| | 30 | *NY* 4 Bos 0 | 2 | 0 | 0 | 0 | 0 | 0 | 0 | | |
| | | Bos 11 *NY* 4 | 2 | 2 | 1 | 0 | 0 | 0 | 1 | | |
| June | 1 | *Bos* 2 Chi 1 | 4 | 1 | 2 | 0 | 0 | 0 | 0 | | |
| | 2 | Chi 6 *Bos* 0 | 4 | 0 | 1 | 1 | 0 | 0 | 0 | | |
| | | *Bos* 10 Chi 8 | 4 | 2 | 3 | 2 | 0 | 0 | 1 | | |
| | 3 | Chi 7 *Bos* 4 | 4 | 0 | 1 | 1 | 0 | 0 | 0 | | |
| | 4 | StL 5 *Bos* 3 | 5 | 1 | 1 | 0 | 0 | 0 | 0 | | |
| | 5 | StL 4 *Bos* 3 | 7 | 0 | 0 | 0 | 0 | 0 | 0 | | |
| | 6 | *Bos* 3 StL 1 | 4 | 1 | 0 | 0 | 0 | 0 | 0 | | |
| | 7 | Det 7 *Bos* 1 | 5 | 0 | 0 | 0 | 0 | 0 | 0 | | |
| | 8 | Det 4 *Bos* 2 | 4 | 0 | 2 | 1 | 0 | 0 | 2 | | |
| | 11 | *Bos* 9 Clev 2 | 4 | 2 | 2 | 0 | 1 | 1 | 4 | 36 | Dobson |
| | 12 | *Bos* 9 Clev 5 | 2 | 2 | 0 | 0 | 0 | 0 | 0 | | |
| | 14 | Bos 5 *Chi* 1 | 4 | 0 | 0 | 0 | 0 | 0 | 2 | | |
| | 15 | Bos 5 *Chi* 2 | 4 | 2 | 3 | 0 | 0 | 1 | 1 | 37 | Dietrich |
| | 16 | Bos 4 *Chi* 3 | 5 | 3 | 2 | 0 | 1 | 1 | 1 | 38 | Lyons |
| | | Bos 14 *Chi* 5 | 5 | 2 | 2 | 1 | 1 | 0 | 2 | | |
| | 18 | *StL* 11 Bos 7 | 4 | 1 | 3 | 1 | 0 | 0 | 1 | | |
| | 19 | *StL* 6 Bos 4 | 4 | 0 | 1 | 0 | 0 | 0 | 0 | | |
| | 20 | *StL* 2 Bos 1 | 3 | 0 | 0 | 0 | 0 | 0 | 0 | | |
| | | *StL* 11 Bos 4 | 5 | 1 | 1 | 1 | 0 | 0 | 0 | | |
| | 21 | *Clev* 7 Bos 4 | 4 | 1 | 1 | 0 | 0 | 1 | 3 | 39 | Milnar |
| | 22 | *Clev* 7 Bos 5 | 5 | 0 | 2 | 1 | 0 | 0 | 0 | | |
| | 23 | *Clev* 4 Bos 1 | 4 | 0 | 1 | 1 | 0 | 0 | 0 | | In 8th on fly to left center, by Ray Mack, Ted and Doc Cramer collided. |

| Date | Score | AB | R | H | 2B | 3B | HR | RBI | Home Run No. | Opp. Pitcher |
|------|-------|----|----|----|----|----|----|----|------|---------|
|  | Bos 2 *Clev* 0 |  |  |  |  |  |  |  |  |  |
| 25 | Bos 11 *Det* 7 |  |  |  |  |  |  |  |  | Ted out next four games |
|  | *Det* 5 Bos 1 |  |  |  |  |  |  |  |  |  |
| 26 | Bos 3 *Det* 1 |  |  |  |  |  |  |  |  |  |
| 28 | Was 4 *Bos* 3 | 4 | 1 | 0 | 0 | 0 | 0 | 0 |  |  |
| 29 | Was 9 *Bos* 7 | 4 | 1 | 2 | 1 | 0 | 1 | 4 | 40 | Hudson |
| 30 | *Bos* 6 Was 5 | 3 | 0 | 0 | 0 | 0 | 0 | 0 |  |  |
|  | *Bos* 5 Was 4 | 4 | 0 | 2 | 1 | 0 | 0 | 2 |  |  |
| July 1 | Phil 9 *Bos* 1 | 3 | 0 | 1 | 0 | 1 | 0 | 1 |  |  |
| 2 | Phil 4 *Bos* 2 | 3 | 0 | 1 | 1 | 0 | 0 | 0 |  |  |
|  | *Bos* 15 Phil 9 | 4 | 3 | 2 | 1 | 0 | 0 | 2 |  |  |
| 3 | *Bos* 12 Phil 11 | 4 | 2 | 2 | 0 | 0 | 1 | 3 | 41 | Dean |
| 4 | NY 12 *Bos* 4 | 4 | 1 | 1 | 0 | 0 | 0 | 0 |  |  |
|  | NY 7 *Bos* 3 | 4 | 1 | 3 | 0 | 0 | 0 | 0 |  |  |
| 5 | Bos 9 *Was* 4 | 5 | 1 | 2 | 1 | 0 | 1 | 2 | 42 | Masterson |
| 6 | Bos 5 *Was* 3 | 4 | 0 | 0 | 0 | 0 | 0 | 0 |  |  |
| 7 | Bos 7 *Was* 1 | 3 | 3 | 2 | 1 | 0 | 0 | 1 |  |  |
|  | *Was* 7 Bos 4 | 5 | 0 | 2 | 1 | 0 | 0 | 2 |  |  |
| 11 | *Bos* 3 Chi 2 | 5 | 0 | 0 | 0 | 0 | 0 | 0 |  |  |
| 13 | Chi 5 *Bos* 0 | 4 | 0 | 1 | 0 | 0 | 0 | 0 |  |  |
|  | Chi 7 *Bos* 0 | 4 | 0 | 0 | 0 | 0 | 0 | 0 |  |  |
| 14 | *Bos* 5 StL 4 | 5 | 0 | 0 | 0 | 0 | 0 | 0 |  |  |
|  | *Bos* 7 StL 3 | 4 | 1 | 1 | 0 | 0 | 0 | 0 |  |  |
| 15 | *Bos* 10 StL 6 | 5 | 1 | 2 | 1 | 0 | 0 | 0 |  |  |
| 17 | *Bos* 8 Det 3 | 4 | 2 | 3 | 1 | 0 | 0 | 1 |  |  |
|  | *Bos* 8 Det 5 | 4 | 1 | 2 | 0 | 0 | 0 | 1 |  |  |
| 18 | Det 10 *Bos* 8 | 4 | 1 | 2 | 0 | 0 | 0 | 2 |  |  |
| 19 | Det 4 *Bos* 0 | 4 | 0 | 1 | 0 | 0 | 0 | 0 |  |  |
| 20 | Clev 9 *Bos* 6 | 3 | 1 | 0 | 0 | 0 | 0 | 0 |  |  |
| 21 | Clev 3 *Bos* 2 | 4 | 0 | 0 | 0 | 0 | 0 | 0 |  |  |

| Date | | Score | AB | R | H | 2B | 3B | HR | RBI | Home Run No. | Opp. Pitcher |
|------|----|-------|----|---|---|----|----|----|-----|------|------|
| | | Clev 2 *Bos* 0 | 4 | 0 | 2 | 1 | 0 | 0 | 0 | | |
| | 23 | *Chi* 8 Bos 7 | 4 | 2 | 1 | 0 | 0 | 0 | 1 | | |
| | 24 | *Chi* 12 Bos 10 | 2 | 3 | 2 | 0 | 0 | 1 | 1 | 43 | Dietrich |
| | 25 | *Chi* 6 Bos 4 | 4 | 0 | 0 | 0 | 0 | 0 | 0 | | |
| | 26 | Bos 14 *StL* 7 | 5 | 2 | 2 | 0 | 0 | 2 | 3 | 44 | Trotter |
| | | | | | | | | | | 45 | Cox |
| | 27 | *StL* 13 Bos 5 | 3 | 1 | 2 | 1 | 0 | 0 | 1 | | |
| | 28 | Bos 3 *StL* 1 | 3 | 1 | 1 | 0 | 1 | 0 | 0 | | |
| | | Bos 13 *StL* 10 | 5 | 2 | 3 | 0 | 0 | 0 | 0 | | |
| | 30 | *Clev* 2 Bos 1 | 4 | 0 | 1 | 0 | 0 | 0 | 0 | | |
| | 31 | *Clev* 12 Bos 11 | 2 | 3 | 0 | 0 | 0 | 0 | 0 | | |
| Aug | 1 | Bos 5 *Clev* 2 | 5 | 1 | 1 | 0 | 0 | 0 | 0 | | |
| | 2 | Bos 12 *Det* 9 | 0 | 1 | 0 | 0 | 0 | 0 | 0 | | |
| | 3 | *Det* 6 Bos 4 | 4 | 0 | 0 | 0 | 0 | 0 | 0 | | |
| | | *Det* 14 Bos 2 | 4 | 0 | 1 | 0 | 0 | 0 | 0 | | |
| | 4 | Bos 7 *Det* 3 | 4 | 1 | 2 | 0 | 1 | 0 | 3 | | |
| | 5 | *Bos* 4 NY 1 | 4 | 1 | 2 | 1 | 0 | 0 | 0 | | |
| | 6 | Bos 8 NY 3 | 4 | 2 | 2 | 2 | 0 | 0 | 1 | | Ted pulled muscle in back missed next six games |
| | 7 | *Bos* 10 NY 7 | | | | | | | | | |
| | | NY 6 *Bos* 3 | | | | | | | | | |
| | 8 | *Bos* 6 NY 5 | | | | | | | | | |
| | 9 | *Was* 6 Bos 5 | | | | | | | | | |
| | 10 | Bos 3 *Was* 0 | | | | | | | | | |
| | 11 | Was 2 Bos 1 | | | | | | | | | |
| | 13 | *NY* 9 Bos 1 | 3 | 0 | 0 | 0 | 0 | 0 | 0 | | |

| Date | | Score | AB | R | H | 2B | 3B | HR | RBI | Home Run No. | Opp. Pitcher |
|------|------|-------|----|----|----|----|----|----|-----|-----|-----|
| | | NY 19 Bos 8 | 3 | 2 | 2 | 0 | 0 | 1 | 2 | 46 | Donald game stopped by dark |
| | 14 | NY 8 Bos 3 | 4 | 1 | 2 | 0 | 0 | 1 | 1 | 47 | Ruffing |
| | 15 | Bos 11 NY 1 | 4 | 2 | 1 | 0 | 0 | 1 | 4 | 48 | Hadley |
| | 16 | Bos 7 Was 6 | 5 | 0 | 2 | 1 | 0 | 0 | 0 | | |
| | 17 | Bos 12 Was 9 | 5 | 1 | 3 | 2 | 1 | 0 | 2 | | |
| | 18 | Bos 4 Was 2 | 3 | 0 | 1 | | 0 | 0 | 0 | | |
| | 19 | Bos 16 Clev 7 | 3 | 3 | 1 | 0 | 0 | 1 | 3 | 49 | Hamphries |
| | 20 | Clev 11 Bos 6 | 2 | 1 | 1 | 0 | 1 | 0 | 1 | | |
| | 21 | Clev 4 Bos 2 | 5 | 0 | 3 | 0 | 0 | 0 | 1 | | |
| | 22 | Det 9 Bos 8 | 5 | 2 | 3 | 1 | 0 | 0 | 2 | | |
| | 24 | Det 12 Bos 1 | 4 | 0 | 0 | 0 | 0 | 0 | 0 | | |
| | | Bos 8 Det 7 | 3 | 3 | 1 | 0 | 0 | 0 | 0 | | |
| | 25 | StL 7 Bos 2 | 2 | 0 | 2 | 0 | 0 | 0 | 1 | | |
| | | Bos 17 StL 3 | 2 | 2 | 1 | 0 | 0 | 0 | 2 | | |
| | 26 | Bos 7 StL 6 | 4 | 2 | 1 | 1 | 0 | 0 | 0 | | |
| | 28 | Chi 3 Bos 2 | 3 | 1 | 1 | 0 | 0 | 0 | 0 | | |
| | 29 | Bos 4 Chi 3 | 4 | 1 | 1 | 0 | 0 | 0 | 0 | | |
| | 30 | Bos 5 Phil 4 | 5 | 1 | 2 | 1 | 1 | 0 | 1 | | |
| | 31 | Bos 10 Phil 6 | 5 | 1 | 0 | 0 | 0 | 0 | 1 | | |
| Sept | 2 | Was 1 Bos 0 | 6 | 0 | 2 | 0 | 1 | 0 | 0 | | |
| | | Was 5 Bos 4 | 3 | 1 | 2 | 1 | 0 | 0 | 0 | | |
| | 4 | Bos 6 Phil 5 | 4 | 0 | 0 | 0 | 0 | 0 | 0 | | |
| | | Bos 5 Phil 4 | 3 | 1 | 1 | 0 | 0 | 0 | 0 | | |
| | 5 | Bos 9 Phil 7 | 4 | 1 | 1 | 0 | 0 | 0 | 0 | | |
| | 7 | NY 4 Bos 3 | 4 | 1 | 2 | 0 | 0 | 1 | 3 | 50 | Russo |
| | 8 | NY 9 Bos 4 | 4 | 0 | 2 | 1 | 0 | 0 | 0 | | |
| | 10 | Bos 6 Det 5 | 5 | 2 | 1 | 0 | 0 | 0 | 1 | | |
| | 11 | Det 11 Bos 7 | 4 | 0 | 2 | 1 | 0 | 0 | 1 | | |
| | 12 | Clev 8 Bos 1 | 3 | 0 | 0 | 0 | 0 | 0 | 1 | | |
| | 13 | Clev 1 Bos 0 | 4 | 0 | 0 | 0 | 0 | 0 | 0 | | |

| Date | Score | AB | R | H | 2B | 3B | HR | RBI | Home Run No. | Opp. Pitcher |
|------|-------|----|---|---|----|----|----|----|-----|--------------|
| 14 | Bos 6 *Clev* 1 | 3 | 1 | 1 | 0 | 0 | 0 | 0 | | |
| 15 | *Chi* 5 Bos 1 | 3 | 0 | 2 | 0 | 0 | 0 | 0 | | |
| | *Chi* 4 Bos 2 | 3 | 1 | 1 | 0 | 0 | 0 | 0 | | |
| 16 | Bos 6 *Chi* 2 | 5 | 0 | 2 | 0 | 1 | 0 | 2 | | |
| 18 | *StL* 11 Bos 2 | 3 | 0 | 2 | 0 | 0 | 0 | 0 | | |
| 19 | *StL* 2 Bos 1 | 5 | 0 | 1 | 0 | 0 | 0 | 0 | | |
| 21 | *NY* 5 Bos 4 | 4 | 0 | 1 | 0 | 0 | 0 | 0 | | |
| 22 | *NY* 6 Bos 3 | 4 | 1 | 1 | 0 | 0 | 1 | 1 | 51 | Russo |
| 24 | Bos 16 *Phil* 8 | 6 | 3 | 3 | 0 | 0 | 2 | 3 | 52 | Caster |
| | | | | | | | | | 53 | Caster |
| | Bos 4 *Phil* 3 | 4 | 0 | 1 | 0 | 0 | 0 | 0 | | |
| 26 | Was 6 *Bos* 5 | 4 | 1 | 0 | 0 | 0 | 0 | 0 | | |
| 27 | *Bos* 24 Was 4 | 5 | 2 | 2 | 0 | 0 | 0 | 4 | | |
| 28 | *Bos* 16 Phil 4 | 4 | 4 | 4 | 1 | 0 | 0 | 2 | | |
| | *Bos* 8 Phil 1 | 4 | 0 | 0 | 0 | 0 | 0 | 0 | | |
| 29 | *Bos* 9 Phil 4 | 4 | 1 | 3 | 0 | 1 | 1 | 3 | 54 | McCrabb |
| | *Bos* 4 Phil 1 | 4 | 0 | 2 | 0 | 0 | 0 | 2 | | |

# Ted Williams' Batting Record
## Boston Red Sox, 1941

| Date | | Game Score | Pos. | A B | R | H | 2 B | 3 B | H R | R B I | B B | S O | Homer No. | Homer Off | Hit |
|------|------|------------|------|-----|---|---|-----|-----|-----|-------|-----|-----|-----------|-----------|-----|
| April | 15 | *Bos* 7 Was 6 | ph | 1 | 0 | 1 | 0 | 0 | 0 | 1 | 0 | 0 | | | |
| | 16 | *Bos* 8 Was 7 | ph | 1 | 0 | 0 | 0 | 0 | 0 | 0 | 0 | 1 | | | |
| | 18 | *Bos* 3 *Phi* 2 | ph | 1 | 0 | 1 | 0 | 0 | 0 | 0 | 0 | 0 | | | |
| | 19 | Bos 7 *Phi* 2 | | | | | | | | | | | | | |
| | 20 | Bos 14 *Was* 8 | ph | 1 | 0 | 0 | 0 | 0 | 0 | 0 | 0 | 0 | | | |
| | 21 | *Was* 6 Bos 5 | ph | 1 | 0 | 0 | 0 | 0 | 0 | 0 | 0 | 0 | | | |
| | 22 | *Was* 12 Bos 5 | lf | 4 | 1 | 2 | 1 | 0 | 0 | 2 | 0 | 0 | | | |
| | 23 | *NY* 4 Bos 2 | | | | | | | | | | | | | |
| | 24 | *NY* 6 Bos 3 | ph | 1 | 0 | 0 | 0 | 0 | 0 | 0 | 0 | 0 | | | |
| | 25 | *Bos* 3 Phi 1 | | | | | | | | | | | | | |
| | 26 | *Bos* 8 Phi 1 | | | | | | | | | | | | | |
| | 29 | *Det* 5 Bos 3 | lf | 3 | 2 | 2 | 1 | 0 | 1 | 1 | 1 | 0 | 55 | Gorsica | |
| | 30 | *Det* 12 Bos 8 | lf | 5 | 0 | 1 | 0 | 0 | 0 | 1 | 0 | 0 | | | |
| May | 1 | Bos 15 *Det* 9 | lf | 5 | 2 | 1 | 0 | 0 | 0 | 1 | 1 | 0 | | | |
| | 2 | Cle 7 Bos 3 | rf | 3 | 0 | 0 | 0 | 0 | 0 | 0 | 1 | 0 | | | |
| | 3 | *Cle* 4 Bos 2 | rf | 3 | 0 | 1 | 0 | 0 | 0 | 0 | 2 | 0 | | | |
| | 4 | Bos 11 *StL* 4 | rf | 5 | 1 | 2 | 0 | 0 | 0 | 2 | 1 | 0 | | | |
| | 7 | Bos 4 *Chi* 3 | lf | 4 | 2 | 3 | 0 | 0 | 2 | 3 | 1 | 0 | 56 | Rigney | |
| | | | | | | | | | | | | | 57 | Rigney | |
| | 11 | *Bos* 13 NY 5 | lf | 6 | 2 | 3 | 1 | 0 | 0 | 1 | 0 | 0 | | | |
| | 12 | *Bos* 8 NY 4 | lf | 3 | 2 | 1 | 0 | 0 | 0 | 0 | 1 | 0 | | | |
| | 13 | Chi 3 *Bos* 2 | lf | 4 | 1 | 1 | 0 | 0 | 1 | 1 | 0 | 0 | 58 | Rigney | |
| | 14 | *Bos* 10 Chi 7 | lf | 5 | 0 | 0 | 0 | 0 | 0 | 0 | 0 | 1 | | | |
| | 15 | Cle 6 *Bos* 4 | lf | 3 | 2 | 1 | 0 | 0 | 0 | 0 | 2 | 1 | | | |
| | 16 | Cle 9 *Bos* 3 | lf | 4 | 1 | 1 | 0 | 0 | 0 | 0 | 0 | 0 | | | |
| | 17 | Cle 12 Bos 9 | lf | 5 | 1 | 3 | 2 | 0 | 0 | 1 | 0 | 0 | | | |
| | 18 | Det 6 *Bos* 5 | lf | 4 | 0 | 1 | 0 | 0 | 0 | 0 | 1 | 1 | | | |
| | 19 | Det 4 *Bos* 2 | lf | 4 | 1 | 1 | 0 | 0 | 1 | 2 | 0 | 0 | 59 | Gorsica | |
| | 20 | *Bos* 4 Det 2 | lf | 3 | 1 | 1 | 0 | 0 | 0 | 0 | 1 | 0 | | | |
| | 21 | *Bos* 8 StL 6 | lf | 5 | 0 | 4 | 1 | 0 | 0 | 1 | 0 | 0 | | | |

| Date | Game Score | Pos. | AB | R | H | 2B | 3B | HR | RBI | BB | SO | Homer No. | Homer Off |
|------|-----------|------|----|---|---|----|----|----|-----|----|----|-----------|-----------|
| | 22 StL 4 *Bos* 1 | lf | 4 | 0 | 2 | 0 | 0 | 0 | 0 | 0 | 0 | | |
| | 23 Bos 9 *NY* 9 | lf | 3 | 0 | 1 | 0 | 0 | 0 | 3 | 2 | 0 | | |
| | 24 *NY* 7 Bos 6 | lf | 3 | 3 | 2 | 0 | 0 | 0 | 0 | 2 | 0 | | |
| | 25 Bos 10 *NY* 3 | lf | 5 | 2 | 4 | 1 | 0 | 0 | 2 | 0 | 0 | | |
| | 27 *Bos* 5 Phi 2 | lf | 2 | 1 | 1 | 0 | 0 | 1 | 2 | 1 | 0 | 60 | Hadley |
| | Phi 11 *Bos* 1 | lf | 4 | 0 | 1 | 0 | 0 | 0 | 0 | 0 | 0 | | |
| | 28 Phi 8 *Bos* 6 | lf | 5 | 1 | 3 | 1 | 0 | 0 | 0 | 3 | 0 | | |
| | 29 *Bos* 6 Phi 4 | lf | 4 | 2 | 3 | 0 | 0 | 1 | 2 | 0 | 0 | 61 | Knott |
| | 30 NY 4 *Bos* 3 | lf | 2 | 2 | 1 | 1 | 0 | 0 | 0 | 2 | 0 | | |
| | *Bos* 13 NY 0 | lf | 3 | 2 | 2 | 0 | 0 | 0 | 1 | 1 | 0 | | |
| June | 1 Bos 7 *Det* 6 | lf | 4 | 2 | 2 | 1 | 0 | 0 | 1 | 1 | 0 | | |
| | Bos 6 *Det* 5 | lf | 5 | 2 | 2 | 0 | 0 | 1 | 3 | 0 | 0 | 62 | Rowe |
| | 2 Bos 9 *Det* 1 | lf | 4 | 2 | 1 | 0 | 0 | 0 | 1 | 1 | 0 | | |
| | 5 Bos 14 *Cle* 1 | lf | 4 | 4 | 3 | 0 | 0 | 1 | 3 | 2 | 0 | 63 | Heving |
| | 6 Bos 6 *Chi* 3 | lf | 4 | 2 | 2 | 1 | 0 | 1 | 2 | 0 | 0 | 64 | Rigney |
| | 7 *Chi* 5 Bos 4 | lf | 4 | 1 | 1 | 0 | 0 | 0 | 0 | 1 | 1 | | |
| | 8 Bos 5 *Chi* 3 | lf | 2 | 0 | 0 | 0 | 0 | 0 | 1 | 3 | 0 | | |
| | Bos 3 *Chi* 0 | lf | 3 | 1 | 0 | 0 | 0 | 0 | 0 | 1 | 1 | | |
| | 12 *StL* 9 Bos 4 | lf | 5 | 0 | 1 | 0 | 0 | 0 | 0 | 0 | 1 | | |
| | Bos 3 *StL* 2 | lf | 2 | 1 | 1 | 0 | 0 | 1 | 2 | 2 | 0 | 65 | Niggeling |
| | 14 Chi 5 *Bos* 2 | lf | 5 | 0 | 3 | 1 | 0 | 0 | 0 | 0 | 0 | | |
| | 15 *Bos* 8 Chi 6 | lf | 3 | 2 | 2 | 0 | 0 | 0 | 1 | 1 | 0 | | |
| | Bos 6 Chi 4 | lf | 3 | 2 | 2 | 1 | 0 | 1 | 1 | 1 | 0 | 66 | Ross |
| | 17 *Bos* 14 Det 6 | lf | 4 | 1 | 1 | 0 | 0 | 1 | 2 | 1 | 0 | 67 | Thomas |
| | Det 8 *Bos* 5 | lf | 1 | 2 | 1 | 1 | 0 | 0 | 0 | 3 | 0 | | |
| | 18 Det 5 *Bos* 2 | lf | 3 | 0 | 0 | 0 | 0 | 0 | 0 | 1 | 1 | | |
| | 19 *Bos* 6 Det 4 | lf | 3 | 0 | 1 | 0 | 0 | 0 | 2 | 1 | 1 | | |
| | 20 *Bos* 4 StL 2 | lf | 3 | 1 | 2 | 1 | 0 | 0 | 2 | 1 | 0 | | |
| | 21 StL 13 *Bos* 9 | lf | 2 | 1 | 0 | 0 | 0 | 0 | 0 | 1 | 0 | | |
| | 22 *Bos* 7 StL 5 | lf | 3 | 1 | 1 | 0 | 0 | 0 | 2 | 1 | 0 | | |
| | StL 12 *Bos* 3 | lf | 3 | 0 | 0 | 0 | 0 | 0 | 0 | 1 | 0 | | |
| | 24 *Bos* 13 Cle 2 | lf | 2 | 2 | 0 | 0 | 0 | 0 | 0 | 3 | 0 | | |
| | 25 *Bos* 7 Cle 2 | lf | 3 | 2 | 2 | 0 | 0 | 1 | 2 | 1 | 0 | 68 | Bagby |

| Date | Game Score | Pos. | AB | R | H | 2B | 3B | HR | RBI | BB | SO | Homer No. | Homer Hit Off |
|---|---|---|---|---|---|---|---|---|---|---|---|---|---|
| 26 | Cle 11 *Bos* 8 | lf | 5 | 2 | 3 | 0 | 0 | 0 | 1 | 0 | 0 | | |
| 27 | *Was* 5 Bos 3 | lf | 3 | 0 | 1 | 0 | 0 | 0 | 0 | 1 | 0 | | |
| 28 | *Was* 3 Bos 1 | lf | 3 | 0 | 1 | 0 | 0 | 0 | 0 | 1 | 0 | | |
| 29 | Bos 13 *Phi* 1 | lf | 4 | 2 | 2 | 0 | 0 | 1 | 2 | 1 | 0 | 69 | Harris |
| | *Phi* 3 Bos 2 | lf | 4 | 0 | 0 | 0 | 0 | 0 | 1 | 0 | 0 | | |
| July 1 | *NY* 7 Bos 2 | lf | 4 | 0 | 1 | 0 | 0 | 0 | 0 | 0 | 1 | | |
| | *NY* 9 Bos 2 | lf | 2 | 1 | 1 | 0 | 0 | 0 | 0 | 0 | 0 | | |
| 2 | *NY* 8 Bos 4 | lf | 3 | 1 | 1 | 0 | 0 | 0 | 0 | 1 | 0 | | |
| 3 | Bos 5 *Phi* 2 | lf | 4 | 2 | 2 | 0 | 0 | 1 | 2 | 0 | 0 | 70 | Dean |
| 5 | *Bos* 5 Was 0 | lf | 3 | 1 | 1 | 1 | 0 | 0 | 1 | 1 | 0 | | |
| 6 | *Bos* 6 Was 2 | lf | 4 | 0 | 1 | 0 | 0 | 0 | 1 | 0 | 0 | | |
| | *Bos* 4 Was 3 | lf | 4 | 2 | 3 | 2 | 0 | 0 | 2 | 0 | 0 | | |
| 11 | *Det* 2 Bos 0 | lf | 4 | 0 | 0 | 0 | 0 | 0 | 0 | 0 | 1 | | |
| 12 | Bos 7 *Det* 5 | lf | 1 | 2 | 0 | 0 | 0 | 0 | 0 | 3 | 0 | | Williams hurt his right ankle while sliding |
| | Bos 10 Det 2 | | | | | | | | | | | | |
| 13 | *Cle* 9 Bos 6 | | | | | | | | | | | | |
| | *Cle* 2 Bos 1 | | | | | | | | | | | | |
| 14 | *Cle* 4 Bos 1 | | | | | | | | | | | | |
| 15 | Bos 6 *Cle* 2 | | | | | | | | | | | | |
| 16 | Bos 2 *Chi* 1 | ph | 1 | 0 | 0 | 0 | 0 | 0 | 1 | 0 | 0 | | |
| 17 | Bos 7 *Chi* 4 | | | | | | | | | | | | |
| 18 | *Chi* 4 Bos 3 | | | | | | | | | | | | |
| 19 | *StL* 9 Bos 3 | ph | 1 | 0 | 0 | 0 | 0 | 0 | 0 | 0 | 0 | | |
| | *StL* 4 Bos 3 | ph | 0 | 0 | 0 | 0 | 0 | 0 | 0 | 1 | 0 | | |
| 20 | *StL* 6 Bos 3 | ph | 1 | 1 | 1 | 0 | 0 | 1 | 3 | 0 | 0 | 71 | Niggeling |
| | *StL* 10 Bos 0 | | | | | | | | | | | | |
| 22 | *Bos* 6 Chi 2 | lf | 2 | 1 | 1 | 0 | 0 | 1 | 1 | 1 | 0 | 72 | Rigney |
| 23 | Chi 10 *Bos* 4 | lf | 5 | 1 | 2 | 1 | 0 | 0 | 0 | 0 | 0 | | |
| 24 | *Bos* 11 Chi 1 | lf | 5 | 1 | 2 | 0 | 0 | 0 | 0 | 0 | 1 | | |

| Date | Game Score | Pos. | AB | R | H | 2B | 3B | HR | RBI | BB | SO | Homer No. | Homer Hit Off |
|---|---|---|---|---|---|---|---|---|---|---|---|---|---|
| 25 | Bos 10 Cle 6 | lf | 3 | 3 | 2 | 0 | 0 | 1 | 2 | 2 | 0 | 73 | Harder |
| 26 | Bos 4 Cle 3 | lf | 4 | 1 | 3 | 0 | 0 | 0 | 0 | 1 | 0 | | |
| 27 | Cle 4 Bos 0 | lf | 3 | 0 | 2 | 1 | 0 | 0 | 0 | 1 | 0 | | |
| 29 | StL 3 Bos 2 | lf | 3 | 1 | 1 | 0 | 0 | 1 | 2 | 1 | 1 | 74 | Niggeling |
| 31 | StL 16 Bos 11 | lf | 3 | 2 | 2 | 0 | 0 | 1 | 4 | 3 | 0 | 75 | Trotter Grand Slam |
| | Bos 4 StL 1 | lf | 3 | 0 | 1 | 1 | 0 | 0 | 0 | 1 | 1 | | |
| August 2 | Det 6 Bos 5 | lf | 3 | 1 | 2 | 1 | 0 | 0 | 0 | 1 | 0 | | |
| 3 | Det 6 Bos 3 | lf | 4 | 0 | 1 | 0 | 0 | 0 | 0 | 1 | 0 | | |
| 4 | Bos 7 Phi 6 | lf | 2 | 0 | 0 | 0 | 0 | 0 | 0 | 3 | 0 | | |
| 5 | Bos 6 Phi 5 | lf | 4 | 1 | 2 | 1 | 0 | 0 | 2 | 0 | 0 | | |
| 6 | Bos 6 NY 3 | lf | 3 | 0 | 1 | 0 | 0 | 0 | 0 | 1 | 0 | | |
| | NY 3 Bos 1 | lf | 3 | 0 | 0 | 0 | 0 | 0 | 0 | 1 | 1 | | |
| 7 | Bos 9 NY 5 | lf | 4 | 3 | 3 | 0 | 0 | 1 | 2 | 0 | 0 | 76 | Gomez |
| 8 | Bos 15 Was 8 | lf | 3 | 2 | 1 | 0 | 0 | 0 | 0 | 2 | 0 | | |
| 9 | Was 8 Bos 6 | lf | 3 | 1 | 1 | 0 | 0 | 0 | 0 | 2 | 0 | | |
| 10 | Bos 7 Was 6 | lf | 4 | 0 | 3 | 0 | 1 | 0 | 0 | 1 | 0 | | |
| | Was 8 Bos 2 | lf | 3 | 0 | 1 | 0 | 0 | 0 | 0 | 1 | 0 | | |
| 11 | Bos 8 NY 0 | lf | 1 | 1 | 1 | 0 | 0 | 0 | 1 | 4 | 0 | | |
| 12 | NY 4 Bos 0 | lf | 3 | 0 | 1 | 0 | 0 | 0 | 0 | 1 | 2 | | |
| 13 | Bos 4 Phi 0 | lf | 1 | 0 | 1 | 1 | 0 | 0 | 1 | 4 | 0 | | |
| 14 | Bos 11 Phi 8 | lf | 5 | 2 | 1 | 0 | 0 | 1 | 3 | 1 | 0 | 77 | Ferrick |
| | Phi 10 Bos 8 | lf | 4 | 1 | 1 | 0 | 0 | 0 | 0 | 1 | 0 | | |
| 15 | Bos 9 Was 0 | lf | 2 | 0 | 0 | 0 | 0 | 0 | 0 | 1 | 1 | | |
| 16 | Bos 8 Was 6 | lf | 5 | 2 | 3 | 1 | 0 | 0 | 1 | 0 | 0 | | |
| 17 | Was 6 Bos 2 | lf | 3 | 0 | 0 | 0 | 0 | 0 | 0 | 1 | 0 | | |
| 19 | StL 3 Bos 2 | lf | 3 | 1 | 1 | 0 | 0 | 1 | 1 | 1 | 0 | 78 | Galehouse |
| | Bos 10 StL 7 | lf | 5 | 2 | 4 | 0 | 0 | 2 | 3 | 0 | 0 | 79 | Muncrief |
| | | | | | | | | | | | | 80 | Muncrief |
| 20 | StL 11 Bos 9 | lf | 4 | 3 | 2 | 0 | 0 | 1 | 2 | 1 | 1 | 81 | Auker |
| | StL 4 Bos 3 | lf | 2 | 1 | 1 | 0 | 0 | 1 | 2 | 2 | 0 | 82 | Niggeling |
| 21 | Bos 8 Chi 5 | lf | 3 | 2 | 2 | 0 | 0 | 0 | 0 | 2 | 0 | | |

| Date | Game Score | Pos. | AB | R | H | 2B | 3B | HR | RBI | BB | SO | Homer No. | Homer Off |
|---|---|---|---|---|---|---|---|---|---|---|---|---|---|
| 22 | Bos 2 *Chi* 1 | lf | 2 | 0 | 0 | 0 | 0 | 0 | 1 | 2 | 0 | | |
| 23 | *Chi* 3 Bos 0 | lf | 4 | 0 | 1 | 0 | 0 | 0 | 0 | 0 | 0 | | |
| 24 | *Cle* 4 Bos 3 | lf | 4 | 1 | 1 | 0 | 0 | 0 | 0 | 0 | 1 | | |
| | *Cle* 5 Bos 2 | lf | 3 | 0 | 0 | 0 | 0 | 0 | 0 | 1 | 1 | | |
| 25 | Bos 1 *Cle* 0 | lf | 2 | 1 | 0 | 0 | 0 | 0 | 0 | 2 | 1 | | |
| 26 | Bos 9 *Cle* 4 | lf | 1 | 0 | 1 | 0 | 0 | 0 | 0 | 4 | 0 | | |
| 27 | *Det* 6 Bos 3 | lf | 4 | 0 | 2 | 0 | 0 | 0 | 1 | 1 | 0 | | |
| 28 | *Det* 8 Bos 7 | lf | 3 | 2 | 2 | 0 | 1 | 1 | 1 | 2 | 0 | 83 | Benton |
| 30 | *Bos* 12 Phi | lf | 3 | 3 | 2 | 0 | 0 | 1 | 2 | 2 | 0 | 84 | Hadley |
| 31 | *Bos* 5 Phi 3 | lf | 3 | 1 | 1 | 0 | 0 | 1 | 3 | 1 | 0 | 85 | Knott |
| | Phi 3 *Bos* 2 | lf | 1 | 0 | 0 | 0 | 0 | 0 | 0 | 3 | 0 | | |
| September 1 | *Bos* 13 Was 9 | lf | 3 | 2 | 2 | 0 | 0 | 2 | 4 | 2 | 0 | 86 | Carrasquel |
| | | | | | | | | | | | | 87 | Zuber |
| | Bos 10 Was 2 | lf | 2 | 3 | 1 | 0 | 0 | 1 | 1 | 2 | 0 | 88 | Anderson |
| 3 | NY 2 *Bos* 1 | lf | 3 | 0 | 1 | 0 | 0 | 0 | 0 | 2 | 0 | | |
| 4 | NY 6 *Bos* 3 | lf,rf | 1 | 1 | 1 | 0 | 0 | 0 | 0 | 3 | 0 | | |
| 6 | Bos 8 *NY* 1 | lf | 4 | 1 | 1 | 0 | 0 | 0 | 1 | 1 | 0 | | |
| 7 | *NY* 8 Bos 5 | lf | 4 | 1 | 3 | 2 | 0 | 0 | 1 | 1 | 0 | | |
| 9 | *Bos* 6 Det 0 | lf | 3 | 0 | 1 | 0 | 0 | 0 | 0 | 1 | 0 | | |
| 10 | *Bos* 11 Det 2 | lf | 4 | 1 | 2 | 1 | 0 | 0 | 3 | 1 | 0 | | |
| 12 | *Bos* 5 StL 0 | lf | 3 | 1 | 0 | 0 | 0 | 0 | 0 | 2 | 0 | | |
| 13 | *Bos* 7 StL 2 | lf | 1 | 0 | 0 | 0 | 0 | 0 | 0 | 3 | 0 | | |
| 14 | *Bos* 9 Chi 2 | lf | 3 | 1 | 2 | 1 | 0 | 0 | 1 | 2 | 0 | | |
| | *Bos* 5 Chi 1 | lf | 4 | 1 | 1 | 0 | 1 | 0 | 1 | 0 | 1 | | |
| 15 | *Bos* 6 Chi 1 | lf | 3 | 1 | 1 | 0 | 0 | 1 | 3 | 1 | 0 | 89 | Rigney |
| 17 | *Bos* 3 Cle 2 | lf | 3 | 0 | 1 | 1 | 0 | 0 | 0 | 1 | 0 | | |
| 18 | Cle 6 *Bos* 1 | lf | 3 | 0 | 0 | 0 | 0 | 0 | 0 | 1 | 1 | | |
| 20 | NY 8 *Bos* 1 | lf | 4 | 0 | 2 | 0 | 0 | 0 | 0 | 0 | 1 | | |
| 21 | Bos 4 NY 1 | lf | 3 | 1 | 1 | 0 | 0 | 1 | 2 | 1 | 0 | 90 | Bonham |
| 23 | *Was* 4 Bos 3 | lf | 3 | 1 | 1 | 1 | 0 | 0 | 0 | 1 | 0 | | |
| 24 | Bos 7 *Was* 2 | lf | 3 | 0 | 0 | 0 | 0 | 0 | 0 | 0 | 0 | | |
| | Bos 5 Was 4 | lf | 4 | 1 | 1 | 0 | 0 | 0 | 0 | 0 | 1 | | |
| 27 | Bos 5 *Phi* 1 | lf | 4 | 1 | 1 | 1 | 0 | 0 | 0 | 1 | 1 | | |

| Date | Game Score | Pos. | A B | R | H | 2 B | 3 B | H R | R B I | B B | S O | Homer No. | Homer Off | Hit |
|------|-----------|------|-----|---|---|-----|-----|-----|-------|-----|-----|-----------|-----------|-----|
| 28 | Bos 12 *Phi* 11 | lf | 5 | 2 | 4 | 0 | 0 | 1 | 2 | 0 | 0 | 91 | Fowler | |
| | *Phi* 7 Bos 1 | lf | 3 | 0 | 2 | 1 | 0 | 0 | 0 | 0 | 0 | | | |